OF SPACE AND MIND

*Cognitive Approaches to Literature and Culture Series*

*Edited by Frederick Luis Aldama, Arturo J. Aldama, and Patrick Colm Hogan*

Cognitive Approaches to Literature and Culture includes monographs and edited volumes that incorporate cutting-edge research in cognitive science, neuroscience, psychology, linguistics, narrative theory, and related fields, exploring how this research bears on and illuminates cultural phenomena such as, but not limited to, literature, film, drama, music, dance, visual art, digital media, and comics. The volumes published in this series represent both specialized scholarship and interdisciplinary investigations that are deeply sensitive to cultural specifics and grounded in a cross-cultural understanding of shared emotive and cognitive principles.

# Of Space and Mind

COGNITIVE MAPPINGS OF
CONTEMPORARY CHICANO/A FICTION

*Patrick L. Hamilton*

UNIVERSITY OF TEXAS PRESS
*Austin*

Requests for permission to reproduce material from this work should be sent to:
Permissions
University of Texas Press
P.O. Box 7819
Austin, TX 78713-7819
www.utexas.edu/utpress/about/bpermission.html

♾ The paper used in this book meets the minimum requirements of ANSI/NISO Z39.48-1992 (R1997) (Permanence of Paper).

LIBRARY OF CONGRESS CATALOGING-IN-PUBLICATION DATA
Hamilton, Patrick Lawrence.
    Of space and mind : cognitive mappings of contemporary Chicano/a fiction / Patrick L. Hamilton. — 1st ed.
        p.    cm. — (Cognitive approaches to literature and culture series)
    Based on author's doctoral thesis (University of Colorado, 2006): Reading space.
    Includes bibliographical references and index.
    ISBN 978-0-292-74397-7
    1. American fiction—Mexican American authors—History and criticism—Theory, etc.    2. American fiction—20th century—History and criticism.    3. Mexican Americans in literature.
I. Title.
PS153.M4H36    2011
813′.60986872—dc22
                                                                    2010026137

First paperback printing, 2012

*To Mom and Dad*

# Contents

# Acknowledgments

I've essentially been working on *Of Space and Mind* since 2004, when it began as my dissertation; that work has been greatly assisted by numerous individuals to whom I owe a great deal of thanks.

I first met Frederick Aldama in his Re-Imagining the Metropolis seminar at the University of Colorado at Boulder, a course that introduced me to the works of Arturo Islas and Alfredo Véa and, really, where this project was born. His dedication to me and this project was immense, as evidenced by his willingness to remain its director even after moving from Colorado to Ohio State. He continues to this day as teacher, mentor, and friend; these few lines are inadequate to express my gratitude for his influence on not only this project but also my career.

Arturo Aldama has been with me and this project since it was only a framework outlined in a prospectus, and he has pushed my approach and argument in better directions than I would have followed without him. He has similarly supported and shepherded the book's manuscript through the publication process and lent it his enthusiastic backing. I am truly grateful for all he has done.

Much of what would become *Of Space and Mind* derives from its origin as my dissertation, and I owe a debt of thanks to those who participated in that process. Drs. Adeleke Adeeko, Karen Jacobs, and John-Michael Rivera rounded out my committee and provided inestimable support and feedback. My dissertation "support" group—Matthew Reiswig, Renee Dickinson, and Lorna Raven Wheeler—read multiple drafts of every chapter over sandwiches and coffee on many a Boulder afternoon and, more importantly, remain my close friends to this day.

Today, at Misericordia University, I enjoy a great deal of aid—informal and formal—from my colleagues and institution. Allan Austin graciously allowed me to invade his office on a regular basis, and he generously lent his thinking to my work and thought. Becky Steinberger, first as a colleague and then as my department chair, has always been in my and this project's corner and has offered without pause her advice and friendship. The Nordstroms—Justin and Alicia—were amongst the first and the fastest to welcome me to my new surroundings, and I must thank them for their exuberant friendliness toward and unflagging encouragement of me and my work. To my fellow faculty in the English department and the College of Arts and Sciences, I give my deepest thanks. Revisions to the manuscript in preparation for initial submission were completed under the auspices of a Faculty Development Summer Grant, and I thank both the Development Committee and the Misericordia administration for this funding. I would also like to thank Joe Curran who, as interim dean of the College of Arts and Sciences, secured funding for my permissions.

Contributing to my revision was the opportunity I had to present early versions of these chapters at conferences. The comments on my discussions of the bildungsroman in Anaya's *Bless Me, Ultima* and Véa's *La Maravilla* at the Western Literature Conference, and those at the International Conference on Narrative on an early version of Chapter 4's treatment of Castillo's *Sapogonia*, were invaluable. In particular, I want to thank Brian McHale for his comments regarding Castillo's novel and its narration, which helped to focus and strengthen my approach.

I could not be happier that *Of Space and Mind* found a home at The University of Texas Press. I'd like to thank Jim Burr of the Humanities division for his tireless efforts on my behalf and answers to my questions, particularly throughout the permissions process; the editors of the Cognitive Approaches to Literature and Culture series—the brothers Aldama and Patrick Colm Hogan—for creating a place for this work; and the anonymous reader and editorial staff—especially Sarah Hudgens and Sally Furgeson—for all their work toward the betterment of the manuscript.

I must save the final thanks for my family, to whom I also send my love. Though I don't get to see them as often as we'd all like, they are always in my thoughts and heart.

# Introduction

## Toward New Mappings of Contemporary Chicano/a Fiction

W hat *can* we understand about cultural differences — race, ethnicity, gender, class, sexuality, and others — from contemporary Chicano/a fiction? Through their constructions of uniquely imagined storyworlds and individual textual aesthetics, what do novels and short stories by Chicano/a authors *ask* us as readers to think?

These are the questions at the center of this study. The emphasis above on the words "can" and "ask" highlights how texts, in the worlds they imagine, act upon a reader's mind. They communicate to that mind a particular meaning, point-of-view, and ethics. Within the field of Chicano/a literature — and U.S. multiethnic literature in general — the tendency has been more to sublimate a text's unique meaning and ethics to an already-existing point of view and ethos. Critics including Marcial González, José Aranda Jr., and Juan Bruce-Novoa previously attest to how a paradigm of "resistance" dominates the study of Chicano/a literature. This paradigm fosters an understanding of cultural interactions based on a binary opposition between dominant and subordinate that is always contextualized by conflict, contestation, and distance. Resistance's ascendancy, however, has the potential to turn against Chicano/a literary study, as it has in other fields such as anthropology, geography, postcolonial studies, and, in particular, cultural studies. In advocating its cognitive approach to the analysis of contemporary Chicano/a fiction, this study seeks to complicate this dominant understanding by placing other textualized conceptions of difference alongside it in an effort to expand the repertoire of intellectual positions within Chicano/a literary study and criticism.

Emblematic of resistance's dominance is one of the governing conceits within Chicano/a literary and cultural study: Gloria Anzaldúa's concept of the "borderlands."[1] Early on in *Borderlands/La Frontera: The New Mestiza*, Anzaldúa powerfully describes the border between the United States and Mexico as "*una herida abierta*," or open wound, "where the Third World grates against the first and bleeds" (25). As this "blood" scabs over, it creates a borderland that Anzaldúa further characterizes as "vague and undetermined" and "in a constant state of transition" (25). The borderlands is, then, a space of First and Third World frictions that is at once hybrid and liminal but also contextualized by violence and conflict. A resistance toward the hegemonic positionalities that partially form the borderlands lies inherent in this image. As well, much work done in the fields of Chicano/a literature and/or Borderlands Studies emphasizes this inherent stance. José David Saldívar's *Border Matters*, for example, comprises a wide range of Chicano/a works—going "beyond literature to examine issues of expression and representation in folklore, music, and video performance art"—that challenge "the homogeneity of U.S. nationalism and popular culture" (ix). Mary Pat Brady likewise notes in *Extinct Lands, Temporal Geographies* how Chicana literature resists U.S. cultural and capitalist hegemony. It "contest[s] the terms of capitalist spatial formation, including the attempts to regularize the meanings and uses of spaces, especially the use of space to naturalize violent racial, gender, sexual and class ideologies" by offering "not just alternative cartographies (or countercartographies . . .) but entirely different conceptualizations of spatiality altogether" (6). Similarly, Ramón Saldívar characterizes Chicano/a works as "one of the most independent cultural and literary 'forms of opposition and struggle' that the dominant culture of the United States has attempted to control, neutralize, and integrate" (10–11). These efforts, and many more like them, define a politically charged approach to Chicano/a cultural production that seeks a more inclusive version of American Studies in general. Their insights successfully created a conceptual framework for Chicano/a literature, music, and video/film in terms of their challenge and opposition to dominant U.S. culture and society.

This study seeks to complicate that framework. It too finds its impetus to do so in Anzaldúa's seminal text. First, it is important to remember that her image of the borderlands is not only textual or metaphoric. It also derives from and encompasses the efforts of real people, residing and laboring in a real, material world external to the literary text. This fact raises the question: what role does the literary text have in such real-world and, yes, political action and change? The tendency under resistance has been to equate the literary text with such action; that is, to see the literary text as not so much representing resistance, but rather *as* resistance and resistant. This study wants to maintain the distinction between the literary text and real-world, material action, an effort in which its advocacy of a cognitive approach plays a significant role. It proposes that we conceive of Chicano/a fiction as a springboard for understanding relations of difference first in textual worlds and secondarily in real ones. That is, that the textual understandings offered by the authors here seek to affect how we think about such differences as race, ethnicity, gender, class, and sexuality within the U.S. nation-space. Those thoughts, then, are the ones with which readers interact and encounter their experiential worlds. Further to this effort, this study proposes that there are other frameworks offered by Chicano/a fiction in addition to that promulgated as resistance. Such alternative narrative and ethical positionings need to be, first, recognized through what this study puts forth as an aesthetic of cognitive mapping and, second, included as other possible relationships toward dominant/hegemonic U.S. culture and society. These textual possibilities reflect on those differences' existence in the experiential nation and world and, ideally, affect how the reader conceives of their existence.

Second, another image from *Borderlands/La Frontera* inspires this study. Anzaldúa begins the prose section of her text with the powerful presentation of the borderlands. She ends it with a similarly powerful call:

> But it is not enough to stand on the opposite river bank, shouting questions, challenging patriarchal, white conventions. A counterstance locks one into a duel of oppressor and oppressed; locked in mortal combat . . . both are reduced to a common denominator of violence. The counterstance refutes the dominant culture's views and beliefs, and, for this, it is proudly defiant. All reaction is limited by, and dependent on, what it is reacting against. Because the counterstance stems from a problem with authority . . . it's a step towards liberation from cultural domination. But it is not a way of life. At some point, on our way to a new consciousness, we will have to leave the opposite bank, the split between the two mortal combatants somehow healed so that we are on both shores at once . . . . Or perhaps we will decide to disengage from the dominant culture, write it off altogether as a lost cause, and cross the border into a wholly new and separate territory. Or we might go another route. The possibilities are numerous once we decide to act and not react. (100–101)

In this image of crossing to the "opposite river bank," Anzaldúa strikingly suggests the need for actual action and change, specifically a change from the acts of "shouting" and challenge that are recognizably resistant.

Though a step on the path toward liberation and understanding, resistance itself is not the end goal of this passage, or of Anzaldúa's text. She lists, toward the end of this passage, multiple outcomes that may result from this "crossing"; resistance, or disengagement, is among these possibilities, but it is not the only one.

To Anzaldúa's voice, Alfred Arteaga adds his. In his *Chicano Poetics*, Arteaga seeks to direct us out of what he terms a "clash of senseless monologues" both within and external to the literary world (78). Both writers express a reduction of life and consciousness—to violence in the former and senselessness in the latter—that results from simply "standing" in opposition, "proudly defiant." Both Anzaldúa and Arteaga theorize a new "territory," "another route," and thus other conceptions of cultural interactions than that defined by resistance. It is, then, a need to take another "step" in how we conceive and understand these cultural differences and relations that both Anzaldúa and Arteaga so vociferously advocate. It is in this spirit that the present study offers its aesthetic of cognitive mapping and analysis of contemporary Chicano/a fiction.

## RESISTANCE IN CULTURAL STUDIES, U.S. MULTIETHNIC LITERATURE, AND CHICANO/A FICTION

The latest battlefronts in the "culture wars" display the continued presence and power of this binary construction of difference. Pundits on the twenty-four-hour cable news channels and politicians haranguing against the "evils" of gay marriage and border policy/immigration do so on the basis of a racist and xenophobic logic. They assert a binary opposition between a dominant self—be it the heterosexual self in the gay marriage debate or the white, Anglo self in that on immigration—and the homosexual or foreign "other." This logic hinges upon both a psychological and literal distance between the parties in its attempted creation of literal and psychological conflict and opposition between them.

The logic behind these virulent positions parallels that underpinning the narrative and ethics of resistance. This reactionary point of view bases itself on the idea that gays and immigrants are something wholly other than an idealized U.S. national "self." Implicit in the challenge both Saldívars and Brady make of Chicano/a literature is the same idea: that Chicano/a culture is wholly other to a homogenous U.S. national and cultural identity. This parallel reveals the resistance model's possible weakness within contemporary cultural debates. Is not resistance too making a similar implicit (if not, in fact, explicit) assertion as dominant U.S. culture when, to paraphrase Anzaldúa, it stands always in refutation and defiance of that nationalist fervor? Would not such a model as resistance, rather than combat such attitudes and beliefs, actually feed into and even exacerbate them? If both "sides" of this debate are, at their respective cores, telling their audiences that "American" and Chicano/a, heterosexual and homosexual, or "citizen" and "illegal immigrant," are in fact wholly other and in irreconcilable conflict with each other, in what other terms are those audiences left to think?

Though these questions may for now seem more theoretical, and thus rhetorical, in relation to Chicano/a literary study, the presence and consequences of the problem they indicate are not so hypothetical elsewhere. Other fields dominated by a paradigmatic binary logic, if not, in fact, an explicit ethics of resistance, have come under fire for just such a consistent position. For example, Linda McDowell, writing about the field of geography, explains how "in common with the other social sciences, binary categorizations structure geographical scholarship"; furthermore, she declares the task of a "feminist geography" to be the "tearing down and re-erecting [of] the structures" of this discipline, "the very ways in which we theorize and make connections between people and places" (11). In the task McDowell sets for herself and other feminist geographers, she points to the continued operation of binary structures—men/women, public/private, to name but two—as a situation to be redressed within the field of geography. Richard Maddox more directly engages with the problematics of resistance and its dominance within the "anthropological community." While noting the "laudable zeal" of scholars looking for "tactics of resistance" in the daily lives of those they studied, Maddox criticizes how "they often seemed to join together under the notion of 'resistance' a disparate array of discourses and dispositions," which "not only appeared to underestimate the forces operating to contain and incorporate counterhegemonic practices but also seemed to obviate the need for direct political action in some subtle way" (275–276). Here, Maddox specifically directs attention to how the dominance of resistance doubly runs counter to its aims: these efforts both underestimate the ways in which power can contain such assumed resistant practices, while also, in the idea that daily life is itself "resistant," short-circuit any more directly resistant or political action.

Aijaz Ahmad similarly objects to just such a circumvention of political action and, more generally, the kind of sweeping paradigm that resistance exemplifies, in his criticism of postcolonial literary/cultural theory. In relation to the former, Ahmad, more pointedly than Maddox, condemns post-

1960s theory as "institutionally domesticat[ing] the very forms of political dissent which the movements had sought to foreground" and displacing "activist culture with textual culture" (1). For Ahmad, the rise of poststructural theory extended "the centrality of reading as an appropriate form of politics" to the detriment of "a broadly Marxist politics" (3–4).

But it is in Ahmad's critique of the categorizations "Third World Theory" and "Third World Literature" that he demonstrates an affinity with those criticisms of resistance above. As he observes, the category of "Third World" simply inverts the "tradition/modernization binary in an indigenist direction so that tradition is said to be better for the Third World than modernist, allowing a defense of the most obscurantist positions in the name of a cultural nationalism" (9). Far from unsettling or destabilizing such a binary logic, this "inversion" simply deploys that logic in a different "direction," if you will. As in resistance, this "Third World" approach is limiting in its selection of and approach to texts. In the first case, as Ahmad explains, postcolonial texts written in English provide "one kind of archive for the metropolitan university to construe the textual formation of 'Third World Literature,'" but neglect the archive of works "in a number of indigenous languages as well" (78). And, for Ahmad, theorists read very narrowly within this category: "The preferred technique among cultural theorists . . . is to look at 'Third World' literary texts in terms always of their determination by the colonial encounter," and so ignoring their "determination" by class, gender, or "the needs of socialist cultural production" (92). Much of Ahmad's criticism of postcolonial literary theory—its sweeping categorization, pre-determined and determining archive or canon, and narrow interpretation—parallels the effect of resistance within U.S. multiethnic and Chicano/a literatures.

But a field even more identified as treating its subjects in predominantly resistant terms is the discipline of cultural studies. Two of its assessors, Winfried Fluck and Thomas Claviez, describe cultural studies in general as a "radical ideological critique of American cultural myths" through "approaches which focus on the critical role of ethnicity, race, gender and sexual preference in American culture" (x). In other words, Fluck and Claviez see the assigning to these differences a consistently "critical role" as putting them in opposition to hegemonic conceptions of American culture, in particular the myths about what is "American" or "America" that dominant U.S. society and culture perpetuate.

Donald Morton likewise identifies such resistance and challenge as the explicit domain of cultural studies. According to Morton, "cultural studies [has become] an intellectual practice aimed at dehierarchizing the gender, the racial, the ethnic, the sexual, and other binaries in which privilege has always been inscribed and which are taken for granted by traditional knowledges and forms of study" (27). Here, he makes it the "practice" of cultural studies to inscribe its subjects within a critical logic that is, at its heart, in opposition to and conflict with a hegemonic U.S. nation-state. To paraphrase Morton even more succinctly, cultural studies by nature inscribes its subjects within a logic of resistance.

Such critiques as those above spur Lawrence Grossberg to call for a transformation of the discipline: "[C]ultural studies needs to move beyond models of oppression, both the 'colonial model' of the oppressor and the oppressed and the 'transgression model' of oppression and resistance . . . . Both models of oppression seem not only inappropriate to the contemporary relations of power but also incapable of creating alliances" (355). Like those mentioned above, Grossberg too sees cultural studies as riven by such a binary logic, and he echoes McDowell in urging the field to alter the same.

But while these more sympathetic treatments call only for change, others are more strident in their critique of the inherent resistant logic of cultural studies. Morton, for instance, explains how cultural studies has been called out for reducing literature to simply one of many cultural practices that relate to our understanding of culture: "[L]iterature no longer has a special privilege when it is placed in conjunction with science, sports, music or any other elements of popular culture" (9). While the surface of this charge betrays an in-itself problematic elevation of literature above other cultural practices, it gestures toward a greater consequence. The paradigm of resistance reduces all cultural practices in assigning them the same relationship to and within culture. None is unique; rather, all are in conflict with dominant U.S. culture. Thus, the function of literature or any other practice has less to do with it *as* a unique practice in and of itself, and more with *how* it works within culture, a practice that is always the same. As a result, within cultural studies, "resistance is everywhere omnivore"; cultural studies scholars, according to Grant Farred, and echoing Maddox from earlier, have "expanded the definition of resistance to problematic lengths . . . , see[ing] working class and marginal communities' resistance in every aspect of their lives. So much so, in fact, that the field is able to identify challenge by oppressed groups in places that are at best unlikely or at worst, implausible" (Farred 86). Resistance thus becomes a kind of shell game. It is what cultural studies is always and only looking for and, thus, always and only finding.

Coinciding with these more acute criticisms against cultural studies are further-reaching "remedies" that bear particular relevance to the study of U.S. multiethnic and Chicano/a literatures. In the name of what they term more transcendent, humanistic values, critics like Richard Rorty and Frank Farrell turn cultural studies' emphasis into a rationale for abandoning it as a critical method. Rorty, for example, laments the current state of literary study, dominated (as he sees it) by the cultural studies model, as "depressing," "antiromantic," "immune to romantic enthusiasm," and devoid of "social hope" and "visions of a better future." Per Rorty, cultural studies has robbed the study of literature of its "romance and inspiration," replacing and "flattening" it with an inferior substitute: "professional competence and intellectual sophistication" (8–9, 12). His "remedy" for this problem is to refocus the study of literature on what he terms the "inspirational value" found in its great works: "[G]reat works of literature all, in the end, say the same thing—are great precisely because they do so. They inculcate the same eternal 'humanistic' values. They remind us of the same immutable features of human experience" (15). There is, of course, an obvious circularity in Rorty's position. We, as critics, should only talk about the "great" literature that reflects these "inspirational" values, and what makes specific literary texts "great" is that they reflect these values. But more chilling is Rorty's recourse to eternal and unchanging "human" values as the basis for literary and cultural study. In a similar vein, Farrell advocates a shift to how literature "allows for experiences important to the living out of a sophisticated and satisfying human life," such a concern being absent in his view from the cultural studies approach: "The cultural studies model holds that all representations are implicated in regimes of social power that are never innocent. . . . So any act of reading must not be neutral or confine itself to the 'literary' but rather must see itself as an intervention in these power processes, as an act of confirming or subverting . . . those cultural representations" (23, 24). In their plea for a return to the "good old days" of a transcendently humanistic literary study, these critics set cultural studies and its paradigmatic resistance in opposition to such immutable values.

The logic behind such a declaration is truly disturbing. In effect, the subjects that cultural studies emphasizes—for example, race, ethnicity, gender, class, sexuality—have no "human value." Farrell perhaps most explicitly throws this baby out with the bath water when he "grant[s] that texts can be usefully read in [the] manner" of cultural studies, but that doing so will "impoverish literary space without offering in return much assistance to those in need of social justice" (23). Though he acknowledges the presence of those who need such justice, his position is that, since cultural studies will not really do anything for them in reality—and has a deleterious effect on the study of literature—we really should stop talking about racial, ethnic, gender, class, and sexual justice(s) in relation to literature altogether. This sweeping claim poses a particular problem for the study of Chicano/a and U.S. multiethnic literature because it implicitly dismisses them. It also neglects what literature can and has done in relation to social justice, which is to effect change in the minds of its readers that can in turn lead to real, material action.[2]

That the same fault lines allowing these critiques of cultural studies exist within the fields of U.S. multiethnic and Chicano/a literatures should be similarly troubling. The dominance of resistance has been noted by multiple critics. Aranda Jr., for example, explicitly identifies "a 'resistance theory' paradigm" that "holds steadfast . . . , strengthened by the sweeping canonization of certain contemporary writers whose works challenged the racist, heterosexist, and other hegemonic foundations of U.S. society" (xxi). He points to resistance's sway in investigations of contemporary writers, citing the canonization of Alice Walker, Toni Morrison, and Audre Lorde, and others who reflect its logic. Aranda Jr. similarly implicates the entry into the canon of rediscovered writers like Zora Neale Hurston, Zitkala-Ša, and Americo Paredes in this promulgation of resistance: its logic similarly determines those earlier and obscured writers that get re-included into this canon. Parallel to Aranda Jr., W. Lawrence Hogue cites numerous contemporary writers—Morrison, Leslie Marmon Silko, N. Scott Momaday, Frank Chin, Toni Cade Bambara, and Paule Marshall—as problematic for how they define an ideology of "racial tradition" that casts racial communities as "cultures of resistance" (4). Formulated as such, Hogue goes on to argue, this racial tradition and its resistant emphasis has "caused certain sectors of the white American population to resist this emerging heterogeneity in the educational and cultural spheres and to attempt to restore to hegemony a codified version of high modernism that is mostly white, male, and upper middle class" (20). Hogue here anticipates precisely what the discussion of the critics of cultural studies should likewise allow us to see. As Akhil Gupta and James Ferguson similarly explain, resistance can "result in reconfirming or strengthening existing identities, ironically contributing to maintaining the status quo" (19). In this case, the dominance of resistance has, according to Hogue, led to a reassertion of those hegemonic values and attitudes it initially combated.

Similarly, both Aranda Jr. and Hogue identify specific consequences to the practice of literary study that result from resistance's emphasis. For the former, it is that the continued privileging of these writers and their narrative interferes with more "comparative and . . . integrated criti-

cal approaches" (Aranda Jr. xxi); for the latter, it is how these works exclude people of color from the experiences theorized as "modernity" and
"postmodernity" through how they construe racialized subjects as different—temporally, spatially, and ontologically—from subjects traditionally
classed as "modern" and "postmodern" (see Hogue 5–6). However, the
consequences of this dominance extend beyond what kind of scholarly approaches are tenable (or not so) under resistance, or within what theoretical constructs differently raced, gendered, sexed, or classed peoples can be
included. The "canon of resistance" and its accompanying logic foster an
understanding of contemporary U.S. culture that separates and distances
the experiences of peoples of difference from that culture. It encourages
readers—always and already—to think of these experiences, these cultures, and these peoples as in conflict with or opposition to U.S. culture,
never as a part of it.

As it is one subset of the U.S. multiethnic literary canon, Chicano/a literature and criticism having resistance at its head is perhaps not surprising.
The dominance of the resistance model further stems from the Chicano
Movement of the 1960s. As Manuel Gonzales explains, "The Chicano
Movement, with its emphasis on cultural regeneration, encouraged the
rise of a vibrant community of authors . . . and *determined their choice of
themes for years to come*" (252, italics added). Wilson Neate further details
the precise alliance between literary criticism and the Movement's cultural
nationalism. The latter "tended to evaluate whether a work constituted ac-
ceptable Chicano/a literature" on whether or not that text included specific elements deemed essential, including "an expression of anti-Anglo
sentiment and resistance to dominant Anglo culture" (12). Such a sentiment led to the designation of Chicano/a literature's "Big Three": . . . *y no
se lo tragó la tierra* by Tomás Rivera, *Bless Me, Ultima* by Rudolfo Anaya,
and *The Valley* by Rolando Hinojosa. "In all of them, despite the constant
contact with Anglo-American culture, the characters seem to exist in a
separate space. All three novels posit the possibility of an alternative other
space of Chicano existence in which the family and individual can survive as an ethnic entity" (Bruce-Novoa 123). Though initially these texts
posited a Chicano space as an alternative for survival, their ascendance
within Chicano/a literature has identified a Chicano/a space as *the* alternative; that is, Chicano/a identity and culture are wholly and only possible
separate from U.S. society.

These texts thus define the Chicano/a canon as one of resistance.
Such a conscription of the canon allows Ramón Saldívar to characterize
Chicano/a literature as continuing "to define itself in opposition and resis-

tance to mainstream social, historical, economic and cultural modalities" (3). It similarly allows Marcial González (much more critically, it should be noted) to claim that "[w]ith borderlands theory, almost anything can be considered an act of resistance" (283), a statement that again resonates with those earlier from Maddox and Farred concerning the ubiquity of resistance. These statements raise the implications cited earlier: when resistance is so pervasive a narrative paradigm that any act—regardless of sociopolitical circumstances or material context—becomes an act of resistance, then the literary text loses its particular significance as a cultural intervention. Conversely, equating actual sociopolitical actions to the aesthetic goings-on of a literary work is similarly flattening.

Chicano/a literary criticism evidences such a tendency to flatten out both the literary and sociopolitical spheres in multifarious ways. It can be found, as González describes, in scholars' inclination to romanticize their own cross-cultural readings as a form of border crossing, which "tends to desensitize the horror of the real conditions of the border" by reducing a "matter of life and death" to "a luxury or an act of resistance" (284). The emphasis in Chicano/a criticism on the borderlands, particularly as a kind of liminal or hybrid space, results in another such flattening. Take for example, *Border Matters'* concept of the "transfrontera contact zone" (adapted from Mary Louise Pratt's own "contact zone"). The text describes this zone as the "social space of subaltern encounters, the Janus-faced border line in which peoples geopolitically forced to separate themselves now negotiate with one another and manufacture new relations, hybrid cultures, and multiple-voiced aesthetics" (Saldívar, *Border Matters* 13–14). The transfrontera contact zone evinces a contradictory "condition of perpetual liminality" (González 280). The actual interactions embodied by or contained in this space all become evidence of its hybridity or liminality, just as all "Third World Literature" is determined by the "colonial encounter," according to Ahmad, giving them an essential sameness that flattens and/or ignores their particular and specific material context and reality.

These examples demonstrate how the same vulnerabilities that have been turned against cultural studies exist within the field of Chicano/a literary criticism. These vulnerabilities are products of how the resistance model has dominated and furthermore encouraged us to equate the aesthetic construction that is the literary text with sociopolitical or material action. Such a move impoverishes not only the act and implications of reading, but also sociopolitical action itself. In order to avoid such consequences, we must maintain a distinction between the literary and the ma-

terial and recognize that the literary's particular intervention into the material or the cultural is through the reader — and his/her mind — and based
on a text's specific aesthetic workings. We must look at how a text's own
particular form(s), style(s), genre(s), storyworld(s), and construction(s) inculcate its judgments and values and, in a dynamic process, affect a reader's
own beliefs, judgments, and values.[3] What, as a consequence, becomes
necessary is an approach or methodology that calls attention to these workings of the text and their cognitive effects. For that, this study turns to the
concept of cognitive mapping.

## TEXTUAL ETHICS AND
## COGNITIVE MAPPING

The term "ethics" has already occurred in this discussion, as
I have referred to resistance as both a paradigm and an ethics. What, then,
is resistance as an ethics?

Ethics, and ethical criticism, has become, in recent years, more and
more of a fashion within literary criticism. However, Adam Newton points
out that ethics and the ethical have always been a part of the novel's development: "[E]thics closely informed the novel's early development as a discourse both accessory . . . and internal . . . to narrative texts. Novels trained
ethical sensibility . . . [and] narrators schooled their readership in the correct evaluation of and response to character and moral situation" (9). The
novel in this sense is inherently didactic. It "trains" one's ethical sense; it
guides how one should react to the characters and situations represented.
Implicit within this description is the notion of a text's ethics being particular to that text and what it represents. The novel trains the reader how to
respond to the specific and unique characters and situations it represents to
him or her. Newton's description does not assign to literature the uphold-
ing of an ethics external to it. Instead, a text defines its ethics through its
storyworld, its events, and its characters' actions and interactions with that
world's characters, situations, spaces, and places.

Contemporary ethical criticism, however, has at times too much imposed just such an external ethics onto a text. In these cases, ethical criticism boils down to judging which works of literature are "good" or "great"
precisely because they uphold a particular ethical or moral position. Rorty
and Farrell, for example, evidence just such a compensatory approach in
their treatments. Jeffrey F. Folks even more explicitly advocates such an
approach: "The basis for an ethics of literature is the recognition that a

shared knowledge of moral conduct exists, that this ethical knowledge is necessary to the survival of human societies, and that *the function of literature is to hold this knowledge clearly before our sight*" (6, italics added). Here, the ethics precedes the text. Folks assumes a universal "moral conduct" that literature must reflect. This function then becomes the standard by which critics deem texts worthy of literary study. The specific texts selected are "important examples of ethical art" because for Folks (who draws from John Gardner's *On Moral Fiction*), they allow "the 'true critic . . . to show what is healthy, in other words, sane, in human seeing, thinking, and feeling, and to point out what is not'" (18). Like Rorty and Farrell, Folks resorts to an assumed universal of what is "human." Substitute Folks's term "important" for "great" or "inspirational," and we have an argument identical to Rorty's. Furthermore, Folks's kind of ethical criticism not only determines what texts get read, but also the critics of those texts. The "true critic" is one who presents literature in this ethically or morally compensatory role.

As should be clear already, this study does not practice this kind of ethical criticism. It does not treat the ethical as a judgment of which texts are "good" or "great" or "important." Nor does it look at them as morally compensatory. Instead, the term "ethics" and the "ethical dimension" of a literary text is something more "descriptive" rather than a "dogmatically prescriptive or doctrinaire form of reading" (Davis and Womack x). A text's ethics are the particular and specific ethical values or meanings encoded in and conveyed through its aesthetic constructions. In other words, texts— including their storyworlds, their characters, their events—communicate unique values and meanings that should not be used as criteria for judging their moral value. All texts, then, are ethical—not in a morally judgmental sense, but in the sense that all texts have an ethical import in what they do. They ask us to judge, value, and think about the specific issues they raise, including issues of cultural differences related to race, ethnicity, gender, class, sexuality, and more. As a result, ethical criticism is necessarily an interactive and dynamic process between the text and its reader. We "engage [texts] in their concrete, formal, narrative particularity. One faces a text as one might face a person, having to confront the claims raised by that very immediacy, an immediacy of contact, not of meaning" (Newton 11). We therefore confront and are confronted with a text's individual, subjective values. Interacting with a text ethically means looking at it as part of this interactive and dynamic process between two unique subjects—the text and the reader—rather than the latter interacting with the morally reified and ethically conscripted former.

When this study refers, then, to resistance as an ethics, it means to indicate two things. First, that resistance is an ethical position regarding cultural interactions and differences communicated by Chicano/a texts. Such an ethics can be conveyed, for instance, through the spatial arrangements of a text's storyworld, as will be shown in the next chapter's discussion of Rudolfo Anaya's *Bless Me, Ultima.* The ethics of resistance can also be conveyed through the aesthetic or formal arrangements of the text itself. Rolando Hinojosa's "Sometimes It Just Happens That Way; That's All," likewise discussed in the next chapter, is an example of precisely this. Second, besides being an ethical position encoded within specific texts, resistance has become *the* ethics of Chicano/a literary study, as well as of U.S. multiethnic literature in general. As was mentioned earlier, the defining of Chicano/a literature through such texts as Anaya's *Ultima* and Hinojosa's *The Valley* has also defined their ethics as *the* ethics of Chicano/a literature. Consequently, resistance's tendency to impose itself on the readings of Chicano/a and U.S. multiethnic works can obscure other possible positionings and the texts that encode them.

As a way to expand our readings and interpretations of Chicano/a literary texts beyond (though, again, not exclusive of) resistance, I propose an aesthetic or methodology of cognitive mapping. Cognitive mapping has grown in its appeal and usage since its origination in the psychological work of Edward Tolman in 1948. The approach was later adopted and adapted by Kevin Lynch for his study of physical urban environments, *The Image of the City* (1960). Cognitive mapping as it is practiced today stems from Lynch's application of the concept to his subjects' impressions of three urban downtown areas: Boston, Jersey City, and Los Angeles. What he posited from their responses was a connection between subjects' inability to mentally map their physical surroundings and their feelings of disconnection, confusion, and even alienation. As he states, "[To] become completely lost is perhaps a rare experience for most people in the modern city. . . . [B]ut let the mishap of disorientation once occur, and the sense of anxiety and even terror that accompanies it reveals to us how closely it is linked to our sense of balance and well-being" (4). The ability to hold a mental representation or understanding of the physical environment—a "cognitive map"—is crucial in Lynch to our ability to position ourselves and make our way through that environment.

This effort to understand or "mentally map" space has since been translated to the study of literary space. To cognitively map a text is to put together its storyworld and that world's meaning and significance from the cues provided through description, character movements and interactions, events, and so on. As applied to literature, cognitive mapping has predominantly occurred in one of two forms oriented externally to the text. Marie-Laure Ryan describes the first such application, its "literal definition," as the generation of a "mental model of spatial relations" (215); in other words, the mental mapping, by the reader, of physical location within a text's storyworld. "[M]ental models of narrative space are centered on the characters and they grow out of them. . . . Out of the movements of characters . . . we construct a global vision . . . that enables us to situate events" (236–237). Ryan demonstrates such an application by having her subjects graphically convey where things are located in the world of Gabriel García Márquez's *Chronicle of a Death Foretold*: what buildings and specific locations were on the town plaza and which were near the river; of the locations on the plaza, which were on the north side, the south side, east and west; and what specific locations were placed away from the town center. This phenomenological approach is prefigured by Gabriel Zoran who, though averring that textual "space is not a neutral material just existing in the [textual] world" as setting or backdrop, still emphasizes the mapping of such worlds in physical terms. He imagines the reader navigating the textual world based on cues relating to its "horizontal structure"—defined as "relationships such as inside and outside, far and near, center and periphery, city and village, etc."—and its "vertical organization" of "up-down" (322, 333). In both cases, the reader's cognitive map yields a literal translation of location within a text's storyworld.

The second application of cognitive mapping to the literary text proceeds by way of analogy and values the text's space for how it reflects an extant reality. Fredric Jameson is perhaps the most famous example of this approach. He applies cognitive mapping to "the realm of social structure . . . in our historical moment, . . . the totality of class relations on a global [or] multinational scale" ("Cognitive Mapping" 353). The result is to cast the "spatial peculiarities of postmodernism" and its associated works as "expressions of a new and historically original dilemma . . . that involves our insertion as individual subjects into a multidimensional set of radically discontinuous realities" (351). Echoing Jameson's approach is Brian McHale's explanation of the "system of structures *en abyme*" in Cervantes's *Don Quixote* as reflecting "the greater Mediterranean's unity-in-diversity." For McHale, then, *Don Quixote* serves as "a cognitive map of the Mediterranean world" and therein lies that map's value ("*En abyme*" 201). Like Jameson's cognitive map of a discontinuous postmodern reality, the map's and text's significance lies only in how it directly reflects an external reality.

Drawing on these externally oriented applications, this study asserts that cognitive mapping can be applied internally to the text as well. The function of textual space is not only to tell us where things "are" in a storyworld, nor only to reflect an extant reality. The literary text can itself be seen as a cognitive map. To put it another way: rather than looking at the text as a space to be (cognitively) mapped, we interact with the text as a cognitive map. Richard Bjornson explains how "[a]ll works of literature must have had a similar origin [that] triggers an individual's desire to create an imaginary space . . . subject to his or her control. This desire impels aspiring writers to devise plans or strategies for achieving their goal" (56). Though Bjornson perhaps too much emphasizes the writer's "control" of the text's imaginary space, he calls attention to what prior efforts to cognitively map texts elide: that the literary text is shaped and arranged to "map" and thus communicate a particular "goal," which can be associated with a text's meaning or ethics. The world mapped by a literary work encodes that text's specific ethical positionings. It is this map that we as readers encounter, not a physical one but rather an aesthetic and ethical one. Thus, the storyworld of a text should not be treated only in a strictly phenomenological sense that conflates it with real or physical space; nor should its value only lie in its reflection of extant realities. In how texts "embody a type of knowledge," they communicate this knowledge to the reader through their various objective characteristics (Bjornson 57).

By paying attention to how a text "maps" its particular world and the ethics inherent within that world, we can begin to open ourselves up to not only those texts communicating a well-established ethics such as resistance, but also to texts that present entirely different conceptions of cultural differences and interactions through their constructions.

## MAPPING ETHICS IN CONTEMPORARY CHICANO/A FICTION

The application of cognitive mapping to the Chicano/a novels and stories discussed in the coming chapters will allow us to perceive how they encode particular ethical positionings into and through their storyworlds. These narrative and ethical paradigms, explicated through the close readings of the works by Rudolfo Anaya, Rolando Hinojosa, John Rechy, Helena María Viramontes, Alfredo Véa, Ana Castillo, and Arturo Islas, concern the relationship between the peoples and cultures of difference they represent and dominant U.S. society. The initial phases of this discussion will focus on two primary methods by which these authors inscribe the particular values and judgments into their storyworlds and communicate them to their readers.

The first method involves characters' relationships to and/or inter-actions with particularly coded or valued places within the storyworld. Linda McDowell explains how our actual built environment encodes "[e]xplicit and implicit rules and regulations about whose bodies are per-mitted in which spaces" (166), and the same is true of fictional spaces and places. Wesley A. Kort in particular describes how the "language of space begins to dominate character and plot when it determines the characters that are likely to appear in certain locations or the kinds of events that occur" (16). Such interactions can also determine a text's ethical import. For example, in placing restrictions, limitations, and conditions on the characters who can inhabit a particular place, textual space also places a value on them. More specifically, characters' associations with specific storyworld institutions symbolic of dominant U.S. society position them in relation to that society and its values.

Such a representation occurs in Denise Chávez's *The Last of the Menu Girls* (1986). Chávez presents her protagonist, Rocío Esquibel, in conjunc-tion with places symbolizing dominant U.S. society—the Drama Factory in "Space is a Solid" and the Altavista Memorial Hospital in the collection/novel's titular story/chapter—and its restrictive effects on peoples of dif-ference, which result from its idealized, homogenous U.S. identity. Nita Wembley, a benefactress of both the Factory and (for a time) Rocío, gives explicit voice to just such a desire: "If you're American, marry an Ameri-can. If you're colored, marry a colored. If you're Chinese, marry a Chinese . . . . None of this other stuff now" (101). Besides her opposition to misce-genation, Wembley also demarcates people of color outside the category of "American." None of that "other stuff" makes its way into her idealization of this cultural identity. The hospital is as limiting, if more subtle in its con-veyance of this fact. Rocío volunteers in this place that is both a space "of order . . . [an] environment of restriction" and a "place of white women, [and] whiter men with square faces" (17). Thus, in this space and its descrip-tions, the novel associates white/Anglo society with feelings of restriction and order from which Rocío is just as clearly differentiated and separated, a fact indicated most clearly by how, upon first entering the hospital, she sees herself reduced to "a frightened girl in a black skirt and white blouse standing near the stairwell to the cafeteria" (17). In both places, Chávez positions Rocío as separate from the dominant U.S. society they symbolize.

Both locations furthermore inscribe Rocío within a subordinate posi-tion to that dominant society. Her job in the Factory's Costume Shop is backstage; she is "responsible for washing the actors' clothes and costumes" and "extricate[es] once-starched shirts and pairs of brown knickers, and a few dark socks" from the male actors' dressing room (104). Rocío does not get to appear onstage; she is relegated to the back of the house, a fact made abundantly clear, to both her and the reader, by her boss Charene when Rocío oversteps these boundaries in her relationship with Mrs. Wembley: "Do you know that Mrs. Wembley's one of the theatre's patrons . . . and . . . can do and say anything she damn well pleases around here . . . ? That means you better the fuck get your priorities and problems and shit together and stop screwing around with members of the 100 Club" (131–132). Not only is Rocío's subservient position to Nita Wembley and the wealthy Anglo society to which she belongs reinforced in this tirade, but so too is the fact that Rocío is not free to do or say "anything she damn well pleases." As for the hospital, it inscribes Rocío within a subordinate position through the identity it imposes as a condition of her entry into this space and the society it represents. Rocío literally encounters the image/ role that will allow her—as ethnic other—to enter into this space: "I stared up at a painting of a dark-haired woman in a stiff nurse's cap and grey tunic, tending to men in old fashioned service uniforms. There was a beauty in that woman's face, whoever she was. I saw myself in her, helping all of mankind, forgetting and absolving all my own sick, my own dying, especially relatives, all of them so far away, removed" (17). The painting Rocío observes and describes here is of Florence Nightingale. Rocío's "fantasy of becoming the etherealized figure that dispenses benediction to a suffering humanity" is also a fantasy that abstracts her out of her ethnic identity (Anderson 239). Such an abstraction is the condition upon her belonging and functioning within not only this space but also the society of which it is an institution. Interestingly enough, she must trade one stereotypically subordinate position—"ethnic other"—for another, "woman tending man." In either case, and even perhaps through the conflation of both, the space of the hospital, like the Drama Factory before it, inscribes Rocío within a subordinate role. In presenting these places and Rocío's interactions with them, Chávez clearly "maps" out their particular values and Rocío's position toward them.

Second, a text's descriptions of spaces are also sources of its ethics and values, making them not only descriptions but also ethical characterizations. A particularly striking example of such is to be found in the opening paragraph of Anaya's *Bless Me, Ultima.* Here, the text presents us with an idealized and idyllic image of the llano that serves as its primary landscape:

> Ultima came to stay with us the summer I was almost seven.
> When she came the beauty of the llano unfolded before my
> eyes, and the gurgling waters of the river sang to the hum
> of the turning earth. The magical time of childhood stood
> still, and the pulse of the living earth pressed its mystery into
> my living blood. She took my hand, and the silent, magic
> powers she possessed made beauty from the raw, sun-baked
> llano, the green river valley, and the blue bowl which was the
> white sun's home. My bare feet felt the throbbing earth and
> my body trembled with excitement. Time stood still, and it
> shared with me all that had been, and all that was to come. (1)

In a variety of ways, this passage places a positive value on the space of the llano. It casts this landscape as a living being through the choice of such active verbs and gerunds as "unfolded," "gurgling," and "throbbing." There is a sense of warmth throughout the passage, not only in the fact that it is summer but also through the particular description of this space as "sun-baked." There is also an emphasis on the vivid colors of the llano, especially in the latter portion of this paragraph. It mentions the "green river," the "blue bowl" that is the sky, and the "white sun," all of which paints and further characterizes this space as vibrant. The effect the llano has on the novel's young narrator, Antonio, further feeds into the ascription of positive value to this space. It exposes him to the power of the earth. It is magical. It not only causes time to stand still, but also opens all of time to Antonio's perception. In sum, this opening paragraph crafts the reader's perception of the llano and the values it embodies. As will be shown in the following chapter's discussion of Anaya's novel as a whole, these positive images of the llano are ethically inscribed within the text's larger world and how it creates a stark contrast and distance between the space of the llano (and its inhabitants) and Anglo-American society.

In sum, the literary world is a constructed world. It is shaped and arranged to reflect and communicate particular values and ethics. Because of its nature, literary space should not be treated in a phenomenological or objective sense; that is, to conflate textual space with real, social space (and vice versa) is to assume equivalence between social reality and textual worlds and reduce both. Literary space is objective in the sense that there are objective aspects of how it is constructed and how it constructs its world: how it is narrated, how it is stylistically presented, how it is generically identified, how its world and spaces are described, and how its characters interact with that world and its spaces. We are not dealing with, reacting to, and evaluating objective spaces when we encounter texts. We are coming to and encountering a space that is subjective in its objective aspects. That is, we are coming to a text that is already constructed with particular, subjective values and ethics within its imagined world and textual arrangements. It thus has it own conception or understanding of the social world and culture that it attempts to communicate through its imagined one. And it is this imaginative, ethical space that we, as readers and scholars, are obligated to decode.

Each of the subsequent chapters is an effort to do precisely that: to demonstrate how each text "maps" and communicates particular ethical positionings in regard to cultural difference. The works at the center of this study—Ana Castillo's *So Far from God* and *Sapogonia*; Arturo Islas's *La Mollie and the King of Tears*; John Rechy's *The Miraculous Day of Amalia Gómez*; Alfredo Véa's *La Maravilla, The Silver Cloud Café*, and *Gods Go Begging*; Helena María Viramontes's "The Cariboo Café"—were all published in the final two decades of the twentieth century, a point at which previous challenges to the Chicano/a canon had already forced it to expand beyond the narrow confines of the male-centered and heterosexist identity and experience noted previously. Castillo, Viramontes, and Rechy would be three prominent figures in this effort, and now-seminal texts like Castillo's *So Far from God* and Viramontes's "The Cariboo Café" are emblematic of its success. But these texts also embody the ways in which other limitations owing to the still-predominant ethics of the canon still impinge upon Chicano/a writers and specific texts, such as Rechy's *Amalia Gómez*. Writers further on the canon's periphery (if even there), such as Islas and Véa, further demonstrate the limiting effects of the canon's basis in resistance.

What these works do in particular is complicate the understanding of cultural interaction guiding the Chicano/a canon, resistance. This established understanding is the subject of Chapter 1, which analyzes Anaya's *Bless Me, Ultima* and Hinojosa's "Sometimes It Just Happens That Way; That's All" for how they "map" resistance within the spaces of storyworld and text, respectively, and so facilitate the shaping power of that ethos. Beginning with Chapter 2, the texts being analyzed offer alternative conceptions and understandings of cultural presence and interaction within the U.S. nation-space and so represent important ethical expansions to the Chicano/a canon. John Rechy's *The Miraculous Day of Amalia Gómez* and

Helena María Viramontes's "The Cariboo Café," both of which are set in Los Angeles during the latter part of the twentieth century, are the first such examples. Both texts have been (mis)read in terms consistent with resistance, showing a further permutation of that paradigm's shaping power. Both works are, rather, constructed in various ways to communicate what I term a "narrative of persistence." That is, both texts speak to (if not depict) cultural differences coming to be an enduring presence within the specific metropolis of Los Angeles and the larger U.S. nation-space and society.

Chapter 3 continues the discussion of persistence in two works set in the rural American Southwest during the mid- and later twentieth century respectively, Alfredo Véa's *La Maravilla* and Ana Castillo's *So Far from God*. These novels go a step further than Rechy and Viramontes in how they present racial and cultural, as well as gender and sexual, differences not only as a presence within the U.S. nation-space but also as a part of and participatory within its culture and society. Furthermore, inhering within both texts' representations is a cosmopolitan ethos that challenges and complicates reduced understandings of such differences. The ontological irreducibility gestured toward in these texts is the crux of the second narrative understanding dealt with in this study, what I term "transformation." The differences represented in these texts' storyworlds, and often mirrored in their narrative constructions and generic conflations, seek to disrupt comfortable and reductive categorizations of differently raced, cultured, gendered, classed, and sexed peoples and spaces that exist within their imagined worlds and parallel the same in the extant world to which they refer.

Chapter 4 begins the effort to map this transformation by mapping the dimensions of Castillo's *Sapogonia* and Arturo Islas's *La Mollie and the King of Tears*. These two novels focus on the consciousnesses of specific Chicana and Chicano protagonists who, over the course of their narratives, transform (or fail to, as in the case of Castillo's male protagonist) themselves from such limited and problematic understandings of difference. These transformations, particularly that of Louie Mendoza in Islas's posthumous *La Mollie*, parallel what the text works to facilitate in its reader. The final chapter concludes this study with an analysis of Véa's second and third novels, *The Silver Cloud Café* and *Gods Go Begging*. These two texts explicitly "speak," in their imagined storyworlds, to the challenge of irreducibility that forms the basis of the narrative of transformation. They furthermore parallel those worlds with a similar irreducibility of text in their conflations of times, spaces, genres, narratives, and/or styles; they thus "push [the reader] to question the traditional and often limiting categorization of his or her experiences of reality" (Aldama, *Postethnic Narrative Criticism* 28). As the Conclusion argues, including these texts and their narrativized understandings of cultural differences alongside that of resistance within the Chicano/a literary canon is important, particularly for how they may speak more usefully to current sociopolitical debates such as immigration reform and gay marriage, which center on a rhetoric and politics of similarity, rather than those of identity-in-difference.

## ONE

*Mapping Resistance in Rudolfo Anaya's*
Bless Me, Ultima *and Rolando Hinojosa's*
*"Sometimes It Just Happens That Way;*
*That's All"*

Resistance hinges on viewing differently raced or differ-
ently ethnic (as well as, for example, differently gendered, sexed, or classed)
peoples and communities as opposed to, in conflict with, and distant from
U.S. society. Implicit within this is a view of these cultures—both hegemonic and marginalized—as homogenous, centered entities. In the specific case of Chicano/a literature, resistance promulgates a view of Chi-
canos/as as a wholly homogenous culture, wholly separate from a similarly
homogenous Anglo U.S. mainstream. Chicano/a culture represents one
state of being (ontology) and/or way of knowing (epistemology), while the
U.S. mainstream represents another completely different ontology and
epistemology. Texts, then, that "map" such a discourse within their storyworlds imagine and construct those worlds in similar terms. That is, the
way specific culturally representative places are described or characterized
and/or characters' relationships to such spaces and places communicate
the sense of Chicano/a and Anglo culture as ontologically and epistemologically homogenous and separate.

Why and how, then, do Chicano/a texts "map" resistance? Answering
the "why" is Chicano/a literature's aforementioned complicity with the
ideologies of the Chicano Movement in the 1960s and 70s. As noted in
the Introduction, Manuel Gonzales and Wilson Neate describe the Chicano Movement as based in an ideology of nationalist resistance. This ideology is exhibited in the third paragraph of "El Plan Espiritual de Aztlán," a
Movement manifesto, which rhetorically unites Chicanos in the "struggle
against the foreigner 'Gabacho,' who exploits our riches and destroys our
culture" (1). And, again like the earlier-cited Juan Bruce-Novoa, Aureliano
Maria DeSoto explains how Chicano/a literature and literary studies became an arm of this resistant effort. She writes, "One of the primary goals
of early Chicana/o Studies was the canonization of a body of literature that
reflected the goals of the Chicano Movement and its radical principles of

cultural nationalism" (43). Primary amongst those goals, and paralleling the Movement's nationalist aims, was its definition of the Chicano/a subject as "antiassimilationist, resistant, and oriented towards an introspective, community-based notion of subjectivity and identity" (43). That is, the Chicano/a subject was, on the one hand, rooted in Chicano/a culture, community, and history while, simultaneously, being placed in opposition and resistance toward a U.S. Anglo society and culture. This sociopolitical definition of the Chicano/a subject was thus given representation in those literary works of the early Chicano/a literary canon.

And as two of the shaping authors and texts of this canon, Rudolfo Anaya's *Bless Me, Ultima* (1972) and Rolando Hinojosa's "Sometimes It Just Happens That Way; That's All" from *Estampas del valle y otras obras/ The Valley* (1972/1983) aptly exemplify how the early canonical texts reflected the aims and values of the Chicano Movement. In doing so, they likewise "map" resistance. Anaya's novel, which focuses on the development and maturation of its youthful narrator and protagonist, Antonio Márez, is ontological in its emphasis. That is, the novel presents its New Mexican Chicano/a community as a centered and complete-unto-itself way of being, one that is then opposed to not only U.S. Anglo society but also the larger world in general. Hinojosa's short work, on the other hand, opposes Chicano/a and Anglo as different epistemologies. Through the story's various testimonies concerning the murder of Ernesto Tamez at the hands of Baldemar Cordero, Hinojosa renders these two cultural positions as wholly separate ways of knowing or understanding reality. Furthermore, the story is constructed so as to value the understanding associated with the Chicano/a characters, just as Anaya clearly values the Chicano/a community he creates around Antonio, over what else exists in the texts' worlds. Not only then do both works create these entirely separate Chicano/a "spaces" but they also value that separation and, in this, evidence resistance, promoting its ethics as an understanding of the social reality of the contemporary United States.

## ONTOLOGICAL OPPOSITION: THE WORLDS AND SPACES OF ANAYA'S *BLESS ME, ULTIMA*

The end of the previous chapter dealt with the opening paragraph of Anaya's *Bless Me, Ultima* and its characterization of the llano as a living, warm, magical space, particularly to the novel's seven-year-old narrator/protagonist Antonio Márez. This characterization also features in the novel's mapping of resistance. The town of Guadalupe, around which much of the novel's action occurs, "is set apart from the greater New Mexican landmass by a river which encircles it" (Kanoza 161). Similarly circumscribed away from the rest of the novel's storyworld are this space and its Chicano/a community. Contrasting the llano's positive coding is the negative value ascribed to the rest of the novel's world. Both U.S. Anglo society and the outside world appear as depredatory toward the space of the llano and destructive to Chicano/a subjectivity. World War II, Anglo incursions into the llano, and the town of Guadalupe, with its specific institutions of school and church, consistently contrast the imagined space of the llano with the world they represent. Simultaneously, the novel values the cultural community identified with the llano over that elsewhere. As Theresa Kanoza states, the "sacred space" and "spiritual presence" of the llano functions in "a world where the Anglo is of little consequence to its . . . Chicano characters" (160). However, the reverse of this is likewise true. The Chicano/a cultural sphere is distinct from and of little consequence to the larger world of the novel. The resistant spatial poetics of Anaya's storyworld, in imagining the Chicano/a community as such radical alterity to both its imagined U.S. nation-space and world, encourage the reader to view its Chicano/a characters and culture as temporally and spatially distant and thus as an anomalous presence within both nation and world.

Factoring further into the novel's "mapping" of resistance is its status as an example of the literary mode of the bildungsroman. In his *A Glossary of Literary Terms*, M. H. Abrams defines this mode as focusing on "the development of the protagonist's mind and character, in the passage from childhood through varied experiences — and often through a spiritual crisis — into maturity, which usually involves recognition of one's identity and role in the world" (193). Antonio Márez's transition from childhood innocence to adult maturity is something for which Anaya's novel has been both celebrated and criticized. Kanoza, for example, praises the novel for showing, through Antonio's maturation, that such does not "[necessitate] exclusionary choices between competing options, but that wisdom and experience allow one to look beyond difference to behold unity" (159). Other critics, as summarized by Marta Caminero-Santangelo, have problematized *Bless Me, Ultima*'s evocation of this literary mode, particularly for how it makes the novel "driven by issues of personal identity that do not seem connected to the larger social and identity issues at the heart of the Chicano movement of the 1960s and early 1970s" (115).

When looked at in conjunction with the novel's ethics of resistance, the bildungsroman in *Bless Me, Ultima* actually subverts both its prior celebration and criticism. A similarly celebratory stance as Kanoza's is offered in Debra B. Black's opening paragraph, a paean to the greatness of Anaya's novel:

> *Bless Me, Ultima* (1972) . . . is a novel that at times sweeps across the mind of the reader with prose that sings with the music of poetry; at times it fascinates the reader with the rich-ness of the ethnic history of Chicano culture, and at times it creates nostalgia for the innocence of youth and the charge to find again one's own identity. Not only is it a novel that contains a rich panorama of visual imagery as it describes the New Mexico landscape of the 1940s, but it is also a novel of realistic concepts about life and living that face ordinary and not-so-ordinary people. (146)

Besides, by the end of the passage, abstracting the novel outside of its ethnopolitical context in ways that Rorty et al. would find appealing, Black, like Kanoza, ignores that the great "unity," "richness," and "panorama" of *Bless Me, Ultima* is wholly circumscribed within its imagined Chicano/a space and community. In doing so, rather than diverting from the social and identity issues of its time, *Bless Me, Ultima* rather replicates them in its telling of Antonio's *bildung*. The novel's mode does not neglect the social and identity issues of the Chicano Movement. Instead, Antonio's *bildung* reaffirms the resistant politics and ethics of the Movement. The "mature" Antonio at the end of the novel is a self completely centered within the space of the llano and thus wholly isolated and distant from U.S. Anglo culture and society and the rest of the world. The novel's explicit valuing of this position, and thus of the end of Antonio's *bildung*, feeds into its re-sistance, encouraging again the reader to similarly view Chicano/a identity and subjectivity as something homogenous and isolated—and thus anoma-lous—within both nation and world.

Within his immediate environment of the llano, Antonio Márez finds himself at the center of various spiritual and philosophical conflicts. The various "sides" of these battles each seek to define in their terms Antonio's identity and destiny. For example, Antonio must deal with the competing ancestral influences represented by his parents. His father "desir[es] for him the free-spirited vaquero life of the Márez," while his mother hopes "he will choose the quiet agricultural life of the Luna" (R. Saldívar 110). Similarly, Antonio feels himself pulled between the teachings of the Catho-lic Church devoutly followed by his mother, and the nature-centered practices and beliefs associated with Ultima's *curandismo* and the legend of the golden carp. By the end of the novel, Antonio decides that he will take all of these influences and combine them, as he declares to his father: "Take the llano and the river valley, the moon and the sea, God and the golden carp—and make something new" (Anaya 261). With this declaration, the novel imagines Antonio as not only making something new out of the collapse of these binarily opposed beliefs and identities but also *being* something new.

However, despite this seeming subversion of his world's philosophical and ethical divisions, a much larger division persists throughout the novel to its end: the division between the space of the llano and the rest of the novel's world. *Bless Me, Ultima* is set during the 1940s, specifically during and following World War II. Rámon Saldívar claims that this allows the novel "to capture ... a critical and complex transition period in the literary-cultural history of the Southwest: the simultaneous existence within Chicano communities of pre-Columbian myths, beliefs, legends, and superstitions, and mid-twentieth century technological, literate, and mass-media culture" (108). However, though historically the novel may be set at such a juncture, its representation of its New Mexican Chicano/a community elides its existence. Far from the sort of technological, media-permeated space Saldívar imagines, Guadalupe and the llano are profoundly rural and pastoral spaces. The "paradoxical" nature of this space, which for Saldívar allows "pre-capitalist social formations" to coexist "within contemporary mass-market economies and capitalist societies" (108), though it may be historically or temporally appropriate, is simply not imagined within the novel's storyworld. Far from allowing such a "paradoxical space" to serve as setting, *Bless Me, Ultima* privileges the temporality and spatiality of those pre-Columbian, pre-capitalist social formations found on the llano, distancing them, spatially and ethically, from the contemporaneous social formations of both its larger nation and world.

The novel accomplishes and reinforces this division on both a global and local level. It first divides the llano from the rest of the world and U.S. Anglo society through its treatment of World War II, during and after which the novel takes place, and the historical incursions of Anglos. Both are presented as depredatory and destructive to the space of the llano and the subjectivity of its Chicano/a inhabitants. Linked to these forces is the town from which the llano is literally separated by a bridge. The town too is distinct from the llano, particularly as a space of sin and moral turpitude that contrasts the llano's perfect morality. Further contrasting the town from the llano are its twinned institutions of school and church, both of which Antonio attends. Located within the town, they initially induce fear in Antonio; even though his initial fear may pass, the descriptions of both places continue this negative characterization. Thus, there is another unity that exists within the world of *Bless Me, Ultima:* a unity among world, nation, and town as ethically corrupt and contrasting the pseudo-utopian space of the llano.

Though World War II serves as a "backdrop of death" in Anaya's novel (R. Saldívar 109), the actual treatment of this event diffuses the connection of the llano and its characters to it. Specifically, the war's treatment absolves the novel's primary community from any responsibility for the war and, in that, removes this community from its larger world. For instance, the war is never actually called "World War II"; rather, it is named as "the war of the Japanese and the Germans" or "this war of the Germans and the Japanese" (Anaya 52). Such labeling makes clear that this war is not a war of the novel's characters. It is a war of other places and other peoples, not of those in this text, even if their sons are taken away in its name.

Later in the novel, Antonio's narration serves to similarly separate its inhabitants from the creation of the atomic bomb, despite its very tangible effects on the llano: "The spring dust storms of the llano continued, and I heard many grown-ups blame the harsh winter and the sandstorms of spring on the new bomb that had been made to end the war. 'The atomic bomb,' they whispered, 'a ball of white heat beyond the imagination, beyond hell.'" Antonio continues, "They compete with God, they disturb the seasons, they seek to know more than God Himself. In the end, that knowledge they seek will destroy us all" (200). Though they scapegoat the bomb for the damage it does to the llano, the people of the llano still see it emanating from people other than themselves. The repeated use of "they" makes this clear: whoever created the bomb, and in that act challenged God and upset nature, it was not them. Interestingly, though Antonio similarly describes how "Man was not made to know so much," it is clear that that "man" is different from themselves (200). Through such devices as these, then, the novel clearly and ethically divides the llano and its inhabitants from any connection to World War II and, consequently, the larger world it inhabits.

Further underlining this distinction between the llano and its world is the novel's treatment of the effect of World War II on those characters drafted into its combat. The war robs, temporarily and permanently, the llano of its young men. Even those who do survive to return are not how they once were. The war changes them in pointedly significant ways. It reduces men like Lupito and Antonio's older brothers to the state of brute animals, thus proving destructive to Chicano subjectivity. The first of these examples, Lupito, appears after he has killed the sheriff and is being hunted by a group of men, including Antonio's father. The elder Márez laments how "the war made him [Lupito] crazy" and Narciso, the town drunk and friend of Ultima, similarly pleads with the men to halt their violence for they "know that the war made him sick" (17, 21). It is, however, Antonio who describes to the reader the actual nature of Lupito's sickness: "The man they hunted had slipped away from human understanding; he had become a wild animal" (20). Antonio similarly characterizes how the war changed his brothers, describing them as "turgid animals who did things mechanically" (68). In both cases, the war (and so the outside world responsible for it) proves destructive to Chicano subjectivity.

Another facet of this destruction is how the war also disconnects Lupito and the brothers from the rhythms of the llano. This change is most clearly demonstrated in Antonio's impressions of his brothers once they return. He notes their nervousness, their "restlessness," the evidence of "*the bad blood*" that "raised from dark interiors the restless, wild urges that lay sleeping all winter" (66, 69, original italics). These no-longer-hidden urges translate into a disdainful attitude toward their former home: Eugene declares, for example, "[T]his hick town is killing me!" León mirrors this sentiment: "Yeah. It's hell to have seen half the world then come back to this" (69). Not only, then, is the war and the world it emanates from coded negatively and in contrast to the llano through its destructive forces, but the novel additionally presents that world as completely different from the llano: temporally, spatially, and ontologically. More to the point, exposure to that world and its forces precludes a return to the rhythms and life of the llano, and the way of being these represent.

Like the war, U.S. Anglo society exhibits similarly negative effects on both the llano and its inhabitants, reinforcing the division between this community and its larger nation-space. The representation of these twinned effects centers on the figure of Antonio's father. As Antonio describes, his father "had been a vaquero all his life, a calling as ancient as the coming of the Spaniard to Nuevo Méjico"; then came the incursions of U.S. Anglo society. "Even after the big rancheros and the tejanos came and fenced the beautiful llano, he and those like him continued to work there, I guess because only in that wide expanse of land and sky could they feel the freedom their spirits needed" (2). The description here establishes two contrasts: the llano as "ancient" versus the more recent arrival of the rancheros and tejanos, and the llano as representing freedom in contrast to the Anglos' fences, which impinge on that freedom. The violations to the land, and thus the spirit of the llano, are repeatedly lamented by Antonio's father. As he reminisces at one point, "The llano was still virgin, there was grass as high as the stirrups of a grown horse, there was rain—and then the tejano came and built his fences, the railroad came, the roads—it was like a bad wave of the ocean covering all that was good" (57). Here, Antonio's father paints the llano in Edenic and virginal terms prior to their metaphoric rape by the penetrating force of U.S. Anglo society, represented by fences, railroads, and roads. Like the tejanos, the "rich rancheros" had a similarly negative effect on the llano. They "sucked the earth dry with their deep wells" (201). According to Antonio's father, the llano responds: "You have used me too much, the wind says for the earth, you have sucked me dry and stripped me bare" (202). These descriptions delineate how U.S. Anglo society has deprived the llano of its resources and spirit; they also cast those interventions in the past tense. In these instances then, a temporal in addition to an ethical line is drawn between the people of the llano and Anglo society. The novel locates the actions, if not the effects, of the latter in the life of the former in the past.

To represent the depredatory incursions of Anglo society into the llano in the novel's present, Anaya uses Antonio's father's job. Like the war's effect on his sons, Gabriel Márez's experiences in the "Anglo world" change him psychologically. He becomes isolated, alienated here, even from those he works with: "He went to work on the highway and on Saturdays after they collected their pay he drank with his crew at the Longhorn, but he was never close to the men of the town" (3). The work also forces Gabriel to compromise his ancestral identity as a vaquero. Antonio explains how it "lowered my father in the esteem of his compadres, the other vaqueros of the llano who clung tenaciously to their way of life and freedom" (2). Like Lupito and his sons, Márez becomes something other than what he once was on the llano through his exposure to U.S. Anglo society, reinforcing the novel's ontological division between the space of the llano and the nation and society surrounding it.

If World War II and the various incursions of U.S. Anglo society represent the more global instances of the novel's ethical circumscription of the llano, then the town and its particular institutions of school and church represent that ethos's more local embodiment. Through Gabriel's work, the novel implicitly contrasts the town to the llano, but it takes Antonio as narrator to make the contrast explicit:

> The two lightposts of the bridge were a welcome sight. They
> signaled the dividing line between the turbulence of the town

and its sins and the quiet peace of the hills of the llano. I felt
somewhat relieved as we crossed the storm-swept bridge. Beyond was home and safety, the warm arms of my mother, the
curing power of Ultima, and the strength of my father. (175)

Antonio reiterates the familiar associations of the llano: quiet, peace, safety,
warmth, health, strength. The town, on the other hand, is associated with
"turbulence" and sin, particularly due to the evil that exists there in the
form of the novel's villains, Tenorio and his daughter-witches.

Of all the specific locations in the town, there is one particular house,
"a large, rambling gray stucco with a picket fence surrounding the weedy
grounds," belonging to a woman known as Rosie, that most fully evokes
the sinful nature of the town (37). Even before he knows this house's precise activities, Antonio already fears it: "I knew that Rosie was evil, not evil
like a witch, but evil in other ways. Once the priest had preached in Spanish against the women who lived in Rosie's house, and so I knew that her
place was bad. Also, my mother admonished us to bow our heads when we
passed in front of the house" (37). When he trails Narciso on his way to
warn Ultima of a possible attack by Tenorio, Antonio learns what no doubt
the reader did at its first mention, that Rosie's is a whorehouse. More dev-
astating is the fact that his one remaining brother, Andrew, frequents this
"house of sinful women" (172). The corruption crystallized here, which
leads Andrew to reject Narciso's fears, precipitating the latter's death, is that
of the town in general. Like the rest of the novel's world, it wholly contrasts
the spirit of the llano.

Besides Rosie's house, two other locations in the town function in the
more local textualization of the novel's ethical division. These are the
school and the church, the two most prominent buildings in the town:
"Towering above the housetops and the trees of the town was the church
tower." Antonio further states that the "only other building that rose above
the housetops to compete with the church tower was the yellow top of the
schoolhouse" (7). Just as they tower over the town, the school and church
are looming presences in Antonio's life. He knows from the earliest pages
of the novel that his destiny, at least in part, involves each: "In the autumn
I would have to go to the school in the town, and in a few years I would go
to catechism lessons in the church. I shivered" (25). Antonio's clearly represented fear is not only due to the ominous presence these institutions seem
to have in his life, but also to their location in the town and corresponding link to its sin. Getting to either of them requires Antonio to cross and
enter the sinful town. The fact that both of these institutions exist within

the environs of the town, and so across the bridge from the warm, safe, and secure llano, taints them with that space's corrupt and corrupting nature.

The novel soon goes on to more explicitly distinguish the school and church from the values and spirit of the llano. Of these two institutions, the school's contrasting dimensions are more subtle. Though upheld by Antonio's mother as where he will be made into the scholar who will one day serve her Luna family, the school is both segregated and assimilationist. His first day of school makes clear how not only Antonio but also other boys like him are marked as different. It begins at lunch when Antonio goes to eat the "small jar of hot beans and some good, green chile wrapped in tortillas" made by his mom; "the other children saw my lunch they laughed and pointed again" (62). Antonio is singled out for his culturally coded lunch that contrasts the more generic sandwiches of the other students, "which were made of bread" (62).

There is also an element of assimilation to the school's negative depiction. Antonio, even prior to his going there, connects what he fears will be the school's effect on him to the war's effect on his brothers: "The war had taken my brothers away, and so the school would take me away" (35). Like the war, then, underlying the process of education is a change to those who undergo it. The most pronounced change occurs with language. As Antonio relates early in the novel, "It was only after one went to school that one learned English" (10). The problems associated with this change are subtly hinted at through what Antonio tells us of his sister Deborah. "She had been to school two years and she spoke only English" (12). Furthermore, she is described as the most problematic of the Márez children. And though Antonio's mother blames Deborah's behavior on the wild Márez blood, her differences from the rest of her family and the life of the llano can also be attributed to her time at school, the one thing that distinguishes her from the rest of her siblings. The resulting isolation and sadness that pervade Antonio's time at school eventually lead him to find others feeling the same. As he describes, "We banded together and in our union found strength. We found a few others who were like us, different in language and custom, and a part of our loneliness was gone" (62). This second passage makes clear how Antonio bonds with those of similar language and custom against the mockery and derision isolating them from the rest of the school. Antonio's recourse here is, on a scale smaller than that of the novel as a whole, to a unified and homogenous cultural community and identity.

Though the Catholic church, like the school, is an always-looming presence in Antonio's life, Anaya only really introduces it a little past the midway point of the novel, coinciding with Antonio's first communion. Almost immediately, it plays into the novel's ethical division. Like everything else associated with the town, the church is presented in profoundly negative terms. Antonio first describes it as he and the other boys enter their catechism class: "The line moved past the water fonts where we wet our fingers and genuflected as we made the sign of the cross. The water was icy. The church was cold and musty" (209). Immediately, the church is unpleasant: the water is not simply cold but "icy"; the building itself is "cold," "musty," and, as Antonio goes on to describe, the "knee boards of the pew[s]" are "rough" and "splintery" (209). These further details only add to the feelings of discomfort and unpleasantness abundant in this much-anticipated space. Even more unpleasant and disconcerting for Antonio are the teachings of Father Byrnes, the priest. When Antonio and the atheist Florence are late for catechism, it is only Florence who gets punished, an inconsistency that proves troubling for Antonio (209–210). The Ash Wednesday before Antonio's first communion, a day he looks forward to like "no other day," is actually undercut, for reader and Antonio both, by what occurs. The morning is "gray," the afternoon "dusty." The faithful are silent, "downcast," with "bony fingers" and preparing for the "shock of the laying of the ashes on the forehead and the priest's agonizing words." The priest's words leave them with "only the dull feeling of helplessness" as Father Byrnes emphasizes the unimportance of the flesh and human life in the face of eternity (214–215). All of this creates a general sense of unpleasantness, pain, suffering, and torment that parallel the negative cast given to the novel's world outside the llano, of which the church, like the school, is another constitutive part.

The question here, then, becomes what does Antonio Márez develop into within this divided world? What is the nature of his mature identity? What role, to borrow from Abrams's definition, does he define for himself in his world? The short answer to these questions is that we do not know. His earlier-referenced declaration to his father that he will "make something new" out of his various influences marks the point at which he decides what he will be. But this declaration comes near the end of the novel. So the "mature Antonio" never actually exists in the world of the novel; the only place where he might be said to appear is in the narration of the story, though even this is complicated. The novel ends with Ultima's death, and in the final paragraph, Antonio-the-narrator explicitly mentions that the next day is her funeral: "Tomorrow the women who came to mourn Ultima's death would help my mother dress her in black, and my father

would make her a fine pine coffin." Furthermore, Antonio goes on to remark how, despite her funeral being tomorrow, Ultima was really buried
with her owl familiar on the llano "Tonight," the final word of the novel
(277). So even if the narrative voice of the novel seems to emanate from
a more mature Antonio, the final paragraph marks the occurrence of the
novel's narration as the night of Ultima's death. Consequently, the "mature
Antonio" remains unrepresented in the novel, as the death occurs immediately after Antonio decides what he will be.

However, the nature of Antonio's world tells us much about what his
mature identity will and in fact can be. Much of the bildungsroman protagonist's identity depends on his or her relationship to that world; as
Abrams notes in his definition, often that identity defines his or her role in
that world. This is especially true in the case of Antonio. He has been literally and figuratively pulled between various influences, be they ancestral,
religious, or moral, and his decision in the end to "make something new"
of them means that his identity will be formed out of their conflict and
confluence.

But the influences Antonio will use to make himself anew are heavily
conscripted. His most profound influence lies in the conflict between his
parents, between his mother's/the Luna's farming tradition and his father's/
the Márez's vaquero lifestyle. In the end, Antonio notes what he learned
from both: "I realized that from these two people I had learned to love the
magical beauty of the wide, free earth." From his mother, he gleaned that
"man is of the earth, that his clay feet are part of the ground that nourishes
him, and that it is this inextricable mixture that gives man his measure of
safety and security." Similarly, from his father, Antonio recognized that
"the greater immortality is in the freedom of man, and that freedom is best
nourished by the noble expanse of land and air and pure, white sky." (242).
In noting what he learns from each of his parents, Antonio establishes the
significance of their conflict to his identity, a conflict that Antonio functions to ameliorate.

However, this also means that the most significant influence on his identity is entirely familial or personal. Caminero-Santangelo notes the same:
"Anaya's representation of identity conflict appears highly personal—a
family matter without larger implications for Chicanos" (115–116). Though
Antonio's conflict remains largely within this familial/personal realm, the
conscription of Antonio's identity to this as well as other narrowly defined
oppositions does have larger implications for Chicanos and the understanding of Chicano/a identity and culture promulgated by this text. These

implications can be seen in Antonio's further declaration and thus explication of the influences feeding into his new identity. Again, this occurs in the penultimate conversation with Gabriel, who advises him that "every man is a part of his past. He cannot escape it, but he may reform the old materials" (Anaya 261). Here, Gabriel makes clear that whatever "new" thing Antonio is going to be, it is still tied to a more ancient past. As becomes immediately clear, this past is that represented by the llano: "Take the llano and the river valley, the moon and the sea, God and the golden carp—and make something new" (261). In this statement to himself, Antonio explicitly lists the often-competing influences he will take and combine in his mature self. And they are all wholly confined to the space of the llano and his familial past. The llano and the river valley—the latter being where the rest of the Luna family is located—again reference his parental conflict, as do the moon and the sea, the emblems of the Luna and the Márez, respectively. The conflict between God and the pagan religion of the golden carp encapsulates the religious/spiritual crisis Antonio has faced all novel long. And though the reference to God might make one think that Antonio is somehow bridging his Catholic upbringing with that of the llano, the circumstances of the novel make it clear that Antonio's God, whoever He is, will not be consonant with the God of agony, punishment, and sin espoused by Father Byrnes. In all of this, then, the novel and Antonio himself, through his narration, completely define and center his nascent mature identity within the space, spirit, and forces of the llano.

Consequently, Antonio defines himself in no way as formed by and thus part of the world(s) outside the llano. Anaya and *Bless Me, Ultima* have previously come under critique for just this conscription, specifically as neglectful of cultural issues relevant at the time the novel was published. "Many critics objected to [the novel] on the grounds that it seemed non-referential even though it was set in a definable historical moment in a New Mexican village" (Padilla 128). In particular, these critics objected to how the novel, unlike its predecessor José Antonio Villarreal's *Pocho* in 1959, failed to highlight the Anglo-Chicano conflict and "issues of assimilation and integration versus cultural preservation" (Caminero-Santangelo 116). At best, in representations such as Antonio's experiences at school, these conflicts seemed sublimated to the novel's larger concentration on more personal, individual issues of identity. As a result, "Antonio is not torn between an Anglo and a Chicano world, but between two ways of being Chicano" (Bruce-Novoa 183), and even then, "it is hard to see how the particular familial choices that are constructed for Antonio . . . might serve this kind of 'referential' capacity" (Caminero-Santangelo 116). However, fundamental to the novel is an opposition between the Anglo culture and world and those of the Chicano/a community centered in the llano. The storyworld and spatial poetics of *Bless Me, Ultima* hinge on this division. However, the reason such a conflict does not seem to factor into Antonio's *bildung* and resulting identity is that Anaya builds the novel on a rejection of this world and culture, both as an influence on Antonio and on the Chicano experience and identity this protagonist comes to represent.

The novel's treatment of Chicano/a identity in relation to U.S. Anglo culture similarly parallels critiques of both the identification of Antonio as a figure of "hybridity" and the novel's treatment of indigenous/Native American beliefs as they affect Chicanos/as. Antonio's struggle "to negotiate a dual inheritance, the elements of which seem incompatible if not mutually exclusive, may call to mind Gloria Anzaldúa's description of the *mestiza* who also negotiates apparently incompatible aspects of identity" (115). But such a resonance proves doubly false. For one, whatever contradictions there are between Antonio's parents and among Ultima, God, and the golden carp, ontologically these all stem from the same "space," that of the llano and its Chicano/a culture. Thus, what is being negotiated or juggled here is, ultimately, part of the same ontological sphere. Second, and perhaps similarly, the novel's overarching theme of unity is not so much a reconciliation between different things, but the recognition instead that those things that seem different or in conflict are actually the same. For example, the petty conflict between Antonio's parents actually sublimates their similar ties and love of the land. Though expressed differently, in farming versus riding, what finally matters and reconciles the two is that love and recognition of the power/spirit of the land. That, in the end, trumps whatever superficial divisions seem to exist. Similarly masked in the novel is the recognition of Chicano/a culture's inheritance from and connection to Native American beliefs and values. How the novel sublimates this connection is the crux of Caminero-Santangelo's critique of *Bless Me, Ultima*:

> A submerged subtext concerning hybrid, *mestizo* identity lies beneath the plot of Antonio's family-based identity conflict, but obscuring this conflict within the narrative is thematically significant and has been overlooked too long. The novel actually concerns the cultural pressures that caused Mexican Americans to deny their Indian heritage in the decades—and

> even centuries—before the Chicano movement.... Struc-
> turally, *Ultima* mirrors those pressures by suppressing issues
> of Native American heritage and masking them with the
> father-mother conflict. In a parallel to Antonio's learning
> process, readers must follow the traces of "Indian-ness" and
> unearth what has been repressed. (117)

This repression can be seen in such things as Antonio's resolution to his religious conflict. He speaks to a "religious syncretism" as something entirely new. Thus, "Antonio fails utterly to recognize that . . . [what] he envisions as a solution to his dilemma has already taken place. A hybrid religion is a reality for Mexicans and Mexican Americans, who routinely incorporate aspects of belief systems inherited from Native American ancestors with the Catholicism imposed by the Spanish conquerors" (118). This repression of indigenous ancestry is another result of the novel's effort to define a pure, absolute, and homogenous Chicano/a identity. In conjunction with how the novel limits Antonio's conflict to combating influences within his cultural sphere, it disappears the influence from forces outside that sphere, such as Native American cultural practices and beliefs that in reality do permeate it.

The same can be said about the novel's treatment of U.S. Anglo culture and society's influence on Chicano/a identity. It absolutely excludes it. The ironic upshot of this effort is how such textual repression actually makes *Bless Me, Ultima* emblematic of the resistance discourse dominant in the Chicano Movement and its prescribed canon that many criticize the novel for not reflecting. The end result of Antonio Márez's *bildung* is to create an autonomous Chicano self, something quite consonant with the goals of the Movement in the 1960s and 70s. However, there is an unfortunate side effect of the novel's foundation in a narrative and ethics of resistance. By so fully and absolutely locating Chicano/a identity as a thing separate unto itself from the larger U.S. nation-space and even world, Anaya's *Bless Me, Ultima* encourages its reader to understand Chicano/a identity, experience, and culture as wholly separate from and anomalous within those spaces, and not, then, as a constituent part. The privileged position of *Bless Me, Ultima* within the Chicano/a literary canon privileges too its spatial poetics, which hinge on an absolute separation of Chicano/a culture and experience from the U.S. nation-space.

EPISTEMOLOGICAL DIFFERENCE:
THE TEXTUAL SPACE OF HINOJOSA'S
"SOMETIMES IT JUST HAPPENS
THAT WAY; THAT'S ALL"

Like Anaya's *Bless Me Ultima*, Rolando Hinojosa's "Sometimes It Just Happens That Way; That's All," from his larger work *The Valley*, bases itself in the paradigm of resistance emanating from the nationalist ideology of the Chicano Movement. Centering on the aftermath of the murder on March 14, 1970, of Ernesto Tamez by Baldemar ("Balde") Cordero at the *Aquí my quedo* bar, this story asserts a similarly irreconcilable separation of Chicano/a culture and experience from that of U.S. society. But where Anaya presents Chicano/a and U.S. cultures as wholly opposed ontologies or ways of being, Hinojosa's emphasis is on the two as radically different epistemologies. That is, each represents a different form of knowing. The murder at the center of this piece is an epistemological hole that representatives of both cultures attempt to fill in for their in-world audiences and the story's reader. Representing mainstream U.S. society's effort are the two newspaper accounts that frame the story. Contrasting these in nature and quality are the testimonies from the accused, Balde, along with those of his sister Marta and her husband Beto. Both sides narrativize the events and thus what they know (or care to/can know) differently. These epistemological differences, then, reproduce the essential distance and conflict between dominant U.S. and Chicano/a cultures underpinning the resistance narrative. It is this story's very structure and construction—its "textual space"—as much as its content that embodies this canonical paradigm and its accompanying ethos.

Preceding the text proper of Hinojosa's "Sometimes It Just Happens That Way; That's All" is a parenthetical description of the work as "A Study of Black and White Newspaper Photographs" (55). These "photographs" are, in a sense, the two separate accounts of the murder published five months apart in the *Klail City Enterprise-News*. Their description as "black and white" is twofold in its meaning. The photographs are literally printed in black ink on white paper; they are also figuratively "black and white" in their conception of the murder. That is, Hinojosa fashions them to represent and communicate the limitations of dominant U.S. society's version of what happened, which is overly simplified, too "cut and dry," and laced with factual errors that encode a disdain toward those involved. Through such textual signals, Hinojosa depicts the U.S. mainstream's willful distance from those events and the Chicano/a persons they involve.

The first of these paired accounts, published the day after the murder, opens the story with its limited perspective:

> Klail City. (Special) Baldemar Cordero, 30, of 169 South
> Hidalgo Street, is in the city jail following a row in a bar in
> the city's Southside. Cordero is alleged to have fatally stabbed
> Arnesto Tamez, also 30, over the affections of one of the
> "hostesses" who works there.
>     No bail had been set at press time. (56)

Several aspects of this passage communicate its distance from the events it describes. Immediately apparent is the brevity of this report. It is "black and white" in its presentation of the facts of the case: who was involved, where the murder occurred, the fact that no bail was set. As a result, there is little beyond a spare presentation of facts, particularly any emotion. Such apparent objectivity speaks in and of itself to a distance and separation from this event and the experience from which it emanates. Similarly, the report signals the narrowness of its associated perspective. Much of its phrasing appears dismissive. Calling the fight "a row," for example, seems to diminish it. Too, the attribution of the conflict to the affections of a "hostess" assigns to it a banal and discrete motivation. Furthermore, inherent in the quotation marks around the term is a winking identification of the woman as a prostitute. In both its distance and narrowness, the passage conveys a lack of interest in and corresponding disdain toward the events, which sets the U.S. mainstream apart from what it describes.

Further telling of these qualities are the errors rampant in the passage. For one, the report misspells the victim's name: he is Ernesto, not Arnesto, Tamez. Similarly misguided is the report's identification of the hostess as the conflict's cause. The reader later learns from both Balde's and Beto's testimonies that she is, at most, tangential to the fight. Balde, for example, explains how the girl only became involved after Ernesto had already begun to verbally abuse him. She likewise contributes little to exacerbate their animus: "[S]he didn't know what to say, what to do; she was half-scared, and embarrassed too, I'll warrant . . . But she just stood there as he [Ernesto] held on to her . . . by the wrist" (60, original ellipses). Beto corroborates: he explains how Ernesto brought "a *vieja* (woman)" over and grasped "the poor woman by the arm," but says nothing of her presence instigating the conflict (68). The choice then to place the hostess at the center of Balde and Ernesto's fight, presenting it furthermore as cold fact, reveals a similarly "cold" disinterest in what happened on the part of U.S. Anglo society.

Hinojosa further emphasizes these same qualities of disdain and distance in the second newspaper account, which closes "Sometimes It Just Happens That Way; That's All." This report appears more than five months after the first and subsequent to Balde's trial.

> Klail City. (Special). Baldemar Cordero, 30, of 169
> South Hidalgo Street, drew a 15 year sentence Harrison
> Pehelp's 139th District Court, for the to the Huntsville
> Judge in State Prison murder of Ernesto Tanez last Spring.
> ETAOINNNNNNNNN
>     Cordero is alleged to have fatally stabbed Ernesto Tanez,
> also 30, over the affections of one of the "hostesses" who
> works there. ETAOIN SHRDLU PICK UP
>     No appeal had been made at press time. (70)

Much of the substance of this subsequent account is unchanged from the first. The paper continues to incorrectly attribute the murder to a fight over the "hostess." Even the phrasing of the report is similar. It begins with the same recitation of Balde's full name, age, and address, and its second paragraph is virtually identical to the original's second sentence. Now, instead of noting the lack of bail, the report ends by noting the lack of an appeal with much the same phrasing. Likewise, errors pervade this report to a more significant extent than the first. The paper has corrected the misspelling of Ernesto's first name but now misspells his last name, Tamez, as "Tanez." It also misspells the Judge in the case as "Pehelp" rather than the correct "Phelps." Even more problematic is the second paragraph's contradictions of the first: if Balde has been convicted of the murder, then he is no longer "alleged" to have done it. Additionally, there are severe grammatical breakdowns in the only wholly new clause, which follows the recitation of Balde's information. Some word, likely "from," is missing between "15 year sentence" and "Harrison Pehelp's." As well, the "for the to the" following soon after this approaches incoherency. Even more so than its predecessor, this second report signals the U.S. mainstream's lack of interest in these events through its manifest sloppiness and inaccuracy.

Another addition to the second report makes clear Hinojosa's judgment of this perspective is lacking. It is the seemingly random series of letters at the end of the first and second paragraphs: "ETAOINNNNNNNNN" and "ETAOIN SHRDLU," respectively. The linotype machines used to set type for printing had their keys arranged by frequency, thus ETAOIN and SHRDLU were the first two lines of keys. When an error was made in the setting, such nonsense type would be set in order to complete the line and allow the metal slug to be discarded. The fact that these lines made it into the printed newspaper further indicates its sloppiness. But, too, their presence can be read as indicating how the rest of what is printed does not matter; it is the same nonsense as what would be generated by randomly and/or repeatedly typing these keys. Given their inaccuracies and errors, these reports' version of events, essentially repeated twice, is the equivalent of randomly striking the keys. As a result, Hinojosa fully undercuts the epistemological perspective of U.S. Anglo society as wholly divorced from the experiences of Chicano/a people and culture.

Complementing how these newspaper accounts reinforce the divisions between these two cultures are the testimonies/monologues of the story's three Chicano/a characters: Balde, Marta, and Beto. Much of the fault in the newspaper accounts of the events, and thus in the epistemological perspective of U.S. mainstream society, lies in their lack of knowledge about the experiences of the story's Chicano/a characters. Balde reiterates this point when he talks about the Reyna brothers and how they drink to mask their drug use. He describes to Romeo Hinojosa, his court-appointed lawyer, how "[c]ops that don't know 'em come up, smell the brew, and they figure the Reynas are drunk, not high" (58). Here, Balde represents the cops, unfamiliar on the whole with the experiences of these Chicano/a characters, as latching on to the most obvious and patently false explanation. The same could be said about the newspaper's version of events. There, too, the writer boiled down the conflict to a simple, discrete, and consequently incorrect explanation. Unfamiliarity thus breeds reduction: what the U.S. mainstream does not know, and is not interested in, it reduces to a lowest common denominator, imposing a false certainty over a situation that, as we discover through Balde's, Marta's, and Beto's testimonies, is much more complex.

Ironically, however, the same epistemological uncertainty and, ultimately, absence to be found in the newspaper accounts also exists within these monologues. As much as each attempt, particularly Marta's, strives to provide a motivation and explanation for Balde's murder of Tamez, none ultimately do. What is important, then, is not any alternative explanation that these monologues provide, but what they represent in contrast to the U.S. mainstream in *how* they try to explain. As a form of "knowing," the narratives created by these Chicano/a characters contrast how the mainstream sought to "know" the events. In this contrast, Hinojosa represents the distance and conflict between the cultural positions from which these epistemological perspectives emanate.

To begin with, the monologues are radically different in form. They are, most obviously, much lengthier than the newspaper accounts. Whereas the articles boiled things down to as few sentences as possible, Balde's, Marta's, and Beto's narratives take up multiple pages. Even Beto's, shorter ostensibly due to the formal occasion—a deposition—and requirement to speak in English, is still more than two pages in length. But even more strikingly different is the tone in these passages. In various ways, Hinojosa appears to, for lack of a better phrase, humanize the stories, contrasting the distanced, "objective" approach that opens and closes the text. Both Balde and Marta are more casual and colloquial in their testimonies, a result of speaking to someone, court-appointed attorney Romeo Hinojosa, already familiar with their experiences. Their tales are peppered with questions to this Hinojosa that reinforce their shared background. Balde, for example, obviates a need to go too much into Tamez's character by asking, and answering, the following: "You knew Tamez, didn't you? What am I saying? Of course, you did?" (57). Marta does the same: "You've known Balde since he was a kid, and, as Pa used to say: What can I tell you?" (62). Far from a need to be objective, both Balde and Marta invoke the personal, subjective knowledge and experience the attorney shares with them to abbreviate their narratives where they can.

Also humanizing Balde and Marta's monologues are how their statements signal their psychological feelings and emotions. Balde appears to still be in shock. He opens his monologue with a telling qualification: "But don't come asking me for no details; not just yet anyway, 'cause I'm not all that sure just how it did happen" (57). But even though his "not just yet" implies his possibly coming to reveal that information later in his speech, such a revelation never actually occurs. Though he returns again and again to the night in question, it is always with a similar caveat. He tells Hinojosa how he "put up with a lot" from Tamez over the years, and then "sometimes something happens, you know" (58). Later on, he claims that Tamez "was always up to something—and then something happened, and I killed him" (59). These are just a couple of several instances where Balde evidences an inability to put into words exactly what the "something" was that happened. After this "something," Balde simply went outside and waited for the sheriff to come, his lack of emotion and resignation signs of the shock he felt immediately afterward and still feels.

Marta, when she gets to tell her story, is clearly plagued by feelings of desperate fear and guilt. She bewails to the attorney, for example, "Oh, Mr. Hinojosa, I just don't know where all of this is going to take us" (65), clearly afraid of where this turn of events leaves herself and family. What explanation she provides hinges on Tamez's unrequited feelings for her and subsequent harassing of Balde and Beto in response. She creates a dramatic tale of how Balde's attack was in defense of her, which places her not only at the center of events, but also centers responsibility for and guilt over the murder on her as well.

As with the two preceding monologues, Hinojosa humanizes Beto's deposition. This most pointedly occurs through how the text signals his struggles to express himself in English. His halting English is made immediately apparent: "I live at 169 South Hidalgo Street here in Klail. It is not my house; it belong to my mother-in-law, but I have live there since I marry Marta" (67). In contrast to the implications of the grammatical errors and misspellings in the newspaper articles, those errors here represent Beto's struggle to express himself. Whereas his wife's and brother-in-law's audience made the telling of their tales easier, Beto's audience makes his more difficult. In many ways, Beto is speaking to a similar, if not the same, audience as that the newspaper articles both spoke to and represented. His difficulty in expressing the essence of his experience to them speaks to the fundamental difference and division between these cultural and epistemological positions.

Further contrasting the newspaper accounts is the effort made in all three monologues to historicize Balde's attack. That is, instead of casting it as a discrete event, one caused by only the present circumstances of the presumed conflict over the hostess, Balde, Marta, and Beto each present it rather as the culmination of a past and thus a process. In both Balde's and Beto's cases, they attribute the murder to Tamez and his pattern of harassing the pair. Beto, for example, describes how "that night he [Tamez] bother Balde again. More than one time Balde has stop me when Tamez began to insult. That Balde is a man of patience" (68). Here, Beto makes clear that this night's harassment is the latest instance of Tamez's abuse, to which Balde never before responded, but rather patiently bore. Balde, in his testimony, goes even further in casting his action as culminating from Tamez's earlier behavior. He describes, for instance, how he and Beto were simply at the bar, drinking and enjoying themselves, when Tamez shows up, "swearing and cursing like always, and I got the first blast, but I let it go like I usually . . . like I always do" (57, original ellipsis). Later on, he adds that "Ernesto was something, though; from the beginning. I'll tell you this much: I put up with a lot—and took a lot, too. For years" (58). Even the hostess becomes a not-unique part of their history. As Balde further on relates to the attorney, Ernesto would "cut in on a girl I was dancing with, or just take her away from me. All the time" (59). In both Balde's and Beto's

cases, the murder of Ernesto Tamez is not an isolated event as the newspaper articles cast it, but rather the result of a historical pattern of repeated
insults and abuse.

Though also historicizing Balde's actions, Marta's monologue differs
strikingly from those of the two men. For one, her knowledge is entirely
hearsay. As she explicitly admits to Hinojosa about midway through her
testimony, "[W]hat I do know is all second-hand. . . . I'm telling you what
I could piece out or what I could come up with by adding two and two
together, but I don't really know; like I told you, I don't have that much to
go on" (63). Of the three monologues, then, Marta's is uniquely plagued
by epistemological problems, as her entire testimony, her knowledge, becomes suspect because of its indirect (at best) basis. This positions Marta
similarly to the newspaper accounts, outside of the events themselves.

But unlike those accounts, her version of events does not keep her in
that distanced position. She instead places herself at the center of the conflict. In fact, she places herself (and her mother) as the cause of all Balde's
actions. Balde remained single because of that responsibility: "[H]e could
have had his pick of any Valley girl there or anywhere else, but because of
Ma's condition, and the lack a money, 'n first one thing and then 'nother,
well, you know how that goes sometimes" (62). He does not fight for the
same reason: "He won't say why he won't fight, but I, Ma 'n me, we know
why: we'd be hurting, that's why" (62). Not only is Marta the cause of
Balde's forbearance, particularly toward Tamez, but she "reveals" to Hinojosa that she is also the cause of Tamez's abuse.

> Listen to this: back when we were in junior high, Neto Tamez
> would send me love notes; yes, back then. And he'd follow
> me home, too. To top this, he'd bully some kids to act as his
> messenger boys. Yes, he would. Now, I'd never paid attention
> to him, mind you, and I never gave him any ground to do so,
> either. The girls'd tell me that Neto wouldn't even let other
> boys come near me 'n he acted as if he owned me or some-
> thing like that. This happened a long time ago, a-course, and
> I'd never breathe a word of it to Balde: but! the very first time
> I learned that Neto Tamez was giving my brother a hard time,
> I knew or thought I knew why he was doing it. (63–64)

As did Balde and Beto, Marta puts the murder within a narrative of long-
standing enmity between Balde and Ernesto, with the added wrinkle of herself as putative cause. Though her knowledge may be suspect, she still dem-

onstrates an effort to put the night's events in a context that contrasts the newspaper's more discrete attribution. This effort to both contextualize and humanize Balde's murder of Ernesto thus runs through all three testimonies. Likewise, their nature signals and embodies a very different epistemology coexisting with that of the newspaper accounts within Hinojosa's text.

The combination of these contrasting forms of "knowing" in "Sometimes It Just Happens That Way; That's All" is how Hinojosa "maps" resistance. It sets the newspaper articles against the monologues, showing how they are epistemologically different: one treats the events with disdain and judgment while the other serves to justify them through the characters' various efforts—conscious and/or unconscious—to historicize and humanize those involved. Furthermore, the form of the text speaks to how the U.S. mainstream is unaffected by the narratives of the Chicano/a characters. Approximately five months separate the two newspaper accounts. In that time, Balde's and Marta's testimonies to Hinojosa were given, as was Beto's deposition, and the trial itself, where likely all of these stories were revealed, occurred. As we see from the final newspaper report, none of this at all altered that view of what happened. What was absent from the articles to begin with remains absent in the end: the stories of the Chicano/a characters actually involved in the events reported in the articles.

And in this is, ultimately, an epistemological irreconcilability. Just as Anaya presented the realm of the llano and Chicano culture as wholly separate and distinct from the larger U.S. nation-space and world, so too does Hinojosa's text present the understandings of Chicano/a and U.S. mainstream culture. They are irreconcilable, wholly separate. In the end, the Chicano/a version of events does not enter into the U.S. mainstream, and so the story replicates the same distancing of Chicano/a culture from the larger nation as that seen in Anaya, though in epistemological terms rather than ontological ones.

Both works serve ably in demonstrating the textualization of the discourse of resistance. And, in their status as two of the "Big Three" in Chicano/a literature, Anaya and Hinojosa are further emblematic of how that same status has been given to their resistant discourse. However, as the subsequent chapters in this study detail, there are other narrative discourses encoded in the storyworld and/or textual spaces of Chicano/a literary works. These other understandings are ones that can stand alongside that of resistance as alternative ways of imagining racial, ethnic, and cultural interactions within these United States, particularly as those real-world interactions have themselves begun to change and occur outside the terms of resistance.

## TWO

*Mapping Persistence in John Rechy's*
The Miraculous Day of Amalia Gómez
*and Helena María Viramontes's*
*"The Cariboo Café"*

> *But under the fake windsounds of the open lanes,*
> *in the abandoned lots below, new grasses sprout,*
> *wild mustard remembers, old gardens*
> *come back stronger than they were . . .*
> LORNA DEE CERVANTES, "FREEWAY 280"

Lorna Dee Cervantes's poem "Freeway 280" imagines its titular freeway as an oppressive and destructive force toward the "wild abrazos of climbing roses / and man-high red geraniums" that formerly occupied its space. However, the grasses and gardens seemingly destroyed by the freeway's construction not only continue to exist underneath its artificial presence, but in fact grow stronger. As the passage above details, there is new growth that is now stronger than before. Later in the poem, Cervantes goes on to further specify what plants and flowers grow back: "Albaricoqueros, cerezos, nogales" and "Espinaca, verdolagas, yerbabuena." The identification of these plants by their Spanish names hints at their symbolism of Chicano/a identity and culture, a connection made concrete when the speaker later scales the fence and reconnects to a part of her identity. That "part" parallels the returning natural growth. Like the listed plants and flowers, the poem's speaker reclaims a part of her Chicana identity that the more dominant/hegemonic world, symbolized by the freeway, sought, directly or indirectly, to eliminate.

In this poem, Cervantes provides an image of "persistence," of the continued existence of cultural differences within and despite oppressive and hostile conditions. Similarly, the works treated in this chapter—John Rechy's 1991 novel *The Miraculous Day of Amalia Gómez* and Helena María Viramontes's "The Cariboo Café" from her 1985 short story collection *The Moths and Other Stories*—map a discourse of persistence into their works' storyworlds and/or textual spaces. The world of both these texts is a late-1980s Los Angeles that starkly contrasts the more rural settings in the works by Anaya and Hinojosa. Too, both texts' imagined city-spaces eerily recall the "postliberal" L.A. that Mike Davis decries in the "Fortress L.A." chapter of *City of Quartz*. Davis's dystopian vision of L.A. as a postmodern, carceral space finds dramatic representation in both Rechy's novel and Viramontes's short story. More pointedly, both works depict their imagined Los Angeles as "full of invisible signs warning off the underclass 'Other'," signs that their Chicano/a protagonists "read the meaning [of] immediately" (226).

However, within these spaces, both authors put forth an alternative understanding of the relationship between Chicano/a peoples and culture and U.S. Anglo society. That is, if writers like Anaya and Hinojosa from the previous chapter represent Chicano/a peoples and spaces as resistant to (and thus wholly separate from) the U.S. nation, Rechy and Viramontes speak to how such peoples and spaces can persist alongside hegemonic society within that larger nation-space and in spite of continued oppression, repression, and violence.

## THE VISION OF PERSISTENCE IN RECHY'S *THE MIRACULOUS DAY OF AMALIA GÓMEZ*

If Anaya and Hinojosa show the shaping power of the ideologies behind the Chicano/a canon, John Rechy perhaps best demonstrates the marginalizing power of the same. From the start, Rechy has had an uneasy relationship with the Chicano/a literary canon that continues to today. Juan Bruce-Novoa identifies, for example, how Rechy "had published three novels by 1970, two of which (*City of Night* and *Numbers*) had attracted international notoriety" surpassing that of José Antonio Villarreal's *Pocho*, Raymond Barrio's *The Plum Plum Pickers*, and Richard Vásquez's *Chicano* combined. Despite this regard, Rechy's works "were not taught in Chicano courses then and for the most part they are still excluded" (120–121). Rechy's exclusion is attributable to his falling outside the ideologically determined topics of the early Chicano/a canon. As Bruce-Novoa explains, "[t]he greatest stumbling block was the blatant homosexuality of the characters"; furthermore, Rechy, particularly in *City of Night*, demonstrates a "lack of a narrow focus on ethnicity" and a denial of "the social values of stability, order, security, and monogamy," and he ironizes "homosexuality's close link with machismo, undermining the chauvinistic stalwart of the male dominated Movement" (121–122). Frederick Aldama further attributes Rechy's slow acceptance into the canon to the queer identities of his characters and plots of his texts, both of which allowed his treatment of Chicano/a identity to go unremarked. Though, as Aldama explains "many of Rechy's first novels had biracial (Mexican/ Anglo) identifying protagonists," his "queer Chicano/a emplotted texts" would not be recognized "within the Chicano/a scholarly community" until the late 1970s (*Brown* 48–49).

Recent years have started to remedy Rechy's inclusion within Chicano/a courses and the canon, but it has been in a limited role. José David Saldívar, for example, describes how Rechy's novels have "yet to be interpreted ... as texts emerging from and responding to his Mexican-American background ... or as cultural critiques inspired and contained by his extended southern California borderlands consciousness" (108). The cause for this neglect is due to the terms in which Rechy has been included within the canon: as a queer writer. That is, the body of criticism that has built up around Rechy's body of works primarily focuses on his treatment of homosexuality and queer experience, to the point that he might be described as "ghettoized" within the canon as a gay/queer novelist.

As a result, Rechy's subsequent inclusion into the canon has yet to lead to much discussion of *The Miraculous Day of Amalia Gómez*, a work centrally concerned with issues of Chicano/a identity and experience and less so with queer identity and experience. A search in the *MLA International Bibliography* turns up only four articles in the novel's first twenty years. The paucity of discussion demonstrates the doubly ironic impact of the canon's limits. As a text by Rechy, *The Miraculous Day of Amalia Gómez* suffers from his general absence from the canon, which is slowly ameliorating. But, as the novel is not centrally concerned with queer topics and homosexual experience, it does not fit into how Rechy has been most often treated—and thus defined—by his appraisers. Despite its focus on issues of Chicano/a identity and experience in general, *The Miraculous Day of Amalia Gómez* remains absent from discussions of these topics because Rechy has largely been absented from them.

This continuing exclusion finds its parallel in Rechy's representation of Chicano/a identity and experience in this novel, which likewise deviates from the paradigm of resistance that dominates the Chicano/a literary canon. Rather, what Rechy maps in his novel and its storyworld is persistence, an understanding encoded in multiple layers of the novel. First, there is the nature of the represented world itself, and how Rechy, like Cervantes, uses the natural world to symbolize the persistence of difference within oppressive and hardening conditions. Rechy positions the titular Amalia similarly. Second, Amalia too strives to persist against the various elements of her larger storyworld, from within as well as outside Chicano culture, that seek to absent her. Within Amalia herself, hope strives to persist despite her prevalent feelings of despair and desperation. In this, Rechy forges another parallel, between the reader and the main character as her interior battle mirrors the reader's own ambiguous feelings toward her: can the reader, like Amalia, believe that hope still persists at the end of the novel despite the goings-on of its larger storyworld?

The imagined storyworld of Rechy's novel comprises two symbolically constitutive elements: "harder" elements such as concrete and iron, which symbolize the oppressive and repressive forces within that imagined nation-space, and "softer" elements prominently represented by the natural world's plants and flowers. These nature symbols attempt to persist within the novel's imagined Southern California environment, as do Amalia and the novel's Chicano/a characters in general. Their relationship, then, to the imagined nation they inhabit forms an overarching symbolic structure for what the novel represents about Chicanos/as' position within that same space. However, the coexistence of these elements may not seem evident to many readers. There is no denying that, for much of the novel, the more oppressive elements of its world are ascendant. José David Saldívar says as much when he describes the novel's Hollywood locale as "another multicultural carceral neighborhood, complete with high-tech Los Angeles Police Department mobilizations, INS raids of undocumented workers in downtown sweatshops, drive-by gang shootings, skinhead hate crimes against gays and people of color, and chauvinist 'Seal the Border' campaigns" (108). Similarly, Saldívar elsewhere states how the novel tells "the lurid story of the 'programmed urban hardening' in Southern California" and, as well, "captures . . . the image of the city proliferating in endless repressions in social space" (*Border Matters* 114, 120).[1] To apply such claims to the entirety of Rechy's world, though, misrepresents it as wholly oppressive, repressive, and violent. Such an interpretation emphasizes what is a single constitutive force in the novel's storyworld as the only one.

Instead, the storyworld offered in *The Miraculous Day of Amalia Gómez* exhibits an oscillation between those ascendant harder elements and the softer consolations represented by the natural world. Rechy textualizes this uneasy balance in the initial description of the novel's imagined environment. The series of paragraphs that compose this description shift between the contrasting elements that compose the novel's world.

> Daily, the neighborhood decayed. Lawns surrendered to
> weeds and dirt. Cars were left mounted on bricks. Every-
> where were iron bars on windows. Some houses were boarded
> up. At night, shadows of homeless men and women, carry-
> ing rags, moved in and left at dawn. And there was the hated
> graffiti, no longer even words, just tangled scrawls like curses.
> (Rechy 6)

The materials most prominently described in this first paragraph are brick
and iron, with a clear emphasis on decay, if not lifelessness. Green lawns give
way to weeds and dirt; signs of human life—homes, cars—have become
empty or still. The only signs of human activity are the furtive movements
of the homeless—who are not even whole persons but rather shadows—
and the incoherent graffiti tags that amount to little more than obscene
scrawls. All of these specific images highlight the symbolic hardening and
growing oppression of the neighborhood Amalia and her family inhabit.

But immediately following this paragraph is one that proffers an alternative sense of it, shifting the perspective to what the environment once was.

> When she had first moved here, the court looked better than
> now. The three bungalows sharing a wall in common and
> facing three more units were graying and in the small patches
> of "garden" before each, only yellowish grass survived. At the
> far end of the court, near the garage area taken over by skele-
> tons of cars that no longer ran, there remained an incongru-
> ous rosebush that had managed only a few feeble buds this
> year without opening. (6)

Though what gets listed in this passage echoes much of the previous—the
no-longer-running cars, the turning of the grass to yellow, the bungalow
walls to gray—the first sentence exhorts the reader to imagine the past that
these details contrast. It used to look better, the first sentence declares. The
walls were not gray, but some more colorful hue; the grass was not yellow
but green, and the "gardens" were more than small patches; the cars used
to run rather than becoming a decayed corpse of their former selves. Paralleling the images from Cervantes's poem, Rechy's here similarly hint that
what the area once was could come back again, if only at this point in the
reader's mind. He even concretely gestures toward such a potential in the
"incongruous rosebush" that clearly still persists, if feebly, within this environment. So too, then, does the brighter, gentler, softer past, of which the

bush's presence remains a single glimpse, lie fallow and dormant but not, perhaps, entirely dead.

The remaining paragraphs of this initial description further oscillate between this world's contrasting elements. The third paragraph continues the second's emphasis on the elements of nature that persist in this environment and goes on to make clear the consolation Amalia draws from their continued presence: "Even the poorest sections retained a flashy prettiness, flowers pasted against cracking walls draped by splashes of bougainvillea. Even weeds had tiny buds." (7). Again, that seemingly past "prettiness" peeks through into the world's present. Nature reasserts itself through the decay: flowers "paste" themselves against the cracks, covering over them, as does the bougainvillea draped and clinging to the walls; the weeds have buds that parallel those on the dormant rosebush. The images in this third passage hearken back to how the neighborhood first appeared to Amalia: "There were flowers and vines everywhere, all shapes, all colors." There were "enormous sunflowers with brown velvety centers" as well as "rows and rows of palm trees" (43). These consolations contrast the realities of hardship that not only Amalia but also other marginalized peoples in this world suffer. The fourth paragraph elucidates how there are "far worse places inhabited by Mexicans and the new aliens—blackened tenements in downtown and central Los Angeles, where families sometimes lived in shifts in one always-dark room" (7). At the same time, though, that this final paragraph returns to emphasizing those harder, oppressive elements of this novel's storyworld, the overall pattern of this description counterpoises the softer elements of the natural world that persist within that oppressive space. They, and these images, reassert their presence— persist—within this world, and also the presence of the "difference" they symbolize, in spite of that world's growing hardness and oppression.

The incongruous rosebush continues as a crystallization of this persistence. It is, as referenced above, the only extant piece of this environment's "brighter past" that still clings to life. It is also apparently succumbing to the oppression and harshness of its world. All it has managed are a few "feeble" but unopened buds, and thus the renewal it offers is, at best, potential. The text repeatedly returns, as does Amalia, to note the condition of the rosebush. Soon after the initial description of the rosebush, Rechy writes how "Amalia continued to water it, though, hating to see anything pretty die" (6); and, later in the novel, we get a fuller description of this effort:

> This early heat would scorch all the flowers, Amalia worried
> as she walked down the narrow cement path that separated

> the three units on one side from the three on the other. She
> stood before the despondent rosebush. Only a few feeble
> buds remained—how sad that they would die without open-
> ing; others had crumbled like long-dry blood. She watered
> the bush anyway. (109)

Adding here to the symbols of oppression is the heat. It is another element
that makes "life" difficult for nature and its softer presence to exist. The
overall state of the rosebush remains unchanged. Its buds are still feeble,
and some have even crumbled, staining the concrete. That Amalia waters
the rosebush "anyway" signals a desperate hope for the rosebush's condition to change, even as the inevitability of its death seems foremost in her
mind.

However, Amalia's hope is rewarded by novel's end. As Amalia returns
home late in the novel, after witnessing a drive-by shooting, she finds "[a]
blossom!" and continues, "[i]t was small, with only a few petals—but it was
alive!" (174). The emphasis in this moment is clearly on the return to life
signaled by the rosebush's blossom. What is important is not the size of the
blossom or the number of petals, but the fact that the blossom exists at all.
It signals, however small, a shift in the relationship between the elements
making up this storyworld. Whereas the world seemed to be growing inevitably harder and harder, more and more oppressive, there too is now growth
in the natural elements that contrast them. However small, the bloom indicates the possibility for something "else," something *different*, to persist
in this oppressive world.

The persistence of the rosebush resonates symbolically with that which
Amalia herself embodies. The longer passage above exhibits a similarity and
sympathy between the two. The "despondent rosebush" mirrors Amalia's
own despondency. Her desperate watering of it, despite the assumption
that her action is futile, parallels her own desperate hopes for herself and
her family. In particular, her watering it to preserve something "pretty" in
her world forges another connection between the two. The same term often
appears in the novel as a description of Amalia. For example, Raynaldo, her
current boyfriend, and Angel, the coyote Amalia meets the night before the
novel opens, repeatedly refer to her as *"bonita"* or "pretty." Amalia's effort
to preserve the rosebush within its harsh conditions mimics her effort to
preserve herself within her difficult environment. She similarly mimics
its relationship to her world/space in her own. That is, like the rosebush,
Amalia exists in a space that is hostile and inhospitable to her presence.
The elements, such as the concrete and the heat, that "oppress" the rose-

bush find their parallel in how Amalia herself is oppressed not only by U.S. Anglo society but also by a chauvinistic/masculinist emphasis within her own culture. Together, these combine into a network of forces that seek to exploit, absent, or otherwise oppress Amalia. It is within such a hostile space that the novel finds a way for Amalia, like the rosebush, to "squeeze out" an existence. This similar positioning thus further "maps" the novel's ethical discourse of persistence.

Rechy's novel is replete with forces of oppression stemming from dominant/hegemonic U.S. society. Amalia sums up the net effect of these forces on her people and culture at the start of the novel's fourth chapter: "Strange that so many people do not realize how beautiful Mexicans are. They just don't see us, Amalia knew" (67). "They," U.S. Anglo society, do not want to see Chicanos/as. Rechy depicts this desire through a variety of efforts to absent Chicanos/as from the U.S. nation-space. Some of these efforts are more subtly insidious. Similar to Anaya's *Bless Me, Ultima*, *The Miraculous Day of Amalia Gómez* presents educational efforts to assimilate Chicanos/as through its delineation of young Amalia's experiences once she enters school. She is told, for instance, by a Catholic nun at the school that God "wants you to speak English" and He "doesn't want you to speak with a Mexican accent" (17). As elsewhere, there are particular terms imposed upon Amalia's entrance into this institutional space, terms that facilitate the erasure of her cultural identity. Other absenting efforts, such as those undertaken by *la migra*, are much more direct: "*La migra* was the Immigration and Naturalization Service; a '*migra*' was one of its agents. Sporadic raids occurred when several *migras* would appear suddenly and one would bark, 'Workplace survey!' The stern men would then interrogate the workers about their 'papers'" (49). In the demand for citizenship papers, *la migra* imposes terms on the identity of Amalia and her people even as the hegemony, of which *la migra* is an arm, exploits their labor.

Rechy similarly establishes Amalia's subordinate relationship to dominant society through her work as a housekeeper to the wealthy Anglos who lock themselves within gated communities. Again, the novel provides an image paralleling Davis's dystopian view of Los Angeles. Real such communities "become fortress cities, complete with encompassing walls, restricted entry points with guard posts," insulating their inhabitants from "ordinary citizens" (*City* 244). In this imagined world, these communities insulate the rich from their cohabitating Amalias. Amalia's function as housekeeper determines her entry into this space. Like Rocío in Denise Chávez's story-chapters, Amalia can only exist here in a service/subordinate role, and the same is true about her existence within the novel's nation-space. "The American woman Amalia worked for asked her why she did housework. 'You could work in a cafeteria or even in a hospital tending to, you know, things'" (Rechy 42). Her employer's statement reveals Amalia's subordinate position in this world: her role must be to "tend things," her labor only to support the U.S. society that both depends on and erases her. Such erasure is evident in how Amalia's employers likewise "berated her with their problems—as if she didn't have any, none" (56). The police who patrol the borders of these communities serve a similar function, making sure of who "belongs" there, and how. Amalia, for example, "learned not to work after certain hours in exclusive areas. From others on the buses she rode, she had heard that Mexicans and black people were routinely stopped and questioned by Beverly Hills Police" (56). Clearly, there are limits, temporal and otherwise, to the access Amalia's labor-based identity provides her, limits that all function to specifically orient Amalia's position toward U.S. Anglo society and foster her exploitation and oppression.

Rechy further represents the police as so oppressive by how they feed into, rather than combat, this world's violence. As Amalia hears "a rising siren, then another" the novel explains how there "were always sirens screaming now. At times it seemed to her that the city itself was shrieking, protesting violence everywhere" (109). The police sirens are themselves harbingers of this violence. So too are the police in general a part of it. No scene demonstrates this more clearly than the violent crackdown by the police on an innocuous street carnival: "[P]olice helicopters hovered over the unofficial parade. Suddenly light poured down in a white pit. Squad cars rushed to block the side exits off the boulevard" (44). Such violence puts the police in parallel with the gangs they should rather contrast. Amalia, for example, notices "sun-glassed Anglo police prowling the area like leisurely invaders in their black cars" (44). Such behavior mimics what Amalia sees in the gangs that threaten her neighborhood. She describes the "young men" who join gangs—which, unbeknownst to her, include her son Manny—as "roaming the streets or idling," their behavior more like than unlike that of the police who "leisurely invade" her neighborhood (71). As a result, Amalia comes to fear the police as she does the gangs: they are both parts of the escalating violence around her.

> Sometimes distant, like echoes or omens, now there were
> more gunshots heard in the neighborhood. *"Las gangas,"*
> older people said, and soon began to add: *"La jura,"* because
> as police cars increased, so did the sound of bullets. In other
> cramped neighborhoods, too, in communities with beautiful

names—Pomona, Florence, Echo Park—violence swept in,
intended victims and bystanders felled by gang bullets, cop
bullets. (71)

The older members of Amalia's community literally speak the terms for the
gangs and the police together, almost like a mantra they have been condi-
tioned to utter. The bullets of both are similarly indiscriminate; intentional
and unintentional targets are hit by the gangs and the police. The police
and the gangs are themselves indiscriminate from each other: one cannot
tell which is the source of the violence, and ultimately, it does not matter.
Both, together, are. Both place Amalia in a vulnerable position through
how she and those like her come to fear the police as much as the gangs,
the former and its society as much as a threat to her/them as the latter.

Reinforcement of Amalia's oppression and subordinate position is not
only from dominant U.S. society and thus external to her culture. She also
encounters similar exploitation, violence, and absenting within her people/
culture. The Catholic Church that is so prevalent a part of Amalia's character and heritage in the novel is similarly exploitative. When Amalia goes
to confess her aborted sexual encounter with Angel, the priest, rather than
offering any kind of absolution for what Amalia feels is her sin, takes advantage of her, making her describe the sordid details of their sex while he
masturbates: "'*Ahhh!*' A gasp a sigh. Then the priest was silent" (157). She
is as sexually exploited and violated by the Chicano men in her life. The
most explicit of these are her relationships with her first husband Salvador,
who rapes her as a young girl, and the coyote Angel, her most recent sexual
encounter, who humiliates her, making her feel beautiful before degrad-
ing her as a whore (137–139). Even the "best" of Amalia's men, Raynaldo,
inflicts pain upon her: "in his awkward urgency, he would hurt her during
his lovemaking, but never deliberately" (63). Raynaldo more intentionally
inflicts pain on Amalia later on when she discovers his sexual advances on
her daughter Gloria.

These specific instances of violence and/or exploitation feed into the
more general absenting of Amalia—and Chicanas in general—by a male-
dominated and patriarchal Chicano culture. The novel gives dramatic representation of this effort to absent women from Chicano culture/history in
a mural Amalia encounters in a plaza.

[T]here was a wall painting that fascinated and puzzled her,
and she went there often to look at it: A muscular Aztec
prince, amber-gold-faced, in lordly feathers, stood with others

> as proud as he. They gazed toward the distance. Behind them on a hill pale armed men mounted on horses watched them. At the opposite end of the painting brown-faced, muslin-clothed men stared into a bright horizon. They were the ones whom the Aztecs were facing distantly. (45)

Upon pondering this mural, Amalia notices the absence of women, asking, "Where were they? Had *they* survived?" (45). As an image of Chicano history, the mural clearly excludes women from that past. But the more immediate question for Amalia centers on the question of those women's survival. An old man explains to Amalia not only how the mural represents the triumph of the *"revolucionarios,* who will triumph and bring about Aztlán, our promised land of justice," but also how this historical event mirrors a later protest about the Vietnam War. The old man describes how he and others marched in the streets in the names of their sons and grandsons, shouting *"No más!* No more abuse. *No more!"* (46). Thus, not only are Chicanas such as Amalia absented from the mythical past that led to Aztlán, but they are also absented from contemporary demands for justice. Literally, Chicanas, and Amalia in particular, are not given a voice to say "No more!"

Summing up Amalia's oppressed position within this world is her friend and coworker Rosario's comment, "[I]t's like living with a loaded gun to your head" (77). The overall effect of such an existence is to inculcate within Amalia an almost total despair and, through that, an acceptance of her subordination and oppression. Even her vision of a silver cross in the sky, the event that opens the novel, in part reinforces how despair and desperation have come to envelop her life. Amalia is "startled to realize that for the first time in her recent memory she had not awakened into the limbo of despondence that contained all the worries that cluttered her life, worries that would require a miracle to solve" (7). From this, it is clear how Amalia's life of worry and fear have made her despondent in the same way as the wilting rosebush. The various forces at play in her world have led Amalia to view her life as lacking possibility.

> So she lived within the boundaries of her existence, and that did not include hope, real hope. She felt that any choice she might have made would have led her to the exact place, the same situation — finally to the decaying neighborhood threatened by gangs in the fringes of Hollywood. (13)

Tied then to her despair is a fatalism that sees her environment as inescapable and inevitable, and herself as its inevitable victim. Such a perception inculcates within Amalia herself a subordinate position to her world. For the bulk of the novel, she sees herself only as something to be acted upon rather than someone who acts. During her childhood, her father's drunken rages were another source of violence, and again Amalia sought to hide from and deny their occurrence: "When his rage erupted, Amalia would huddle frozen in a corner, motionless, soundless, even holding her breath, too terrified to cry. That was the only response she knew to violence" (16). In the present, when earthquakes—another constant violent threat—strike, she simply crouches in a corner waiting for them to pass, "as she always did at the prospect of violence" (5). Further critiquing such passivity is how it reiterates her subordinate relationship to the network of forces that make up her world. In this variety of ways, Rechy presents the array of forces—social, cultural, and even natural—that function to oppress and/or erase Amalia and the difference she represents. The question, then, of whether or not Amalia can persist within this world, and thus this novel's textualization of "persistence," depends upon altering, for herself as well as for the reader, the role these forces and their world enforce on her and her reaction to them.

Amalia's opportunity to do so, and thus the novel's moment to promulgate a different positioning and understanding of what she represents, comes in its climax. Here, the various forces at play in the world of *The Miraculous Day of Amalia Gómez* come together in a single location, "a huge shopping complex at the edge of Beverly Hills" that at first seems much like the gated communities Amalia elsewhere entered (199). It is "full of unsubtle signs warning off the Amalia Gómezes of the world" and thus demonstrates how "malls such as the one Amalia finds herself in reinforce urban apartheid" (Saldívar, *Border Matters* 120–121). Amalia quickly becomes cognizant of how people are looking at her as out-of-place; likewise, she clearly notes the presence of a security guard with "a gun in a holster by his side," a "prop of violence" that, along with his stare, sends a chill down her spine (202). However, just like within the novel's larger storyworld, these signs of oppression/violence are not the only dimension of this space, and so the mall does not function within the novel solely as another such representation.

Rather, the mall is simultaneously akin to Michel Foucault's concept of heterotopia. Foucault most extensively defined this concept in a lecture delivered in 1967 and later published as "Des Espaces Autres" in *Architecture-*

*Mouvement-Continuité* seventeen years later in 1984. He links the concept of heterotopia to utopia, describing both as possessing "the curious property of being in relation with all the other sites, but in such a way as to suspect, neutralize, or invert the set of relations that they happen to designate, mirror, or reflect" (Foucault, "Of Other Spaces" 24). Though utopias "present society itself in a perfected form" and thus are inherently "unreal spaces" or ones "with no real place," heterotopias are "real places—places that do exist and that are formed in the very founding of society" (24). Amongst the various "real" places in society that Foucault marks as heterotopias are boarding schools, rest/retirement homes, psychiatric facilities, prisons, cemeteries, theaters and cinemas, and even gardens (see Foucault 24–25). What all these places have in common is their function as "counter-sites" or a "kind of effectively enacted utopia in which the real sites, all the other real sites that can be found within the culture, are simultaneously represented, contested and inverted" (24). As an example of this function, take the theater. As Foucault describes, this space "brings onto the rectangle of the stage, one after the other, a whole series of places that are foreign to one another" (25); in other words, the space of the theater can represent various "real" spaces in what it presents on stage, spaces that might themselves be incompatible or contradictory. Instead of deriving verisimilitude through an Aristotelian unity of space, the theater-as-heterotopia derives its power from how it disrupts this unity and juxtaposes several spaces upon a singular stage. Shopping centers, too, can be thought of in heterotopic terms, particularly for how they juxtapose such sites Foucault individually lists as heterotopias—gardens and theaters, for example—within their confines. Through such conglomeration and juxtaposition, the "normal" relations of societal space are inverted, contested, and subverted.

What Rechy's imagined shopping center specifically inverts are the "normal relations" of his novel's storyworld. In that "normal" world, for example, violence is omnipresent while nature only appears in sporadic splashes. In the shopping center, this relationship is reversed: the violence is a sporadic presence within an overall peaceful environment. The gun in the guard's holster is one such instance, as is Amalia's description of what she sees while passing a Hard Rock Café: "As she crossed the street toward the shopping center, Amalia noticed for the first time that over a restaurant situated at one corner was what looked like the rear half of a car, inclined, as if it had crashed intact through the roof" (199–200).

Amalia goes on to note the oddness of this image of violence within a space "where everything was so peaceful" (200). Unlike the rest of her world, the pervasive sense of this space is of peace and tranquility, inverting the more normal omnipresence of violence. Similarly, nature, which is only a feeble presence outside the mall, is here prevalent: Amalia remarks on the "real plants and exotic flowers" that grow "in encircled areas at regular intervals on the floor" and how "people sat casually, surrounded by cascades of flowering vines" (201). Here, the presence of nature is "regular," rather than sporadic; specific places, the "encircled areas," exist for plants and flowers that, in the outside world, squeeze through whatever cracks occur within the concrete and brick. In all of this, the shopping center is presented not just as another unwelcoming and threatening space to Amalia, but rather as a convex image of her world and its relationships.

And in this heterotopic inversion, the shopping center provides the necessary setting for Amalia's own perceptions of her world, and her relationship to that world, to likewise be subverted and challenged. For one, Amalia fully realizes the invisibility or absenting the outside world forces upon her. In the shopping center, Amalia becomes "aware of herself" and how she stands out in this "glittering palace": "So many people . . . Did they see her? Yes, they saw a woman who looked out of place, tired, perspiring. But did they see her? She felt invisible" (203, original ellipsis). Coinciding with her being in this space is Amalia's burgeoning awareness of her position in the outside world. She might have been aware of others not seeing her, but instead of a resigned acceptance of that invisibility, Amalia implicitly seems to question it. Furthermore, the society around her—the wealthy, consumerist wing of U.S. society—confronts the reality they have tried to ignore or absent: Amalia herself and, by extension, those of their world like her.

Subsequent to this interrogation of her invisibility, the shopping center also facilitates Amalia's overcoming of her despondency and passivity. As she continues to explore and experience the mall, a weariness that recalls her overwhelming hopelessness starts to intrude upon her. She at first rests on a bench and then props herself against a wall, telling herself, "*I have to think.*"

> She breathed deeply, deeply, to gather some energy so she could walk on. *I have to fight this weariness—to face—to cope with—What? Tomorrow, and the next day . . . if I can find the strength to move!* At the same moment, she felt the paralyzing fatigue she recognized so well, which came with fear and then surrender. Why now, when there was no discernible

threat—just these strange thoughts? *If I can push this tired-*
*ness away, thrust away this*—But a feeling of defeat was in-
vading her. (203, original italics, original ellipsis)

As Amalia explains, the weariness she begins to feel is familiar to her,
particularly for what normally follows it: fear and surrender. In this way,
the novel makes clear how what Amalia experiences here parallels her experience in the outside world, and her reaction to this feeling is the same:
passivity and surrender. At the same time, however, Amalia's thoughts in
the italicized portions make clear that, at least mentally, she is trying to
overcome, and thus act against, these forces. For one of the first times in the
novel, Amalia speaks of her need to "fight," to "face" or confront the worries that are fatiguing her, to "push" and "thrust" them away, rather than
simply let them wash over and paralyze her. She again realizes a pattern
of her life—fatigue followed by fear and eventual surrender—that invokes
her subordinate position to these forces. Here, too, she surpasses the ques-
tioning of each in her expressed (mentally if not verbally) desire to break
out of both.

The shopping center eventually provides Amalia with the means to act
on these realizations when she is taken hostage at gunpoint. This moment
crystallizes what has been the pattern of Amalia's life, her friend Rosario's
earlier image of a loaded gun to the head having become strikingly literal:

> Within a strange, long, loud silence, she heard a tiny click at
> her ear and she knew that a bullet had slid into position to kill
> her. She would succumb, yes, finally, to the weariness of this
> long, terrible day that contained the weight of her whole life,
> she would surrender—
> "*No more!*" she screamed.
> And she thrust the man away from her with ferocious
> strength and she flung her body on the concrete. (205, origi-
> nal italics)

In this instance, Amalia pushes back against all the oppressive forces in her
life in her literal shoving of the gunman. Both this day and this moment
contain the "weight" of her life. They contain or embody all that pushes
down on or oppresses her: Anglo domination and oppression, violence, as
well as her absenting by Chicano culture. Telling of the latter is how she
recovers what the mural's representation of history denied her. The *revo-*
*lucionarios* in the painting were standing up to their conquerors, saying

to them "No *más!* No more!" Amalia's voice, the voice of the Chicana, was not included in that protest. But, in this climactic moment, Amalia voices the same protest, taking those words for her own. Not only, then, will Amalia "surrender no more," she also "no more" succumbs to the position dominant society imposes on her. This day that began with the first sign of an impending miracle—Amalia's vision of the silver cross that opens the novel—ends with that miracle's arrival. Amalia, in the flashbulbs of the media gathered around her, sees *"[t]he Blessed Mother, with her arms outstretched to her"* (206, original italics). But this miraculous vision is followed by a further miracle, the sudden "surge of energy" that sweeps "away all [Amalia's] fear" and makes her feel "resurrected with new life" (206). She, like the rosebush, has found new life, and with it, new hope. When one of the medics asks her if she is all right, Amalia is able to answer triumphantly and exultantly, "Yes!" followed by "I am sure!" (206). Despondency has been replaced by hope, and a resignation to being destroyed by the forces arrayed against her has been superseded by a determination to persist despite them.

Germinating with this transformation of Amalia's relationship to and position within her world is the novel's textualization of persistence. She, and the difference she represents, acts and decides to persist within her world's conditions. The novel demands a corresponding transformation in the text's reader. Like Amalia, Rechy asks his reader to have hope for the persistence of both her and what she represents, a hope that verges between fleeting and gleaming as the novel progresses. But in titling his novel *The Miraculous Day of Amalia Gómez*, Rechy would seem to drive his reader to focus on the miracle realized at the novel's end, and its alteration of Amalia and how she positions herself within that world, rather than on the manifest difficulties and challenges that clearly remain in her life. What appears important is the new understanding of herself and her world with which Amalia will confront these and new challenges, an understanding and confrontation vested in a will to persist within her U.S. nation-space.

## SURFACE AND DEPTH: PERSISTENCE IN HELENA MARÍA VIRAMONTES'S "THE CARIBOO CAFÉ"

On the surface, Helena María Viramontes's "The Cariboo Café" speaks to the tragedy of its characters. The story ends with a Central American refugee washerwoman shot in the head and killed by the police. Two children, Sonya and Macky, become lost in the streets after losing their house key. They will likely be returned to their Popi; however, his reporting of their disappearance would seem to necessitate exposing the family's status as undocumented immigrants, with deportation a likely consequence. The Anglo owner of the titular café loses his clientele of exploited immigrant laborers, who blame him for the shooting. In its litany of tragic outcomes, "The Cariboo Café" seems the direct antithesis of persistence. Its characters, quite simply, do not persist within its imagined U.S. nation-space, particularly as they appear placed at odds with each other. The washerwoman precipitates Sonya's and Macky's exposure when she mistakes Macky for her lost son Geraldo and effectively kidnaps the pair. The owner endangers not only the woman but the children as well when he calls the police to report where they are. And the owner likely loses his livelihood due to this trio's repeated visits to his establishment.

However, proving counter to the events of the storyworld and the divisions between the characters are the resonances between them that Viramontes builds within the text of the story. Specifically, her invocations of both the first-person narrative tradition of *testimonio* and the La Llorona legend position them similarly within the U.S. nation-space, particularly the washerwoman and the owner/operator. They share a marginalization and resulting oppression that often proves strikingly similar not only between them but also to that witnessed in *The Miraculous Day of Amalia Gómez.* But though Amalia's narrative builds in persistence as a transformative potential, Viramontes's encodes it as a lost one. The losses within the storyworld and plot of "The Cariboo Café" lament the conditions that cause them, but Viramontes's structural motifs allow the story's reader to perceive the similarities that existed between the characters, and thus perceive how the text values the kind of persistence that the story's literal events undermine.

Perhaps not surprisingly, approaches to the storyworld and textual space/structure of "The Cariboo Café" most often negatively characterize both. Ana Maria Carbonell, for example, echoes Davis by describing the story's setting as the "fragmented, multi-ethnic world of Los Angeles in the 1980s," which "[brings] together people from various social backgrounds in[to] this postmodern city." However, the U.S. nation-space proves inhospitable to their survival, "disrupt[ing] familial unity" and "creating extreme conditions of poverty" (59). Ana Patricia Rodríguez likewise explicates how the denizens of this storyworld, the "undocumented workers . . . , the homeless, the poor, the drug addicted, and the lonely," search for "freedom and safety" but at best find only a "temporary asylum" from their enforced plight in the story's central locale, the run-down Cariboo Café (398).

The structure of the story has been read in concordance with this fragmentation. The story is divided into three explicitly marked sections: the first is a third-person narration focused on Sonya and Macky as they lose their house key; try to make their way to a neighbor's home, only to become lost; and end up seeking oasis at the café as night falls. The second section shifts to the narrative perspective of the café's owner/operator. It also shifts in time: the owner's mention of how he "tried scrubbing the stains off the floor, so that [his] customers won't be reminded of what happened" and the "crazy lady and the two kids that started all the trouble" clarify that he is speaking some time after the story's tragic end (Viramontes 64, 65). The third section of the story is the most disorienting. It begins in the voice of the refugee washerwoman, from her search for her lost son Geraldo amongst the children arrested by her country's police[2] to her undocumented immigration into the United States. However, once she encounters Sonya and Macky, the perspective shifts to a third-person account in indirect free style that moves back and forth among her, Sonya's, and the owner's perspectives, changing back again to the washerwoman's first-person perspective for the story's final paragraph. The effect of this "interplay of focus" has been seen as "disturb[ing] reader perception," causing the reader to focus on the "problem of expanding fragmentation in our cultures" (Moore 277). Barbara Harlow similarly parallels the story's structure to those refugees within the world it contains: "Much as these refugees transgress national boundaries . . . so too the story refuses to respect the boundaries and conventions of literary critical time and space and their disciplining of plot genre" (152). Despite differing orientations, Deborah Owen Moore and Harlow aptly demonstrate how the fragmentation of the story's structure has been found consonant with its events.

Likewise, critics of "The Cariboo Café" have emphasized the fragmentation between the story's various characters. Most often, the refugee washerwoman and the two children have been diametrically opposed to the Anglo café owner, who is taken as a representative of U.S. society and hegemony. Though Rodríguez initially characterizes "[a]ll the story's characters" as "part of a large group of undesirables" (398), she later excludes the owner from this group, labeling him simply "a racist" (399).[3] Rodríguez also equates him to the other oppressive forces in the story: "The owner, along with the polie, la Migra, and the soldiers . . . are part of the global order protecting private property and policing capitalist interests. They are responsible for the 'human-induced disasters' that displace and trauma-tize people" (400). Sonia Saldívar-Hull also implicates the owner with U.S. hegemony, casting him as a "mouthpiece of the dominant society. While his speech places him in the working class, he spouts the ideology of the dominant class" (218). Roberta Fernández, too, intractably opposes the owner and the washerwoman: "Although both adults have suffered the loss of a child . . . , they will never be able to communicate this to each other, for in the Cariboo Café they are natural antagonists" (72). Thus, the apparent disjunction within the structure of "The Cariboo Café" correlates to that between the owner-operator and the story's immigrant characters.

However, Viramontes does more than depict these characters as "natu-ral antagonists"; in fact, she shows their antagonism not as natural but as artificial. The story, once all its workings are taken into account, just as much laments the factors that create and foster that antagonism. Gestures toward such a theme appear somewhat less frequently in the criticism. For example, Moore's treatment of the story presents all the characters as victims of the storyworld's escalating fragmentation, though at times the discussion threatens to too much aestheticize this aspect of the story.[4] Car-bonell's assessment of the characters further marks their similarities. As she describes, "Viramontes links U.S. foreign policy [in Vietnam] with Latin American dictatorships by showing the interrelated effects they both have on ostensibly unrelated characters. . . . All of these characters either lose or are threatened with the loss of a child or dependent, and actively attempt, with varying degrees of success, to recuperate or prevent that loss" (59). Carbonell makes two moves here that place particularly the owner and the washerwoman in similarity to each other. First, she links the Vietnam War, in which the owner lost his son JoJo, to the political dictatorships in Latin America that rob the woman of Geraldo. Both are victims of a same or similar force. Second, their shared effort to deal with/recuperate from the loss of a child would allow both to replicate the figure of La Llorona. However, Carbonell's discussion only treats the washerwoman in either of these regards. So, though her work gestures toward the reading being put forth here, it stops short of actually explicating what are important similari-ties between these characters.

These similarities begin with how Viramontes's imagined U.S. nation-space, like that in *The Miraculous Day of Amalia Gómez*, is both oppres-sive and violent toward its ethnic/immigrant inhabitants, often suddenly so. The police/*la migra* serve again as the clearest embodiment of this op-pression. Avoiding the police is one of Sonya's three rules, dictated by her father: "Rule two: the police, or 'polie' as Sonya's popi pronounced the word, was La Migra in disguise and thus should always be avoided" (61). However, avoiding them proves impossible, as they swoop in unexpectedly and violently: "[B]efore she [Sonya] could think it all out, red sirens flashed in their faces and she shielded her eyes to see the polie" as they accost a "tall, lanky dark man" Sonya mistakes for the father of a classmate (63). The police exhibit a similar suddenness when they close in on the café near its tragic climax: "Two black and whites roll up and skid the front tires against the curb" without warning; their lights "carousel inside the cafe" and then the police enter with "their guns taut and cold like steel erections" (74). In both instances, juridical oppression and violence is swift, sudden, and unrelenting.

Furthering this depiction of U.S. law enforcement as oppressive and violent are Viramontes's parallels between their actions and those of the Central American police. The Central American police disappeared the washerwoman's son Geraldo, while Sonya witnesses the police swoop in and disappear the tall man. Both symbolize the "repressive machinations of culture, politics, and economics that run her [the washerwoman's] country as well as the United States," which silence and displace her and the peoples she represents (Rodríguez 400). Viramontes makes this similarity explicit when, before being shot, the washerwoman curses the police with "you're all farted out of the Devil's ass," a phrase earlier used to describe the Central American police: "[T]hese men are babes farted out from the Devil's ass" (75, 71).

How Viramontes imagines the U.S. nation-space as oppressive and violent toward peoples ethnically or racially different from its Anglo hegemony is patent; however, that the café owner suffers from a class-based marginalization of his own is just as explicit a point. Like Sonya and the washerwoman, the owner suffers from police oppression. He describes, for example, how "[c]ops ain't exactly my friends, and all I need is for bacon to be crawling all over my place" (66). But the intrusion of the police is unavoidable. The overdose of one of his customers, Paulie, leads them to harass the owner: "That's the thanks I get for being Mr. Nice Guy. I had the cops looking up my ass for the stash; says one, the one wearing a mortician's suit, We'll be back, we'll be back when you ain't looking" (67). Here, the individual officer explicitly states what is true about U.S. law enforcement for all these characters: they show up and swoop in when least expected. As well, the owner is similarly struck by their violence. When *la migra* follows three undocumented workers into the café to arrest them, the owner, "didn't expect handcuffs and them agents putting their hands up and down their thighs," nor the use of handcuffs on one of the workers that looks "old enough to be [his] grandma's grandma" (68). That the story first introduces the owner as he is cleaning the blood left on his floor after the story's violent climax highlights again how he, like the washerwoman and Chicano family, is surrounded by and subject to the violence of dominant U.S. society.

Adding to these characters' similarities is the effect of this violence and oppression on all of them: disorientation. Again, the disorientation of the minority characters is explicit. For instance, Sonya confuses the "tall, lanky dark man" for her classmate's father. Looming larger is her disorientation when she tries to navigate the city's streets to Mrs. Avila's. What she demonstrates is an inability to cognitively map (in Lynch's originating sense) her surroundings.

> At the major intersection, Sonya quietly calculated their next move while the scores of adults hurried to their own destinations. She scratched one knee as she tried retracing their journey home in the labyrinth of her memory. Things never looked the same when backwards and she searched for familiar scenes. She looked for the newspaperman who sat in a little house with a little T.V. on and selling magazines with naked girls holding beach balls. But he was gone. What remained was a little closet-like shed with chains and locks, and she wondered what happened to him, for she thought he lived there with the naked ladies. (62–63)

Though Sonya tries to calculate their path, she finds both her surroundings and her memory frustrate those efforts. Both prove labyrinthine, as the path seems unfamiliar when reversed, and her benchmarks are not where or what they should be.[5] Her and Macky's disorientation only worsens: when they approach a music store that seems familiar, Sonya does not "remember if the sign was green or red" nor does she "remember it flashing like it was now"; when forced to flee the dreaded presence of the police, the pair enter "a maze of alleys and dead ends" from which they emerge wholly lost (63).

Lost in more figurative terms is the refugee washerwoman. Once she immigrates, she finds herself at a loss for how to function and survive. She expresses a desire to work, but the "machines, their speed and dust, make [her] ill" (72). She likewise finds herself marked by the loss of her son, both in her original country and in the United States. Back in her former home, people whispered around and avoided her, for "[t]o be associated with [her] is condemnation" (70); she is similarly ostracized by her nephew's wife, whom she suspects will not let her hold her impending child once born, "for she thinks [the woman is] a bad omen" (72). The woman's disorientation reaches its peak when her path intersects with that of Sonya and Macky, and she mistakes the latter for her lost Geraldo: "Why would God play such a cruel joke, if he isn't my son? . . . I've lost him once and can't lose him again" (72).

In the cases of Sonya and Macky and the washerwoman, their disorientation coincides with the fracturing of their families. The café owner shares both this disorientation and its source. His monologue reveals that he has lost not only JoJo but also his wife Nell. With this subsequent loss came the loss of the owner's certainty. This is what Nell provided. "See, if Nell was here, she'd know what to do" (66). After Paulie's overdose, the owner elaborates not only on the effect of Nell's presence but also of her absence: "That's why Nell was good to have 'round. She could be a pain in the ass, you know . . . , but mostly she knew what to do. See, I go bananas. Like my mind fries with the potatoes and by the end of the day, I'm deader than dogshit" (67). Bringing to a head the owner's "going bananas" are the moments in the story when he is confronted by the police and those they pursue. When the undocumented workers hide in his bathroom, the owner relates how "by that time, my stomach being all dizzy, and the cops all over the place, and the three illegals running in here, I was all confused, you know" (68). Similarly, when the washerwoman returns with Sonya and Macky, the owner breaks out in a sweat, his "hands tremble," and he feels like vomiting as again he is unsure what to do. His one certainty—that "[c]hildren gotta be with their parents, family gotta be together," which prompts him to call the police—also precipitates the story's tragedy, such irony further undermining the owner's sense of what he should do (73).

Through all of this—their mutual oppression, their suffering of sudden violence, and their disorientation—Viramontes forges concrete similarities among her various characters. Not only do they inhabit the same world, but they also experience the same negative effects of its forces. However, these are not the only ways Viramontes's story encourages the reader to see all these characters as connected. They do not only exist within, nor are they only similarly affected by, the tension that pervades the story's storyworld and surface. Additionally, they resonate with each other in subtle ways that ultimately speak to a correction of this imagined world's destruction of its marginalized peoples, one that, though forestalled in this particular text, gestures toward their persistence within and despite their world.

The deeper resonances between the minority characters in "The Cari-

boo Café" and the Anglo owner/operator present themselves in two textual patterns or motifs. The first is the story's evocation of the Latin American tradition of the *testimonio*.[6] However, the presence of this tradition
has been localized entirely within the figure of the refugee washerwoman.
This focus ignores the ways in which the owner/operator's monologue can
also be said to evoke elements of the *testimonio* tradition, particularly what
William G. Tierney describes as the parameters and purpose of such texts.
The second textual pattern unifying the Anglo owner with the other characters is the legend of La Llorona, or "the weeping woman." Like the *testimonio* tradition, La Llorona's explicit role in "The Cariboo Café" has
been discussed solely through the figure of the washerwoman, even though
there is much in the story that allows us to see the owner/operator as another textual exemplar of this legend. Viramontes deploys these two textual
patterns—and the characters contained within them—against the storyworld's context of divisive oppression and violence.

One important quality of the *testimonio* tradition that both the washerwoman and the Anglo owner embody is the position of such a text's speaker
to his or her larger society. As Tierney explains, "those who are most often
the providers of testimonio are those . . . on the margins—the poor, minority people of color, indigenous peoples" (105). Both characters fall into
one or more of these marginalized categories. Their association with the
Cariboo Café further reinforces their shared marginalized status. Twice,
the story describes how the sign on the building has faded so that only the
"oo" of its first word is visible, prompting Sonya and the owner to describe
the café as "the zero zero place" and "the double zero café," respectively
(Viramontes 64). As Carbonell explains, this label identifies this space as
"the endpoint of human survival where the most abysmal of human conditions exist" (62). It likewise identifies the café as a locus for those undesirables of society: undocumented immigrants like Sonya, Macky, and the
washerwoman, as well as poor whites like the owner. It is what Foucault
terms a "heterotopia of deviation," places "in which individuals whose behavior is deviant in relation to the required mean or norm are placed" (25).
Literally, the café is on the outskirts of the city, where, "[e]xcept for the
rambling of some railcars, silence prevailed and . . . shadows stalked . . .
hovering like nightmares" (Viramontes 63–64). So too are these characters, their experiences and their lives, pushed to the outskirts or margins of
their environment, similar to those lives and experiences documented in
traditional *testimonios*.

Like the voices of the *testimonio*, these characters are on the margins of a dominant world that their experiences are meant to contradict: "The point [of *testimonios*] is not simply to bring to light the mangled and distorted histories of the subaltern, but to claim that the present and future must be different, that not only is the subaltern able to act in a different manner by claiming voice, but that the dominant must readjust the ways they have interpreted and lived in the world" (Tierney 106). Both the washerwoman and the Anglo owner accomplish the first of these goals, the "claiming" of a voice. Viramontes literally gives them one in their respective mono- logues/testimonies. But, too, both speak against their positioning within the United States and thus toward the need for change. The washerwoman does so in a dramatic fashion somewhat similar to Amalia Gómez. She lit- erally "speaks out" against the representatives of her dominant and domi- nating society, the police. She screams at them, curses them to hell, and even throws hot coffee in their faces (Viramontes 74–75). How the Anglo owner does so lies in the ironies revealed in the aftermath of the washer- woman's death. His acting in concert with U.S. hegemony leads to the de- structive result. In calling 911 when the woman and kids reenter his estab- lishment, the owner can be said to act in concert with dominant society, even if his intentions — to reunite another broken family since he cannot repair his own — might be considered benign if not generous. The result of his action, though, is tragic. And the effects of the tragedy continue to haunt him. As much as he tries to clean away the literal blood stains on his floor, and the figurative guilt they represent, he cannot. His customers will not let him, as he mentions "they keep walking as if my cafe ain't fit for lepers. And that's the thanks I get for being a fair guy" (64). More to the point, it is the "thanks" he gets for acting in accord with a dominant society that marginalizes him and sets him against his fellow outcasts. Both characters, explicitly in the case of the washerwoman and implicitly in the owner/operator, voice a need to act outside the strictures and ideologies of dominant society, which allows their fictionalized *testimonios* to parallel actual works in this tradition.

An even more pervasive textual motif unifying the experiences of these characters is the figure of La Llorona. The text explicitly invokes this legend in the first part of its third section, through the voice of the washerwoman after she has lost her Geraldo: "It is the night of La Llorona. The women come up from the depths of sorrow to search for their children. I join them, frantic, desperate . . . . I hear the wailing of the women and know it to be my own" (68–69). All the story's characters play some role figured within this legend. Sonya and Macky provide instances of the lost children themselves, while the washerwoman and owner/operator figure as La Llorona in how they mourn their respective losses.

Besides fitting the general parameters of the legend, the characters simulate its more specific permutations. La Llorona can be a figure of "maternal betrayal" who "murders her own children, usually by drowning" for a variety of motivations: "insanity, parental neglect or abuse, and/or revenge for being abandoned by a lover" (Carbonell 54). She can also be a ghost who lurks by bodies of water to snatch other children as she bewails her own (see Moore 283). Further revisions of the legend have emphasized La Llorona's status as a victim of her social context:

> By emphasizing the lover's betrayal and locating his actions within a social context [of conquest], these ethnographic accounts highlight the hostile forces influencing La Llorona's life and provide a social reason for her behavior. In describing La Llorona's race or class position and claiming the lover abandons her to marry another woman of his own higher social status, these interpretations register the unegalitarian structure of colonial society and shift the onus of responsibility for the tragic outcome of the tale . . . from La Llorona to the lover. (Carbonell 56)

At play within these varying definitions and revisions of La Llorona are diametrically opposed paired readings of her as betrayer/victimizer or as betrayed/victim. Both readings are possible for both the refugee washerwoman and the Anglo owner/operator in "The Cariboo Café" and thus further determine them both as textual permutations of this legend.

Within the betrayer/victimizer reading, Carbonell notes that La Llorona becomes a "murderess who continues either to commit treacherous behavior or eternally and impotently weep for her sins"; this further depicts women as "either safely passive or dangerously active" (56). The washerwoman and the owner/operator embody both of these possibilities at various points in the story. They both "continue" their treachery and do so unintentionally. The washerwoman, for example, feels she "betrayed" her child Geraldo by sending him out for a mango she wanted; it was during this excursion that Geraldo was "disappeared." She continues this betrayal in mistaking Macky for her lost son. First, this imposes the identity of her first son onto Macky, a kind of figurative "murder" of his own being. Second, she endangers him during the final scene by clinging to him the entire time the police are attempting to arrest and eventually kill her. Finally, her alleged kidnapping has the effect of betraying the entire family of Sonya, Macky, and Popi. A direct consequence of her act is likely the revelation of the family's undocumented status. The day of the story's climax is, for the owner/operator, a continuing succession of betrayals. The police harass him after Paulie's overdose. However, this harassment does not stop him from pointing out the hiding place of the three undocumented workers when *la migra* invades later that day. And, despite how shocking he finds this moment, he still betrays the woman, Sonya, and Macky when he calls the police again upon their return. Both characters also demonstrate at other times La Llorona's safer passivity. Both can only weep for their lost children. The washerwoman's direct invocation of La Llorona includes her in the weeping of her fellow women. Too, the owner/operator is reduced to tears: "He can't believe it, but he's crying. For the first time since JoJo's death, he's crying" (Viramontes 73). These tears are spilt upon the woman's return with the lost children and are an expression of the owner's frustration over what he feels he must now do. He cannot resist the dictates of dominant society. He can only passively weep over this exigency and its consequences.

The two also share in the second reading of the La Llorona pattern, the betrayed/victim pairing. As Carbonell notes above, in this interpretation, La Llorona and those who figure her are not the betrayer or victimizer themselves, but are rather betrayed/victimized by their social context. This pattern is easy to see in the experiences of the washerwoman. Geraldo was literally taken from her, disappeared by the police in her Central American country. Her fellow countrywomen turned against her, stigmatized her for her loss, a stigma that continues even after she enters the United States, where she finds its institutions, particularly the police/*la migra*, operating against her. When she sees Macky initially and takes him for her son, for example, she explains that she cannot "take my eyes off him because, you see, they are swift and cunning and can take your life with a snap of the finger" (Viramontes 72). The use of the "they" in this passage signals how the woman views herself as a victim of her society and its forces, the "they" that snatch children away from their mothers. She echoes the same feeling when the police confront her at the end. She runs from them "because they will never take him [her "son"] away again" (74). The owner/operator has also been betrayed by his social context. Like the woman, he too lost a son, JoJo, as a result of the Vietnam War and U.S. society's intervention there and then. He is betrayed, as well, in the end, when his actions in accord with the rules of his social context actually make life harder for him. He mentions in his monologue how his customers—the "scum," the "out-of-luckers, weirdos, whores," the "five-to-lifers," and "illegals"—are the crux of his business (64). These are the same customers, particularly the "illegals," who no longer frequent his establishment after his compulsory betrayal.

What both these textual patterns/motifs—the *testimonio* tradition and La Llorona legend—share in common is an effort to speak against the dominant forces and ideologies that determine society in order to change them, and thus that society. So, too, then do the figures in this story who evoke these patterns share in this effort. "The Cariboo Café" uses its characters and what they evoke to critique the efforts of U.S. society to marginalize and eliminate the class-based and/or race/ethnicity-based differences embodied in its characters. The story's titular space stands for both these efforts. At the same time, such a space makes explicit how these forces are operating in the storyworld and, by extension, the material world it represents. Such a concentration and thus evidencing of these forces would seem to be a necessary step toward recognizing them, on its own a first step toward altering them and allowing those peoples and the cultures/differences they represent to persist within this imagined and representative space.

However, "The Cariboo Café" appears to stop short of fully textualizing this discourse of persistence. Most obviously, this is because of how persistence actually fails to happen for any of its characters: the refugee woman is likely dead, Sonya and Macky are likely to be deported along with their Popi. Even the owner/operator will struggle to persist now that his customers are deserting him. All of this is because the characters fail to achieve what Carbonell describes as a "psychic transformation." Though entering into this heterotopic space allows them to grasp "the magnitude of their oppression and respond with resistance" (58), they do not grasp how much of their oppression stems from failing to perceive their similarities, from failing to see themselves in sympathy with the other characters. Rather, they remain subject to the divisive thinking propagated by their society, seeing themselves as wholly separate and different from each other, rather than similar and, furthermore, similarly a part of the U.S. nation-space.

It is left then to the reader to make the realization that the story's characters cannot. Instead of being led to a similar realization as a text's character(s), as was the case in Rechy's *The Miraculous Day of Amalia Gómez*, in "The Cariboo Café," Viramontes constructs the text so as to foster in the reader a different realization than that of the story's characters about the story's worlds, its imagined one and the material world to which it refers.

By recognizing the deeper similarities between the characters, and the groups/cultures they represent, the reader of Viramontes is positioned to understand how such differences can persist within and despite an explicitly hostile national space, even if such persistence fails to happen in the events of the text itself.

## THREE

*Cosmopolitan Communities in*
*Alfredo Véa's* La Maravilla *and*
*Ana Castillo's* So Far from God

Both published in 1993, Alfredo Véa's *La Maravilla* and Ana Castillo's *So Far from God* textualize a discourse of persistence surpassing that in Rechy and Viramontes. First, differentiating Véa's and Castillo's texts is where they locate persistence. In Rechy, persistence inheres within a lone individual, Amalia, and only at the close of the text; like Antonio's mature identity in *Bless Me, Ultima*, Amalia's persistence remains nascent within the text. In "The Cariboo Café," persistence is precisely what does not happen in the story. It remains an implicit discourse behind the story's explicitly tragic events. Véa and Castillo, on the other hand, explicitly emphasize communities of ethnic and cultural differences as the embodiment of persistence.[1] Both Buckeye Road, Arizona, in Véa and Tome, New Mexico, in Castillo are conglomerate spaces, the first a space where different peoples, cultures, and histories combine, the second conflating conflicting ideologies. Second, the texts establish a reciprocal relationship between these communities and mainstream or dominant U.S. society. Véa and Castillo imagine the peoples and cultures contained within these spaces as a participating part of the U.S. nation-space alongside mainstream/dominant Anglo society. They no longer imagine differences persisting within the U.S. nation as isolated, anomalous presences, but as participatory within, and thus a part of, that nation and society.

In representing a world in which such peoples and differences are persistent and participatory in the U.S. nation, both texts encourage in their readers an understanding of that nation different from the rigid binary oppositions underpinning both U.S. racism and resistance. Both temporally and philosophically, then, both novels are rooted in and/or participate in the debates over the value of multiculturalism that were particularly acute in the 1990s. At first, the temptation might be to identify what Véa and Castillo represent as multiculturalism and/or cultural hybridity. However, either designation proves problematic. As Stacy Alaimo points out, multiculturalism often only "serves to distance, contain, and control the very 'cultures' it presumes to promote" by essentializing them, "flattening them out into easily consumable icons that contain difference and make it less threatening" (163).[2] The concept of cultural hybridity has likewise proven flattening to the differences it too intends to celebrate. It falls prey to a similar critique of postmodernism made by Román de la Campa: ethnic, cultural, racial, gender, and sexual differences get decontextualized as "hybridity," becoming a free-floating, uncritical mash of very materially, politically, and historically grounded identities (see de la Campa 11–19). Patrick Colm Hogan similarly criticizes how hybridity has become, in recent years, the "authentic" identity for peoples and cultures of difference. He particularly targets Homi Bhabha and Judith Butler, writing that their classification of difference as "sites of 'disruption, error, confusion, and trouble'" to dominant identity categories is itself an imposition of categorical identity: they define what for them is the "right" kind of raced or gendered subject, and that definition—hybridity—becomes in turn its own "regulatory regime" (Hogan, *Empire* 6–7).[3] Furthermore, such definition vacates those differences, rendering them politically and historically divorced and empty. To identify the differences represented in both Véa and Castillo in such terms would be to contradict the understanding generating their storyworlds' construction.

The understanding of cultural differences undergirding those worlds is, rather, akin to the ideal of "cosmopolitanism." Timothy Brennan outlines cosmopolitanism's popular evocation as "among other things, the thirst for another knowledge, unprejudiced striving, . . . supple open-mindedness [and] broad international forms of civic equality" ("Cosmo-Theory" 659). Kwame Anthony Appiah likewise notes two intertwining ideals within the larger one of cosmopolitanism: "One is the idea that we have obligations to others . . . . The other is that we take seriously the value not just of human life but of particular human lives . . . [and] the practices and beliefs that lend them significance" (xv). Both definitions speak to the recognition of those peoples and cultures of difference in subjective or ontological terms; that is, cosmopolitanism means to view them as living beings, not as flattened, reified objects.

But in spite of its ideals, cosmopolitanism often falls short of its laudatory aims. Appiah explicates how so-called cosmopolitanism has not always coincided with enlightenment (see Appiah's discussion of Richard Burton, 1–8). It has similarly proven self-congratulatory. Proponents of cosmopolitanism view it as "an ethical stance that . . . grows inexorably out of exciting and revolutionary new material conditions: the mode of proper social conduct appropriate to a heretofore unseen age" (Brennan, "Cosmo-Theory" 662). As Brennan here encapsulates, it is assumed that the age of globalization automatically, "inexorably," gives rise to an attitude both open and respectful toward the differences such conditions inevitably require. In positing cosmopolitanism as the inevitable consequence of our globalized conditions, though, these proponents prematurely applaud themselves. Because they participate in a globalized, transnationalized world, they assume their possession of the respect and openness toward alterity such conditions require. What such logic elides is how such an understanding of cosmopolitanism often functions instead as "a relay for the center's values" as "one—benevolently, of course—expands his or her sensitivities toward the world while exporting a self-confident locality for consumption as the world" (660). In the same way that, then, celebrations of multiculturalism and cultural hybridity ignore their problematic applications and implications, so too does Brennan here decry a self-congratulatory cosmopolitanism viewed as the inevitable consequence of contemporary material conditions. What is truly being celebrated here is not cosmopolitanism, but rather a hegemonic or dominant center's assumed assuredness of its own cosmopolitanism and benevolence, both of which often fail to be exhibited.

The cosmopolitan ethos generating the worlds in *La Maravilla* and *So Far from God*, on the other hand, puts the center and differences/alterity together into a whole, without downplaying or eliding the dynamics of power that exist between them. The peripheral spaces in these texts persist in a reciprocal relationship with U.S. hegemony as parts of a larger whole. Cosmopolitanism inheres in these storyworlds not as a center extending itself out unalterably toward its larger world and differences, but rather in how the center and those differences mutually exist and interact as the world or cosmos. Both Véa and Castillo encourage and even seduce their readers to understand their imagined national and world communities as one in which differences coexist and persist, as well as apply the same to their material ones.

## WORLDS WITHIN WORLDS: THE SPATIAL ETHICS OF ALFREDO VÉA'S *LA MARAVILLA*

At first glance, Véa's Buckeye Road, the central space and community in *La Maravilla*, appears remarkably similar to the café in Viramontes's story. It too can be characterized as a heterotopia of deviation, a place where dominant society relegates and marginalizes those outside of its imposed norms. But though the two spaces might share a common origin, Buckeye Road is ultimately a very differently imagined space from Viramontes's café, with a very different import. For one, the community that remains unrealized by the characters in "The Cariboo Café" exists in Véa's central space, if not always easily. In particular, Véa notes a generational divergence between the adults in the novel who, sometimes at best, tolerate the differences around them, and the younger generation (symbolized by the novel's protagonist, Alberto, also called Beto) that more easily coexists with and accepts the racial, ethnic, cultural, and sexual differences around them. Furthermore, Buckeye Road establishes a very different relationship between itself and its inhabitants and the novel's imagined U.S. society and nation. Though marginalized, it/they persist as a reciprocal part of the U.S. nation, as Véa symbolizes umbilical connections between this space and its nearest U.S. metropolis, Phoenix, Arizona.

How Véa shapes the spaces of *La Maravilla* consequently gives rise to its ethos of cosmopolitanism. Within Buckeye Road, Beto most clearly embodies this ethos. He contrasts the more rigid, close-minded beliefs of the adults in the novel, including his Catholic *curandera* grandmother, Josephina, and Yaqui grandfather, Manuel. However, Beto further speaks to an ethos of cosmopolitanism in how his development contrasts that of Anaya's Antonio. Beto's narrative track likens itself to the bildungsroman in general and *Bless Me, Ultima* in particular. Like Antonio, Beto stands at the center of conflicting influences amongst which he tries to define himself. Where the two strikingly differ is in the nature of the worlds within which this process occurs. *La Maravilla* occurs in the American Southwest and predominantly in the 1950s, putting it just a few years removed in time from *Bless Me, Ultima* and its similarly Southwestern locale. However, Antonio's environment in Anaya is culturally homogenous and distanced both from Anglo culture/society and the world at large. Beto's surroundings are heterogeneous and, by the later stages of the novel, he finds himself — unwillingly, it must be said — confronting his larger society and world as well. In the end, whatever Antonio may end up being, it will be based on a limited, if not stunted, world.[4] Beto's mature identity, which Véa, also unlike Anaya, actually represents in a flash-forward to Beto's post–Vietnam War return to a now-gone Buckeye Road, contrasts that of Antonio in how it derives from a network of influences not limited to even the single-yet-conglomerate space of Buckeye Road but, rather, the novel's world as a whole. Defining himself within such a conglomerate space requires Beto to develop a worldview that reflects the ideals of cosmopolitanism, which

Véa uses to communicate a need for a similar understanding and ethos in the extant world to this novel's reader.

At the center of *La Maravilla*'s effort to foster cosmopolitanism in both its characters and reader is the imagined space of Buckeye Road, Arizona. It shares with Rechy's Amalia the effort to persist within a U.S. nation-space and world whose dominant, capitalist society is, at best, dismissive and, at worst, hostile toward the peoples, cultures, and differences it contains. The marginal position of Buckeye Road results from these very attitudes. Early on, Véa characterizes it as one of many "small squatter communities forced outward into the desert by malls and convalescent homes and peewee golf courses for the retired old gringos who had come down for the air" (Véa, *La Maravilla* 24). This description makes clear Buckeye Road's location on the periphery of dominant society. The "outward" process mentioned in the passage is a continuous one. As dominant/capitalist U.S. society needs greater room for the trappings of its consumerist society—its malls and peewee golf courses—it pushes these squatter communities farther and farther away. As a result, the inhabitants of Buckeye Road are doubly marginalized: they are first consigned to this space for their deviance from normative U.S. society, but then that space itself is further marginalized as a space of such "deviant behavior" and "difference." As Erin G. Carlston notes, "Véa joins a host of other critics of the 1950s in his focus on the suffocating normativity . . . enforced by the burgeoning Anglo bourgeoisie he identifies with Phoenix" (118). Not only is that enforced normativity suffocating to those in Phoenix, but it also proves distancing toward those "deviant" from the bourgeois norms of a growing capitalist and consumerist society.

The end result of this process is to make Buckeye Road a conglomeration of racially, culturally, sexually, gender-, and class-different peoples. Buckeye Road becomes a space of multivalent and kaleidoscopic difference, aptly summarized by Alaimo:

> Yaqui, Papago, and Pima Indians, African Americans, Mexican-Americans, a Spanish *curandera*, a wandering Jew/ Fuller Brush Man, a sprinkling of gringos and Okies, a Chinese family, an old white woman spouting Andrew Marvell's poetry, the men who inhabit broken down cars at the "Cadillac Ranch," lesbian prostitutes, transvestites, and homosexuals all coexist, and shop at the "Rainbo Market" which "held everything twenty races could want." (166–167)

Nothing and no one appears excluded from this space. Counted amongst its inhabitants are dispossessed Anglos alongside people of Native American, African, Mexican, Asian, and Jewish ancestry. All are excluded from and by dominant society. Coinciding with this conglomeration of peoples and cultures is a parallel conglomeration of histories and times. Buckeye Road is as much a combination of times as it is of people, as these various inhabitants carry with them particular histories: Harold, the Jewish salesman, bears the scars of imprisonment in a Nazi concentration camp; Buckeye Road's "gringos," the Okies and Arkies, signal the western migration from the Dust Bowl; the Chinese family likewise carries into this space the history of Chinese immigration to the United States, just as the Native American and Mexican peoples bear their historical treatment at the hands of U.S. hegemony.

In Buckeye Road, then, multiple peoples, histories, and times coexist within a single space. Such a linkage between time and space is fundamental to Véa's text. Of particular importance is Einstein's notion of singularities, which Véa uses Harold the salesman to introduce explicitly into the novel. In talking to Josephina about God and Einstein, Harold connects the concept of singularities postulated by the latter to the mysteries of the former: "What is it that the physicists call unmeasurable, ununderstandable things? Things that become less measurable with each attempt to measure? Singularities? Well, I think God is a singularity" (204). For Harold, God and singularities share an immeasurability that results, in the latter, from a collapse of time into space and space into time. Buckeye Road, in its own temporally and spatially collapsed nature, should be a similarly immeasurable space. That is, it is something that exceeds normal ways of reckoning with reality, the normative structures and categories used to explain—and thus contain—phenomena. In *La Maravilla*, these structures and categories are the blinkered and narrow-minded ones perpetrated by dominant society. Gabriele Pisarz-Ramírez specifically identifies these categories as binarily based ones, characterizing Buckeye Road as "a community where binarisms of white and non-white, civilized and barbaric, colonizer and colonized, center and periphery are constantly subverted" (69). Important to this function is how the subversion of these epistemological categories happens through the juxtaposition of peoples and histories within Buckeye Road. This is the ironic result of how those attitudes marginalize these peoples and histories together. Doing so effectively negates the separation not only between those peoples/histories but also between them and dominant society. Buckeye Road exposes and challenges the operation of those attitudes by rendering them visible through how it is a product of them.

However, it is not just, nor primarily, as a space of category-challenging, or resistant, difference that Buckeye Road exists in this text. What the novel emphasizes about Buckeye Road surpasses such a characterization. Of particular concern is the relationship the novel constructs between this space and Phoenix, which mimics the relationship between this space and dominant U.S. society. Not only does Buckeye Road stand for or symbolize the persistence of differences within the U.S. nation-space, but it also further represents these differences as reciprocally related to and part of a larger "whole" along with Anglo society. Buckeye Road exists in an inverse or complementary relationship with U.S. society that implies a mathematically reciprocal relationship. As defined by mathematics, reciprocal numbers are any pair of numbers the product of which is one. So, for example, $2/3$ and $3/2$ would be defined as reciprocal numbers because, when multiplied together, they produce a product of one: $2/3 \times 3/2 = 6/6$ or $1$. To put it another way, the two "parts" that produce a unity or whole are flipped or inverse images of each other. This is precisely the relationship the novel creates between Buckeye Road and Phoenix. As a result, the "whole" of the novel's imagined U.S. nation-space, and indeed world, is the product of these inverse and complementary parts.

The novel's textualization of this reciprocity stems initially from the umbilical connections it creates between Buckeye Road and Phoenix. One such connection is the literal road itself, which begins as "just a fanciful extension of the real 14th street that ended with the asphalt just outside of Phoenix. The dirt passage that continued on into the desert and ended at Buckeye Road just north of the market was given the same name for lack of a better one" (Véa, *La Maravilla* 64). This street's description casts it as a physical link between the two spaces of Phoenix and Buckeye Road, even if it is a vestigial tether. Similarly, the novel emphasizes the economic ties between the two sites as another symbolically umbilical connection: "Phoenix acknowledged Buckeye in only one way: each morning at four o'clock its *jefes y potentados* sent buses and flatbeds rumbling down Broadway past the tract homes and into the desert to load on workers by the hundreds" (24). In this description, there is an interesting reversal of the typical umbilical pattern. It is actually the cast-off "offspring" that is Buckeye Road that economically "feeds" its progenitor, Phoenix. The narrator goes on to explicate Buckeye Road's economic necessity to dominant/capitalist society:

Cauliflower pickers waited over by the tire dump, brussel sprouts lined up at the church, cotton at the side of the store, and rice across from the bus stop. Roofers would come for Mexicans to work the ovens on days when the sun alone would melt the tar plugs together by midmorning. Construction companies would come for Indians to work as lumpers, setups, hod carriers, and screeters. Local 23 came for dishwashers, and the motels from the main highway wanted young dark-eyed maids and old janitors. The Liquid-Ox plant came for men to clean up and bury the chemical spillage. They handed out impressive, new white cotton gloves and paper masks to attract their workers. (24–25)

Like Amalia Gómez in her work as a maid, the peoples of Buckeye Road represent an unacknowledged but vital part of the U.S. economy. In fact, its distance from and invisibility toward dominant society is likewise "essential" (Carlston 127). The novel provides a litany of roles that ethnic and racially "other" people play in the U.S. economy: field workers to supply a variety of agribusiness concerns, construction and chemical workers to add to the preponderance of service providers from maids to dishwashers and janitors. Further revealed in this passage is the deployment of those normative, objectifying categories upon which dominant society relies. The people as individuals are not acknowledged. They are either identified by race or ethnicity—for example, Mexicans and Indians—or by their jobs. They become the "brussel sprouts," the "cotton," or the "rice" that they pick. This lack of acknowledgment likewise speaks to the guilty secret of dominant society, its dependence on those it has marginalized and so remains necessarily connected to.

These are, however, but the merest of connections. "Otherwise, Phoenix stayed away. Its police cars, its fire departments, its ambulances all stayed away" (Véa, *La Maravilla* 25). As these economic connections are ambivalent and limited, Véa creates metaphoric connections between Buckeye Road and Phoenix to further highlight their reciprocal relationship. The two have, for example, inverse or complementary rhythms. Twice in close succession, the narrator describes Buckeye Road as "coming to life" at night. With the heat of the day past, "Buckeye stirred to life; the asphalt streets were only now walkable for the shoeless; the upholstery and skins of dead Cadillacs touchable" (23). Similarly, at night, life in Buckeye Road no longer appears so deprived. Its broken-down cars seem instead to have just been parked, the dust covering everything becomes invisible, and the "nightmarish" makeup on its prostitutes becomes "alluring" (26). Again, space and time feed into each other. Changes in time transform the space; as well, the expectations of that time—night—alter according to how the space itself "awakes" when the sun goes down. In this transformation, Buckeye Road is the inverse of what is "normal," as represented by Phoenix. "When streetlights went on in Phoenix, Buckeye stayed in the dark" (23). For normative society, the night is a time for dormancy, for activity to relent and the day to end. But "in the dark" has a different meaning for Buckeye. It is when the "day" and life in some ways truly begin.

Véa similarly figures the inverse and reciprocal relationship between Buckeye Road and Phoenix through the voice of Beto's Yaqui grandfather, Manuel. Ironically, Manuel reciprocates the disdain of U.S. society that he suffers with his own. "Manuel asserts . . . a clear opposition between ethnic rootedness, purity, cultural authenticity, and a precapitalist economy on the one hand, and rootlessness, cultural inauthenticity, and capitalism on the other hand" (Carlston 124). In such assertions, Manuel parallels the spatial poetics in Anaya's novel, which privileged the similarly coded llano over its larger nation and world. Such a division appears in how he explains to Beto the differences between Yaqui and gringo society: "A gringo will go to the edge of his city to look 'out' into the desert, while a Yaqui will go to the edge of the desert and look 'out' into the city" (Véa, *La Maravilla* 31). Manuel means this image to make concrete the separation and division between the "gringo city" and Buckeye Road. Alaimo similarly characterizes this image as signaling how Buckeye Road's "kaleidoscopic abundance . . . pushes the hegemonic monoculture far into the distant horizon," making Buckeye Road a "space of resistance in part because it suggests the possibility for something else" (167, 169). Likewise, Pisarz-Ramírez focuses on this moment and how, through it, Manuel attempts to translate Anglo loneliness into Yaqui terms, as symbolic of how "[p]erspectives on things change with language/culture, as . . . . [s]ome concepts which exist in Spanish and English are unknown in Yaqui" (70). These critical assessments replicate the irreconcilable difference and distance that is the surface content of Manuel's imagery and betokens a narrative of resistance that is consistent with Manuel's explicit portrayal in the novel.

However, coexisting with this resistant image is one more consistent with the novel's textualization of persistence and its accompanying ethos of cosmopolitanism. Read in temporal terms and within the context of the two spaces' reciprocal relationship, this image becomes a moment of mutual regard. Such a reading hinges on understanding the word "while"

not as emphasizing difference — a "gringo does this, *but* a Yaqui does this" —
but simultaneity: "a gringo does this *as* a Yaqui does this." Specifically, the
image becomes one in which the gringo looks out into the desert at the
Yaqui and Buckeye Road, while, simultaneously, the Yaqui looks out at
the gringo and Phoenix. Simultaneously, the two communities each regard
the other. Contextualized by their reciprocal relationship, this becomes
not a moment of two wholly different and disconnected spaces and times
viewing each other, but, rather, complementary parts of a single whole,
be it a nation or a world, sharing not only a similar experience but also a
similar feeling of loneliness that, though lacking a single word to describe,
this more complex image successfully conveys. It sets up not a distinction
between these two spaces and their inhabiting peoples and cultures but,
rather, a resonance. Ultimately, the complementary rhythms and umbilical connections between Phoenix and Buckeye Road make them seem
not like two different worlds but different hemispheres on a single globe.
They are, in essence, two halves of this text's world or cosmos. Imbricated
within this moment of mutual regard and feeling, then, is an openness
to each other that further signals this text's ethical concern to engender a
cosmopolitan ideal.

Véa's mapping of persistence within the world of *La Maravilla* is similarly bound up in the communication of this ideal. Through the construction of its storyworld as a space of persistence, *La Maravilla* also "maps"
cosmopolitanism; that is, the novel promulgates this ethos both for its characters and to its readers in how it depicts cultural differences as mutually
coexisting. Such a world demands an ethos that correspondingly appreci-
ates this positioning. In this, the world of *La Maravilla* serves as both cognitive map or "situation model," what, as Hogan further puts it, "we take the
world to be" (*Cognitive Science* 40). These maps/models are the complex
architecture we develop for understanding our environment. They develop
based on our cognitive accommodation and assimilation of our experiences, and ultimately "[guide] our responses to and actions in the world"
(40). Véa's novel supports the cosmopolitan ideal as an ethical map/model
for encountering the world and its differences in place of the blinkered,
narrow views more prevalent within the novel's storyworld and outside it.

As a result, Véa and *La Maravilla* are profoundly concerned with the
ways people understand or perceive their world. The novel's opening "Prólogo," voiced by Josephina, the now deceased Catholic *curandera* and
Beto's grandmother, manifests the primacy of this concern. Josephina directly critiques the self-centered worldview that runs counter to cosmopolitanism. As she speaks from beyond her grave to Beto, Josephina initi-

ates this critique using the image of a swimmer below the surface of a still pond who is *"hard-pressed to tell whether you were beneath the surface or above it."*

> *You could reach above your head to touch the margin between air and water and see your own reflection reaching. Then you could fragment it, touch the surface, make the margin chaos. Are you above or below? It does no good to look around because things are moving with you. It gets even more complicated when you realize that neither man nor woman is the measure of all things.* (Véa, *La Maravilla* 1, original italics)

This image immediately destabilizes the binary distinctions founding normative perception. The "first image we are given is that of a line between the living and the dead, between air and water, between divine and human, and between past and present. In none of these cases can we determine clearly what is center and what is margin" (Carlston 117). Furthermore, Josephina's final sentence points out the error of privileging such either/ or thinking. It arrogates human perception as the arbiter of reality. It looks at the world only in the terms by which it knows itself, a centered self extending itself out into the world, confident of its priority, yet mistaken. The image of the swimmer's action plays into this point as well. His or her effort to reach toward the surface reflects back in the pond. Touching the surface makes it erupt in chaos, but was this touching from above or below? That remains unanswered and unanswerable as nothing around the swimmer is stable or objective. All efforts then to render this experience in objective terms prove futile, and thus those terms themselves, human perception itself, prove lacking.

As the "Prólogo" unfolds, Josephina even more explicitly critiques the assumption that human perception is capable of encompassing all it encounters:

> *Imagine the same still pond with yourself standing on it, not even breaking the surface tension; on it like a breath, with the softness of a maidenfly. Beneath you are your feet, and below that, your face. All of you—and your universe beyond that. An absolute symmetry. Which is real? As far as you are concerned, both are. Now I don't mean to be condescending, but human language is as limiting as human eyesight or human thought. Think about it. How much of the light spectrum can you see?*

> *Not much. How much of the spectrum of ideas can you understand or speak? Far, far less.* (Véa, *La Maravilla* 1–2, original italics)

Again, Josephina begins with a binary opposition, that between the real and image. Her image again frustrates such a model. Both images/universes appear equally real and equally image. The larger or "absolute symmetry" between the two lies outside the limits of human thought/perception, just as the full spectrum of light encompasses much more than the human eye is capable of perceiving. In fact, the passage seems to evoke the idea that a larger universe or cosmos comprises the two here. Their symmetry, their complementarity, their reciprocity create something beyond human limits, or at least the limits human thought has defined for itself.

The relationship between the two universes contained in this image, of course, explicitly mirrors that between Buckeye Road and Phoenix. These two locales are themselves reciprocally constitutive of a larger "cosmos," the U.S. nation. Consequently, the normative divisions between peoples and cultures dominating this nation equate to the faulty "objective" perceptions Josephina casts into doubt. She specifically calls out such normative thinking by declaring how, "*Most mortals have a mind-closing function that works so much better than the mind opener*" (2, original italics). The explicit mention of closed/open reasserts that ideal of cosmopolitanism, with its constituent "openness" toward differences. This novel's effort is, in essence, to "jump-start" that mind-opening function in its characters and readers. In other words, *La Maravilla* encodes and encourages an ethical stance or worldview that does not reduce differences to predetermined categories and structures. It complicates and expands such a cognitive architecture by mapping a world in which such difference persists, ideally, as an equal state of being.

Buckeye Road and its conglomerate nature attempt to engender precisely this kind of openness in its inhabitants; such an effect is an equal part of this space's significance as its reciprocal relationship to dominant U.S. society. Buckeye finds particular success in its younger inhabitants. For ethnically and culturally marked children like Beto, living in such a space, particularly with its lower-class whites, makes them open-minded toward those representatives of Anglo society: "Mexican or black or Indian kids whose first experience of the white race was the migratory Arkies could never thereafter harbor a categorical hatred of white people" (66). At the same time, those poor white children do not appear subject to their own "categorical hatred" of the nonwhite children and cultures they encounter.

"But best of all, no Arkie kid ever turned down an invitation to dinner or ever asked what he was eating. Arkie kids ate chitlins and tripe, goat brains or mountain oysters, then sat quietly hoping for more" (66). The reciprocal effect is clear here: both groups of children come to accept not only each other but also each others' cultures and cultural differences, rather than closing themselves off from those experiences and peoples.

The children like Beto contrast the attitude we see embodied in the adults of *La Maravilla*. These older characters, to varying degrees, are representative of the more common, divisive attitudes toward difference that are part of the storyworld's hegemonic processes. Manuel is, of course, one such example. Beto's itinerant mother, Lola, is a more extreme representation of these hegemonic attitudes, particularly in how she serves to implicate capitalism and consumerism within them. As she explains to Beto as she takes him away from what has been his home, "You're going to live with me now. You won't be living in the desert anymore. In California, Indians are history and Sunday is for football, not for church" (293). Soon after this statement, Lola continues, "This is the twentieth century and this is America. Nobody believes in their stupid superstitions and dumb stories anymore" (293). Lola's comments make clear how Buckeye Road is, to her, a wholly separate time and space than the mainstream/dominant America to which she has apparently assimilated. It is a past: she lives in the twentieth century, the present, unlike her parents and their cohabitants. Lola similarly moves her son spatially, from the empty and desolate desert to the plenty of California, enacting in miniature the western migration. Also missing from this "desert" are the material goods she likewise identifies with mainstream America. She lists to her mother the things she can now possess as an American: "three sliding aluminum windows with real glass," . . . "a refrigerator," and a "real toilet" (22). These further comments make clear how Lola has not only assimilated to hegemonic American attitudes toward cultural difference, but likewise has inculcated U.S. materialism and consumerism as both part of herself and what it means to be "in America." The two appear as inextricably linked.

However, as much as the novel seems to clearly condemn Beto's mother for the views and attitudes she espouses, such blinkered attitudes are not limited solely to her.[5] In fact, the woman to whom she is most diametrically opposed, Josephina, shares her own narrow-minded conceptions even as she exists in the cosmopolitan space of Buckeye Road. They are, for example, the source of her own internal struggle. As Manuel explains to Beto, "Whenever someone gets sick or has bad dreams, she is a bruja first and a Catholic second, and she knows it" (34). Her Catholicism and her *curandismo*—the two parts of Josephina's identity—conflict, particularly because her Spanish/Catholic heritage disdains the "superstitious" practices of the *curandera*. That she voices such terms about herself reveals how such attitudes determine Josephina's perceptions. The same divisions cause what strife there is in her marriage to Manuel, someone of whom, again, her upper-class, Spanish heritage would/does not approve. She fears eternal damnation for her marriage to him. She refused the "Yaqui part" of her wedding ceremony, where the bride is taken by her groom's relatives and brought before her husband for both to say, "Only you" or "*Solamente tú.*" As Josephina declares, "It's certainly not a Catholic ceremony!" (16–17). Similarly, she looks down on the African-American men who congregate at the Blue Moon bar in Buckeye Road, while simultaneously, and thus ambivalently, enjoying blues and jazz recordings by African-American vocalists and musicians. These ambivalences—toward herself, toward her husband, and toward other peoples/cultures in her environment—demonstrate a deeper similarity between Josephina and her estranged daughter.

The difference between these two women is that Josephina eventually overcomes her attitudes. Upon Manuel's death, she pours her scorpion water into his ears, allowing him to hear her apology for her intolerance. She goes on to tell him, "I now see that all waters are confluent and all graves are congruent" (238). Here, Josephina not only repudiates the intolerance that plagued her, but makes a further realization that, in its water imagery, hearkens back to the "Prólogo." The image of waters being confluent is an image of things divided or separated coming together into a unity, and it is this confluence that Josephina now realizes is natural, the way things "are." The final reconciliation between Josephina and Manuel comes when Beto returns as an adult to their gravesite, returning the *chapayeka* mask of Manuel's that Josephina had hidden. Having restored the mask, and thus completed this final reconciliation of his grandparents (whose graves are literally divided by a third one mistakenly buried between them), Beto hears amid the other voices, peoples, and histories that envelop him, "*Solamente tú,*" the voices of his grandparents completing the Yaqui ceremony (279). In all of this, then, the novel gives symbolic representation of Josephina transcending those narrow- or close-minded views.

But no figure in the novel is more an embodiment of its cosmopolitan ethos than Beto. He exists at the confluence of the various peoples, cultures, and histories within Buckeye Road, beginning with those represented by his grandparents. "He sat between the shafts of dusty light that were his grandfather's preference and the flicker of the red votive candles that was his grandmother's. Unaware and unresisting, Beto became part of the flux that radiated between the two magnetic poles that were his abuelitos" (40). As this description makes clear, Beto inhabits the flux created between his oppositely-charged grandparents and inhabits that space naturally, unresistingly. The same can be said about his position in Buckeye Road. He exists at the confluence of all its constituent cultural forces. He is drawn to the Blue Moon bar and its African-American patrons. He interacts with the two lesbian prostitutes who service the downtrodden men of the Cadillac Ranch. He plays amongst the transvestite hairdressers, the Arkies and Okies, and is babysat by Vernetta, the former prostitute living next door to his grandparents. Amongst all of these, Beto exists comfortably, unaware, or unconscious, of any tension between them or between them and him.

Beto's positioning amongst these forces, and their formative effects upon him, feed into this novel's replication of the bildungsroman and in particular *Bless Me, Ultima.* Beto's development of a mature identity starkly contrasts that of Anaya's Antonio. The two novels are, at the same time, remarkably similar. Both concern, in whole or in part, young Chicano protagonists growing up in spatially and temporally distinct spaces within the American Southwest. Both protagonists are pulled between very similar ancestral heritages. Antonio stands between the farmer existence of his mother's family and the free, vaquero life of his father. Beto's grandfather Manuel, and the Yaqui traditions he represents, are similar to Antonio's father and the traditions of the Márez. Beto's grandmother Josephina can be seen as combining the Catholicism of both Antonio's mother and Ultima with the latter's *curandismo.* Josephina's family, like the Lunas, is of a higher class than that of her husband; she, like Ultima, strives to balance her Catholicism and her role as *curandera.* One could even go so far as to compare the Luna-Márez struggle after Antonio's birth to the conflict between Yaqui traditions and those of Josephina's family that occurred at her wedding. However, despite these similar situational conflicts, the end result of their influence — what Antonio and Beto become — ends up being quite different.

Both their worlds and the formative power of those worlds upon them clearly differ. Chicano/a society and culture in *Bless Me, Ultima* is in various ways spatially and temporally distanced from mainstream U.S. society. More to the point, the novel is constructed in such a way as to reinforce this distance. As a result, Antonio's understanding of himself and his place forms only from the influences at play within his smaller community. To use Brennan's terms, Antonio's identity is entirely localized or "centered" within this homogenous space. Antonio can, then, only be a wholly centered self extending itself out to its larger world (assuming he ever does). The differences he may encounter—in particular, U.S. Anglo society—would thus be encountered as something completely separate and distant from him, something, in other words, that he is closed off to rather than something he approaches with openness, paralleling that world's disdain with his own. Such a centered and closed-off sense of self as that exhibited in Anaya's Antonio contrasts with the more open sense of self Beto achieves in *La Maravilla*. The effect of Buckeye Road on its younger inhabitants, the subversion if not complete elimination of "categorical hatreds," is most pronounced in Beto. His growing up in such a racially, ethnically, culturally, and sexually heterogeneous space makes him naturally open toward such differences rather than distant from them. Very often, Josephina sends Beto out into Buckeye Road to run errands for her, errands that require him to move between and amongst its constituent differences. Beto, then, does not grow up nor does he develop in an environment wholly centered on him. To refer back to the novel's opening image of the still pond and submerged swimmer, there is much more going on and moving around him than just that which relates to or is encompassed by him.

Also unlike Anaya's *Bless Me, Ultima*, *La Maravilla* actually represents to its reader the mature/adult Beto all these influences feed into. The novel's penultimate chapter flashes forward to Beto post–Vietnam War, when he returns to his grandparents' gravesite. At the same time that his return and walk to their graves is detailed, the text is interspersed with a history of Buckeye Road transcribed by Boydeen, an African-American girl who lives underneath the Rainbo Market. As this interspersed history persists within the text, the voices of Buckeye Road persist, around and within Beto:

> There were words about him now. The silence of the outer cemetery gave way as he walked to the poorer section—soft whispers in Spanish and every Indian language. The Mexican graveyard. There were conversations flying now, recipes exchanged and letters reread in flashes of energy. There were love songs hanging as wafts of perfume in the ionized air. There were curses and flirtations flying like neutrons and cutting at the hushed center of an airy confessional. There were chains of morose words here and the spliced couplets of

lovers there. As he walked he passed through pockets of lives, caresses, slaps, communions and extreme unctions, haircuts and catheters. There were old voices. Deepest among them were voices that knew this land by other names. Above these there was a voice reading a shopping list while another, forever moribund, composed a farewell. The voices dazzled him as he walked—a priest recanting a blasphemy, the giggling of children. And a single, dry, rice-paper voice among them. (278–279)

Persisting alongside these voices are images from this space's history of, for example, "*Federales* cowering," peppered by arrows, who "were turned back again and again by the barbarians in Sonora, the *chichimecas*" (279, original italics). Beto carries with him his grandfather's *chapayeka* mask that holds not only Manuel's history but also Beto's:

Manuel's *chapayeka* mask had gone with Alberto into the Imperial Valley and north to the San Joaquin Valley. He had carried it with him from labor camp to labor camp, from bunkhouse to quonset hut. *Braceros* had asked about it in Calexico. It had seen the Pinoy bachelor societies in Stockton and San Jose. It had witnessed I.N.S. raids and welcomed a manong's shy mail-order bride.

In Vietnam it had peeked out of his flak vest while he waited in the bush to shoot at a smoking mirror, to hunt dark-skinned, black-haired people. (280, original italics)

In all of these images, the text signals the heterogeneous times, spaces, histories and experiences that Beto hears and, crucially, feels in his blood.

In this, the text further signals Beto's emergence as a product of these multifarious influences. He, in a way, carries with him, in him, his entire world. As he prepares to leave Buckeye Road with his mother, Josephina advises Beto "to remember what" Manuel had taught him, that the world his mother "wants you to belong in is a lonely, greedy and seductive world" (303). Beto's adult representation precedes this advice in the text, and so the reader knows that Beto does not wholly belong to the world of his mother, the world of materialist, secular U.S. society. But nor does he reject it, as the voices and histories permeating him clearly demonstrate the presence of this part of U.S. society. Rather, Beto belongs to the larger world of the text. Beto carries with him and has been formed by all the influences of his experience and cosmos. He persists within it as a conglomeration of those influential cultural times, spaces, and differences in the same way Buckeye Road once did. His *bildung* has brought him to, made him a representation of, cosmopolitanism.

However, Buckeye Road itself has disappeared from the world of *La Maravilla*, making its representation nostalgic. That is, Véa looks back to a time when a space like Buckeye Road, with its concomitant effect, might have existed and literally persisted. However, its presence persists and even comes to infiltrate the cultural sphere of Phoenix. Josephina passes on her *curandera*'s bag and thus her practice to "a little girl living in Tucson." In this succession, "Josephina forcibly introduces Buckeye Road's space/time into Tucson's urban, rational, capitalist time, and her prophetic vision of the little girl's reaction to the bag suggests that in this contest of worldviews, America is going to have to continue to deal with Buckeye Road" (Carlston 132). Beto too remains a presence within the novel's America, and he carries the legacy of Buckeye Road not only on his excursions there but also throughout his world. More crucially, Beto mirrors the novel's reader. Just as he persists in his cosmopolitan ethos despite the absence of the space that most fully influenced his development, the reader too stands to be influenced by the novel now that it is completed. Also, the novel seeks to position its reader as similar in relation to its textual space as Beto was to Buckeye Road. The narrative structure of the novel mirrors this locale's diverse and conglomerated nature.

To again contrast with Anaya's novel, where everything in the text centers around Antonio's development, *La Maravilla* comprises multiple narrative strands, of which Beto's development is only one. There is, for example, the plot concerning the death of Hiawatha at the hands of his girlfriend Boydeen, who later comes to live underneath the Chinese-owned Rainbo Market and to record the events (and eventually history) of Buckeye Road on her court typewriter. Too, there is the plotline concerning Vernetta and her recovery of her son Danny/Danelo, which carries within it a substantial flashback to Vernetta's past—her affair with Danny's African-American father, J. D.; his subsequent lynching by Vernetta's father and brothers; and Vernetta's rejection by J. D.'s family who raises her son. And, of course, there is the ongoing struggle between Beto's grandparents that, prior to Beto's return from the Vietnam War, appears to end with Manuel's death and Josephina's self-imposed isolation, which she takes on as a penance. As similarly heterogeneous spaces, then, both Buckeye Road and *La Mara-*

*villa* simultaneously speak to the persistence of cultural differences within the U.S. nation-space as well as within the reader's mind and strive to cultivate a resulting cosmopolitan ethos in inhabitant and reader respectively.

### IDEOLOGICAL CONFLATION AND COSMOPOLITANISM IN ANA CASTILLO'S *SO FAR FROM GOD*

Ana Castillo's 1993 novel *So Far from God* opens with the death of its central family's youngest daughter, La Loca. La Loca's death is short-lived, as she is resurrected during her funeral and immediately flies up to the roof of the church, the first of several magically real moments that pervade the world of the novel. Simultaneous with its narration of this singular event, this chapter encapsulates the experiences of La Loca's mother Sofi and her three other daughters, Esperanza, Caridad, and Fe, starting from the doomed marriage that gave birth to the girls to the present. Their father Domingo's absence at the funeral provides the narrator her opportunity to describe how Sofi's "marriage had a black ribbon on its door from the beginning" (Castillo, *So Far from God*, 21), being forbidden by her parents and plagued by Domingo's itinerant gambling and eventual departure.

Likewise, La Loca's resurrection gives way to the encapsulation of her sisters' lives and how they each had "gone out into the world and had all eventually returned to their mother's home" (25). The oldest, Esperanza, was the only one to complete college; this was followed by her relationship with Rubén (self-named Cuauhtemoc) and eventually her "landing a job at the local T.V. station as a news broadcaster" (25–26). The second child, Caridad, "tried a year of college, but school was not for her" and followed this effort with pregnancy and marriage (in that order). Upon learning of her husband Memo's infidelity, Caridad aborted the pregnancy and further began to sleep with "anyone she met at the bars" (26–27). The third daughter, Fe, "was fine": twenty-four, with a job at a bank, a hard-working fiancé, and a meticulously maintained image. Fe's revulsion at La Loca's illness and her mother's superstitions returns the reader to the narrative present that began with La Loca's death and miraculous resurrection (27–29). Here, "filtered through the parodic voice of a Chicana-identified narrator," then, are the experiences of *So Far from God*'s central family of characters (Aldama, *Postethnic Criticism* 76).

Their conflated narrativization here and throughout mirrors this novel's textualization of a cosmopolitan ethos toward differences within the U.S. nation-space. The novel's narrator presents the relationship between the text's central community of Tome, New Mexico, which contains the specific "home-space" of Sofi and her girls, and a larger U.S. nation-space that is dominated by a "society of the spectacle [that] peddles a patriarchal nationalist ideology" (81). Like Véa, Castillo does not simply oppose these two cultural/ideological spaces. Rather, she too imagines them as reciprocal parts of a larger whole, be it the specific U.S. nation or, more generally, the world. Different from Véa is how the novel links these cultural spaces. *So Far from God* features less a conglomeration of peoples within its imagined community and more locates both at a nexus of values and ideologies: those of its homogenous Chicano/a community and those of dominant U.S. society. At first it may seem that the novel opposes the former to the latter. But the narrative lives of the four sisters point to the difficulties stemming from locating oneself ideologically solely within either. It is then left to Sofi, their mother, to straddle both cultural/ideological camps as she carries her daughters' legacies into various political actions and organizations. Within, then, the conflation of the girls' experiences, as well as Sofi's subsequent reform efforts, lies this novel's textualization of an idealized cosmopolitan ethics that transforms the characters' and the readers' understandings of cultural difference.

In *At Home in the World*, Brennan elaborates on cosmopolitanism as an ethical stance between the U.S. nation-state and its world. He writes, "Formed in the confluence of official strategies and fresh inclusivist openings, cosmopolitanism . . . becomes a way of talking and seeing, unanchored and flexible. Its ethical postulates arise as descriptions and its implicit policies arise as ethical postulates" (37). Implicit in this description is the nature of cosmopolitanism as de-centered. Such a position lies inherent in the use of terms like "unanchored" and "flexible," as well as in the replacement of prescriptive certainties with "descriptions" and "postulates." The U.S. nation is not a self-assured center extending itself out to other, lesser positions and subjects in its world or "cosmos." Its ideally cosmopolitan subjects extend themselves out—tentatively, openly—to a world of other positions and subjects. It accepts the possible challenge and change these cultural positions offer. Such cosmopolitanism assumes that there are peoples, states, and cultural formations existing in the world with different, to use Brennan's terms, "rhythms" than those of the United States. But such difference does not become a reason to reinforce a jealously centered subject and national position (see Brennan, *Home* 308–312). It is, rather, to see one's position—and the particular position of the U.S. nation-state—as one of many cultural and national formations, as one cog in a larger machine, not as the central cog of the cosmos or world.

To put it another way, cosmopolitanism predicates a subject that views itself as within a "world reality" composed of "world subjects" (38). A similar cosmopolitanism ethos is the result of what Castillo's *So Far from God* "maps," which is, again, persistence. The novel depicts the differences embodied within its pages as various subject positions within the United States alongside that of Anglo, heterosexual, patriarchal, and capitalist society. Castillo specifically sets up the values and ideologies of her Chicana characters and Chicano/a community alongside the competing values and ideologies of dominant U.S. society. *So Far from God* conflates these competing values to engender a cosmopolitan ethos that is itself transformative within the novel's storyworld.

However, such is not the way critics have treated the relationship between the ideologies of the novel's imagined home-space and nation. Instead, critics have most often read the home-space of Tome as a site of resistance and thus in keeping with the Chicano canon's dominant narrative and ethics. Roland Walter, for example, claims "Castillo's narrative instantiates counterhegemony . . . as a substance of Chicano/a thinking" (82). Similar to Ramón Saldívar in *Chicano Narrative*, Walter presupposes "Chicano/a thought" as "counter" and thus resistant toward U.S. hegemony. Similarly, Mayumi Toyosato and Theresa Delgadillo posit the home-space as a requirement for "survival" in this novel, resultantly implying that cultural survival is not possible outside of that space in *So Far from God*. Toyosato declares that the novel "suggests the potential for survival in . . . locally-based, culturally-conscious actions, developed in a particular place" (308). Again, this would seem to mirror the anti-cosmopolitanism view that privileges a centered self, here local, Chicana, and "home." Likewise, Delgadillo relates how the home-space "is revealed to be a center of survival, recovery, and self-knowledge" (905), again delineating that such self-survival cannot be found outside of that space's values.

Those critics more centrally concerned with the specific role of the home-space in *So Far from God* similarly replicate the discourse of resistance. Carmela Delia Lanza, for example, echoes the critics above in defining the home-space in such terms: "In this novel, Castillo . . . constructs the home as a 'site of resistance' for the women of color living in a racist and sexist world" (65). Drawing from bell hooks, and by way of a contrast between this novel and Louisa May Alcott's *Little Women*, Lanza at first sums up the four girls' imperative to "construct a home space that will offer them sustenance, security and spirituality in order to move into a white world as subjects" (66). In Lanza's conception, the self must be wholly centered within the values of the home-space before it extends itself into the world and then as insulation from that world. She identifies the girls as only "experienc[ing] loss in the collision of their . . . home space with the destructive forces outside" (68); furthermore, she privileges Sofi and La Loca over the other women (Caridad, Esperanza, and Fe), claiming that neither of the former pair "desire[s] the objects, the static role or the sterile, domestic environment of mainstream white culture" but are instead "rooted in their own history" (75). Such a statement contradicts Lanza's later claim that Sofi and La Loca "accept their world in its playful state of constant change, and contradictions" (75). The world they accept in this conception is circumscribed by the values of Tome. Such positioning precludes interaction with U.S. Anglo society, as it clearly locates the characters in a homogenous and distinct set of values.

The home-space proves equally constraining in Kelli Lyon Johnson's treatment of the novel. Relying on the traditional version of Anzaldúa, Johnson explains the home-space as a kind of borderlands created by the imposition of borders on women through patriarchal violence. It is from this "in-between space" that the women in this novel negotiate, as Johnson describes (based on Homi Bhabha), "'the intersubjective and collective experiences of *nationness*, community interest, [and] cultural value'" (39–40, original italics). Such a negotiation gestures toward a more cosmopolitan ethos in how it links female community and identity with nation. But Johnson in the end reiterates a fundamentally anti-cosmopolitan stance. The home, for her, becomes "a safe space, redrawing a geography of empowerment independent of paradigms of statehood and nationalism," and more local: "By locating political action . . . in the home space, Castillo elaborates and enlarges the space between the binary divisions of public and private" (40–41, 56). Again, the home signals a safety and security that presupposes that such can only be achieved away from the U.S. cultural and national mainstream. Johnson expands the space between the opposed locales of private and public, home and nation. Rather than an expansion of this opposition, though, the novel's imagined home-space works to collapse its private space into the public/political space of its larger nation and world, and vice versa.

This collapse or conflation begins in the overlapping discourses of the four daughters' narrated experiences. At first glance, the narratives of Esperanza, Caridad, Fe, and La Loca might seem to promulgate a binary opposition between the novel's imagined U.S. mainstream and Chicano/a community. Esperanza and Fe, the two daughters who most fully reject the values of their home-space and, in turn, subscribe to the values and ideologies of the novel's dominant, capitalist, masculinist, and spectacular U.S. mainstream, are tragic figures. The daughters most fully centered in the home-space, Caridad and La Loca, too end tragically but appear more sympathetic in their tragedy. Though all four meet untimely deaths, Caridad and La Loca have a lingering literal and/or figurative presence, and while Esperanza returns, Fe remains, simply, dead. The differences between these pairs ostensibly replicate the opposition of the resistance paradigm, which privileges the values and ideologies of Chicano/a culture over those of mainstream U.S. society.

However, the relationship between the daughter-pairs, and so the ethical discourse encoded within their narrative experiences, are not so cut-and-dry. The novel expresses its ethos not through the bifurcation of these pairs but through their conflation, which establishes a reciprocity between them. Despite their differing relations to the values of mainstream U.S. society, all four daughters encounter the divisive, exploitative, and violent forces of sexism and heterosexism stemming from this part of their world. But those problematic forces are not exclusive to the U.S. mainstream. They also exist in Chicano culture. At the same time, the novel and its narrator problematize all of the daughters' relationships to their home-space, whether it be Esperanza's and Fe's rejection of that space and its values, or Caridad's and La Loca's centering in them. Through the conflation of their experiences, then, the novel asserts a necessary reciprocal, interactive relationship among the values, ideologies, and actions of both its imagined spaces, showing those values not as atomized and distinct from each other within their larger nation and world but, rather, persisting together.

Sofi's first and third daughters, Esperanza and Fe, most directly interact with the novel's imagined U.S. mainstream. However, their function in the novel is not simply to expose the U.S. mainstream as sexist, exploitative, and violent. The same destructive sexism and exploitation is to be found in both sisters' relationships with Chicano men. Castillo thus genders their destruction as male and so parallels that U.S. mainstream to Chicano culture. The daughters' destruction comes not just at the hands of the U.S. capitalist spectacle, but also as a product of each daughter's rejection of the values of the Chicano/a community represented by Tome and the home-space created by their mother. Both eventually return too late to that community and its values as a refuge. That return itself speaks to the necessity of that space and its values alongside those of dominant U.S. society within the U.S. nation-space.

In Esperanza's case, the exploitative and sexist nature of the U.S. mainstream appears most fully in her job as a local T.V. newscaster. In this job, she herself becomes a part of the "spectacle" of U.S. society, becoming a flattened image on the television screen. Parallel to this literal "flattening" are the compromises to her identity that this job imposes on Esperanza. As mentioned earlier, Esperanza was the one daughter to complete college, even going on to receive a Masters of Arts in communications that eventually lands her the newscaster job. However, as the novel's narrator explains, she still "felt like a woman with brains was as good as dead for all the happiness it brought her in the love department" (Castillo, *So Far from God* 27). More pointedly, her experiences in this job condition her to feel that her identity as an intelligent woman is counter to the complete or fulfilled woman that is stereotyped as one who is paired with a male lover. These patriarchal ideologies make her feel, as a result, that a part of her—her intelligence—if not her entire self, is disposable. Such self-perceived disposability demonstrates one way in which Esperanza's identity is flattened. The U.S. mainstream similarly views Esperanza as disposable. When the narrator describes this daughter's return home after receiving a dangerous assignment in Saudi Arabia during the Gulf War, Esperanza's newly returned and horrified father asks "How come they don't send someone with more experience, like la Diana Sawyer" (48). Esperanza replies "Papi, it's part of my job," after which the narrator sums up, "And that was that" (48). The reasons for Esperanza's disposability are implicit within this exchange. In Domingo's desired substitution of Diane Sawyer is an assumed disposability of women; whoever goes to this dangerous site, it will be a woman. Furthermore, it is not just Esperanza's newness that features in her disposability but how also, versus the Anglo Sawyer, she, as an ethnic subject, becomes more disposable in the eyes of the U.S. mainstream.[6]

Esperanza's paired sister, Fe, is similarly exploited by the forces of U.S. capitalism, represented initially by her bank job. Alongside her steadfast effort to maintain a professional image, she "considered herself the steady and dedicated worker type, always giving her one hundred percent." She does this despite the fact that "she was passed up twice for promotion" (177). The bank benefits from Fe's hard work and effort. She does not. Fe exhibits the work ethic commonly evocative of the American Dream, but receives little of its reward. As well, she is easily disposed of when she no longer proves so useful. When the breaking off of her engagement leads to a prolonged screaming that compromises her ability to interact with the public, she is unceremoniously fired, "and that was that" (177). The finality to the narrator's description of Fe's dismissal repeats that of Esperanza's. Both are in the end disposable within the roles dominant society offers them, and that is that.

However, it is not just the U.S. mainstream that views these women and women in general as so disposable. These same patriarchal attitudes appear within Chicano culture in the form of Esperanza's and Fe's male paramours. Esperanza's relationship with her boyfriend Rubén—"who, during the height of his Chicano cosmic consciousness renamed himself Cuauhtemoc"—is just as deleterious to her identity (25). For one, Esperanza's effort to rekindle her romance after Rubén dumps her requires her to turn down a sought-after promotion. Instead of pursuing her own career in Houston, she accompanies Rubén to "the teepee meetings of the Native-American church" where she is taught "the role of women and the role of men and how they were not to be questioned" (36). The description here makes clear Esperanza's secondary role in the proceedings: she is someone to be taught in this clearly male-centered and dominated space. The narrator's final statement on the role of women points to how Esperanza is doubly dominated by the men here, particularly Rubén. The specific roles of men and women are not to be questioned, so, at the same time, the privileged role of men in general remains intact. Reinforcing her subordinate role are Esperanza's feelings of objectification. Her relationship with Rubén makes her "feel like part of a ritual in which she herself participated as an unsuspecting symbol, like a staff or a rattle or medicine" (36). Here, Castillo's narrator describes how Esperanza feels, in essence, "flattened" by her identity within this circle. She is an object in their rituals and set aside when that time has passed.

As the novel's narrator describes Esperanza's disposability within this space and its rituals, she also sarcastically mocks them. Rubén's activities in this space include "singing and drumming, keeping the fire, watching the 'door'" (36). The quotations around "door" signal how there really is no door to be watched in a canvas teepee. These same sarcastic quotations, however, appear soon after around the "lodge 'etiquette'" Rubén teaches to Esperanza (36). The narrator employs them again later to describe Rubén's so-called "pilgrimage" to Mexico, a journey Esperanza was "not invited to join" but which really amounts to nothing more than a sightseeing trip (39). In both these cases, the narrator undercuts and belittles the aggrandized beliefs and activities of Rubén and his compatriots, and so too, then, the patriarchy they represent.

Like Esperanza, Fe too is disposable to the man in her life. Part of what makes her fine to start the novel is her "hard-working boyfriend whom she had known forever," Tom Torres, and their recent engagement (27). However, on the day of her dress fitting, she receives a letter from Tom breaking off their engagement and begins the "bloodcurdling wail" that earns her the title of "la Gritona" (32). As with her older sister, Fe's dismissal is a result of Tom's inherent male privilege. He writes in his letter "*I just don't think I'm ready to get married. Like I said, I thought about this a long time. Please don't call and try to change my mind*" (30, original italics). In all of this, Tom's needs, wants, and desires, though clichéd, supersede those of Fe. He, in fact, preemptively disposes of them just as he does Fe herself. Neither Esperanza nor Fe ever completely recovers from this treatment. Though Esperanza does manage to initially break up with Rubén, she eventually reunites with him, turning down the job offer in Houston. Fe is even more scarred by her treatment: her voice remains compromised even after her shouting ends.

The relationship these two sisters have with patriarchal ideology mirrors their relationship with the U.S. capitalist spectacle: "Castillo ... emplace[s] her characters within a late-twentieth-century world dominated by capitalism that naturalizes as normal the estrangement these characters feel in an increasingly spectacularized society" (Aldama, *Postethnic Criticism* 79). Esperanza's "sense of estrangement" is clear in her resignation to the Saudi Arabia job. Her response to her father's horror indicates how she accepts such treatment as normal. Her disappearance goes on to become news itself and thus adds to the spectacle. She is deemed "an American hero" and given a posthumous medal, even as Sofi and Domingo are run around Washington, D.C., looking for answers to their daughter's fate (Castillo, *So Far from God* 159–160). Esperanza has become spectacularized, as much a part—objectified, ritualistic, flattened—of the U.S. spectacle as she was in Rubén's circle. Fe, too, estranges herself by buying into an economically and materially defined American Dream. This ideology—perhaps more than actual feeling—was the original impetus behind her engagement to Tom. Through it, Fe imagined herself getting out of both her home and Tome "with a little more style and class than the women in her family had" before (29). Despite the break-up and ensuing tragedy, Fe remains committed to this materialist ideology, as evidenced by what she achieves in her successful marriage to her cousin Casimiro: "Fe got the long-dreamed-of automatic dishwasher, microwave, cuisinart and the VCR" (171). As a result of her continued commitment, Fe too "remains vulnerable to the consumerist American Dream" that she associates with heterosexual coupling

(Delgadillo 908). Fe's conception of marriage is estranged from feeling and, thus, empty in how her joy stems from these material goods. Love has been replaced by consumerism.

And, just like her relationships with men, Fe's relationship to U.S. capitalist society and its ideologies proves destructive. In order for Fe to purchase her material success, she takes on a job with weapons manufacturer Acme International. Because she is "intent on moving up quick," and, as always, a hard worker, she takes on whatever jobs are thrown her way (Castillo, *So Far from God* 178). Her effort is doubly ironic. Fe figuratively destroys herself by making herself just another anonymous if efficient cog in this capitalist machine; she also literally destroys herself. Her diligence requires Fe to turn a blind eye to the cancerous chemicals her job requires her to use, at least until those symptoms can no longer be ignored. This tunnel vision, which Fe only sees beyond once it is too late, indicts Fe for allowing herself to be exploited. The narrator generalizes this critique when Fe returns to the plant after her diagnosis and finds the Acme factory and its female workforce changed:

> The whole plant had been completely remodeled in the short time since she had been let go, down to the replaced sheet-rock. And all the stations, not just the foreman's, which used to be open to everybody and everything, were partitioned off. Nobody and nothing able to know what was going on around them no more. And everybody, meanwhile, was working in silence as usual. (189)

Here, the narrator mourns these women's estrangement. Her labeling the silence of the women as "usual" again speaks to this as a norm of dominant society. She regrets not only how these women labor under silent, isolated conditions, but also indicts them as culpable in those conditions. The factory has changed, yes, but only to facilitate how these women isolated and silenced themselves as a product of the ideology they, like Fe, slavishly follow(ed). The changed factory floor spatially represents how Fe's and these women's devotion to their consumerist values and the society from which they derive facilitates their own destruction.

As a result, much of Esperanza's and Fe's suffering does in fact stem from their distance from and rejection of their home-space. Again, the normative ideology of dominant society features in this rejection. Both women separate themselves from a family they see as too outside the American mainstream. Fe turns to the pop psychology of the *Oprah Winfrey Show* to explain her family's idiosyncrasies (119). Esperanza similarly reads "a flurry of self-help books" to help her rationalize the oddities she feels exist in her family (38). Both these efforts become highly ironic. Fe, who sees her family as unambitious and self-defeating, is herself defeated by her own ambition. Esperanza's rationalism not only fails in the face of her family, but is in turn the hard and cold logic that forces her to her disappearance and death. In this irony lies an apparent binary division between the two ideological spaces of nation and home: it is both sisters' rejections of the home-space and its values that make them vulnerable to the ideological forces of capitalist U.S. society.

But contrasting this apparent and easy division are the narratives of the two remaining sisters, Caridad and La Loca. What differentiates the second sister, Caridad, and fourth, La Loca, from Esperanza and Fe is their complementary distance from the mainstream/capitalist U.S. society. The novel's narrator emphasizes the pair's contrast from the start. Caridad, for example, directly contrasts Esperanza, the latter having completed college while Caridad "tried a year of college but school was not for her and never had been, for that matter" (26). The narrator's physical description of Caridad further highlights how the larger world in general is not for Caridad. The narrator remarks on Caridad's "porcelain complexion," her "perfect teeth and round apple-shaped breasts" (26). These images cast Caridad as a doll, making her seem too fragile for the harsh, outer world to which her contrasting sisters fall prey. La Loca shares this sentiment, believing that nothing like Caridad "could last in the vulgarity of the big world very long" (152). But even as she notes this aspect of her sister, La Loca, too, shares in it. La Loca's withdrawal from what she terms the vulgar world is voluntary. The narrator summarizes how La Loca "had grown up in a world of women who went out into the bigger world and came back disappointed, disillusioned, devastated and eventually not at all." As a result, she "did not regret not being a part of that society, never having found any use for it" (151–152). As the narrator further describes, La Loca, throughout her life, healed her sisters from the damage their excursions into the world caused, a "society she herself never experienced firsthand" and that, apparently, she wishes to never so experience (27).

As a result of their separation, if not aversion, to the novel's imagined U.S. mainstream, Caridad and La Loca dwell, literally and ideologically, within the home-space of Tome. However, despite this centering and separation, neither sister is able to escape the attitudes and ideologies of main-

stream society. Events of the novel do not allow them to remain so disconnected. In how dominant society and its attitudes impinge upon the lives of
these remaining two daughters, the novel makes its complementary point
to the lives of Esperanza and Fe. Just as the previous pair was critiqued for
their separation from the Chicano/a community and its values, the novel
critiques in Caridad and Loca a self wholly centered away from the U.S.
mainstream and even world.

Of the two, Caridad is the most wounded by the sexist and judgmental
attitudes within her community. Just as the men in Esperanza's and Fe's
lives reflect patriarchal attitudes, Tome as a whole is similarly patriarchal in
how it judges Caridad for her sexual promiscuity. As the narrator explains,
there were those around her "for whom there is no kindness in their hearts
for a young woman who has enjoyed life, so to speak" (33). Even the narrator seems to blanch a bit at Caridad's activities, euphemizing and thus
obscuring them with the phrase "enjoyed life," which even she points to as
a wanting phrase with her ending caveat ("so to speak"). These pervasive
attitudes find their personification in the figure of Francisco El Penitente,
who develops an eventually fatal obsession with Caridad. When he first
sees her, Francisco envisions her as "all that was chaste and humble," imposing on her a gender-specific requirement of purity (192). Consequently,
he reacts with violence when he learns of Caridad's lesbian relationship
with Esmeralda, a relationship that violates both his categorization of her
and the patriarchal and heterosexist attitudes from which those categories
derive. In both the town and Francisco, those sexist (and heterosexist) attitudes of the U.S. mainstream find a corollary in the Tome community.

The novel further figures these attitudes and their violent effect on Caridad in the physical force that attacks her and leaves her "for dead by the
side of the road" (33). The damage inflicted by this force is clearly gendered; according to Caridad's doctor, her "nipples had been bitten off. She
had also been scourged with something, branded like cattle. Worst of all,
a tracheotomy was performed because she had also been stabbed in the
throat" (33). Her attacker mutilates her breasts, a marker of both woman-
hood and potential motherhood. Her branding reduces her both to the level
of animal and property. The stabbing can be read as an attempt to silence
her, paralleling even the vocal damage suffered by Fe. These wounds, then,
are graphic reflections of patriarchal attitudes and their damaging, objectifying, and silencing effects. When Caridad's attacker is finally identified
by the narrator as what she calls "a *malogra*," Castillo metaphorizes these
attitudes as a violent force that is:

> a thing, both tangible and amorphous. A thing that might
> be described as made of sharp metal and splintered wood,
> of limestone, gold, and brittle parchment. It held the weight
> of a continent and was indelible as ink, centuries old and yet
> as strong as a young wolf. It had no shape and was darker than
> dark night, and mostly, as Caridad would never ever forget, it
> was pure force. (77)

As Delgadillo describes, one dimension of the *malogra* is its embodiment of those attitudes that "foster disregard for women at every level of society" (907). Its tangibility and amorphousness reflect this: the attitudes, beliefs, and ideologies are amorphous in their being mental or psychological, but tangible, as we see dramatically here, in their effect. The *malogra* is furthermore a representation of all the forces and attitudes historically present in the United States that inflict themselves on those it sees as weaker, vulnerable, and different. Its composition—the "sharp metal" and "splintered wood"—recalls the hard materials of Amalia's environment in *The Miraculous Day of Amalia Gómez*. The references to ink, the U.S. continent, and, most particularly, "brittle parchment" invoke the history of treaties made and broken between U.S. society and native peoples. The *malogra* makes "visible the misogynistic and racist violence that a society of the spectacle seeks to normalize . . . . The mysterious event is the violence of a society that . . . brands, maims, and disfigures gendered bodily sites— and it silences" (Aldama, *Postethnic Criticism* 80). The *malogra*'s "mysterious," magically real presence and effect further speak to the pervasive power these attitudes have to permeate all areas of the U.S. nation-space, even those places and peoples ostensibly withdrawn from it. The *malogra* is a culmination of both societies' manifest patriarchy, thus intertwining both rather than distancing them.

Like Caridad, La Loca comes into contact with the novel's larger world in spite of her more pronounced withdrawal from it. In La Loca's case, though, these encroachments have a very different quality. The first of these comes in the form of the peacocks being bred by "Mr. Charles," one of many Anglo outsiders who more and more inhabit Tome. Though the presence of these outsiders may carry with it a subtle sense of menace, the peacocks do not. The narrator describes how La Loca saw them as "the most splendid thing on two claw feet." The narrator continues: "She imitated the peacock's walk and tried to make the peacock talk, but it didn't go along with any of her playfulness, not because it was stupid like a chicken or ornery like a rooster. The peacock, Loca concluded, was just not an imitator" (Castillo, *So Far from God* 151). The singsong quality of the narrator's description here—the rhyming of "peacock's walk" and "peacock's talk," for example—evokes the childlike and playful consciousness of Loca. This encroachment of the outer society and world is a much gentler and even benign presence, playfully prideful in how it will not reduce itself to Loca's games. Furthering this shift is how the presence of the peacock contrasts other encroachments of the novel's world, such as chemical poisoning or the Gulf War. Instead of violent and dangerous, the peacock, to Loca, is "splendid" with a "tremendous turquoise blue tail that opened at whim like the Spanish fan her mother used" (150–151). Not only is the peacock unique in its loveliness, but it also resonates with an image from Loca's own experience, Sofi's fan. Loca's interactions with the peacock differ from the bulk of the sisters' interactions with the novel's larger world; it is an aspect of that world that actually resonates with the community of Tome, setting up a consonance rather than difference between the two.

More similar to the experience of her sisters, and Caridad in particular, is Loca's contraction of AIDS. Representing another inadvertent but inevitable incursion of the larger world on Tome and its inhabitants, the virus's infection of Loca is also comparable to the *malogra*. Both are, in different ways, amorphous, particularly given that there is no rational way for Loca to have contracted the disease, making it another magically real instance in the novel. It also can be said to connect Loca's experience with that of her two contrasting sisters. Like Fe, Loca finds herself suffering from a disease that ravages the U.S. nation and world. In the latter sense, Loca too gets swept up by the course of world events, not unlike how Esperanza is disappeared by the Gulf War.

But the significance of Loca's disease is not only for how it connects her to the same violent and exploitative forces that disposed of her sisters. Rather, it has a much more transformative effect within the world of *So Far from God* on how the various peoples, spaces, and accompanying attitudes relate to each other. One can see this effect prior to Loca's death in the interaction of her two doctors, Dr. Tolentino, a psychic surgeon, and *la doña* Felicia, a local *curandera*. Though the two practitioners are initially opposed to each other, their experience treating Loca breaks down those divisions. The narrator describes, for example, how *doña* Felicia "put aside pride regarding her knowledge and relented to every tratamiento known to the Rio Abajo curanderas" as well as male doctors (232–233). Inherent in this passage is *la doña*'s transcending of the professional, philosophical, and gendered divisions, a shift that is reciprocated by Dr. Tolentino when he notes, for example, his familiarity with and respect for her practices. Furthermore, the narrator highlights how both maintain "the practice of praying before they did anything. So it may be said in the end that they did have much in common" (235). Their larger similarity of prayer, one of several commonalities the two share, makes them not competing systems, but two parts of a larger system, unique and distinct from each other, yes, but not distant and unrelated. Loca's death brings these doctors, and the novel's reader, to this realization.

The Holy Friday Procession of the Cross that Loca participates in prior to her death is another instance of unity proceeding from commonality. That commonality is the struggle by peoples, traditions, and cultures against the violent and exploitative forces at play in their nation and world. As Delgadillo claims, this moment manifests "a commitment to alliances with other marginalized groups . . . creating a bridge between the divergent populations it describes" and exemplifying "the emergence of a Chicana subjectivity that defined itself within the context of community and in league with the struggles of others" (910, 912). But it is not just an aware-ness of an alliance-in-difference that this procession indicates. In how it brings together the experiences of the four daughters with the similar ex-periences of all the women in the novel's world,[7] it also collapses its entire world into this moment, making these characters aware of themselves not just as allied in their marginalization as gendered, raced, sexualized sub-jects, but as world subjects. The unity evidenced between these women also unifies them with, makes them part of, and participatory within their world. They, in this moment, recognize themselves as world subjects rather than as distant and disconnected presences in that world. Loca, who so much separated herself from the big, vulgar world of the novel, becomes, in the end, the one most responsible for bringing not only herself but also others into a relationship with that world.

If the four daughters represent the two ideological sides of the novel, then it is their mother, Sofi, who most stands at the point of their over-lap and interpenetration. Thus, she, more than any other character in the novel, crystallizes both the novel's representation of persistence and its cos-mopolitan ethos. However, she does not start out so. Like Rechy's Amalia, Sofi initially lives a life of limited possibilities, simply enduring "the par-ticular life she had been given" (Castillo, *So Far from God* 85), especially the traumas suffered by her daughters. Her relationship with her husband, Domingo, after his return, lacks passion; the narrator describes how they "had become so used to each other that they didn't even notice one another anymore, like an old chair in the corner of the room or a table passed on

from one generation to the next that is there for the purpose of eating off"
(109).

Too, her community of Tome, New Mexico—with which she, above all
the other characters, is connected—mirrors the situation of Buckeye Road
in Véa's *La Maravilla*. The narrator describes how Tome "wasn't even an
incorporated village like Los Lunas or Belen," in the same way that Buckeye Road did not officially exist to its mainstream United States (137). Tome
also appears to share the same fate as Véa's imaginary community, to be
disappeared from the U.S. nation-scape. Sofi's *comrade* notes to her how
their land "just gets smaller y smaller," and the novel's narrator continues
on to delineate the precise forces furthering this diminishment:

> there were a lot of outsiders moving in, buying up land that
> had belonged to original families, who were being forced to
> give it up because they just couldn't live off of it no more, and
> the taxes were too high, and the children went off to Albu-
> querque or even farther away to work or out of state to college
> or out of the country with the Army, instead of staying home
> to work on the rancherias. (139)

Not only does this passage provide a litany of depredatory factors, but it
also implicates the members of this community in this process along with
those outside factors of U.S. society. The same passivity, the same acceptance of this process as inevitable, which we saw in both Véa's and Rechy's
novels, is evident here in the people of Sofi's community. As she herself
declares, "That kind of attitude was just the reason why things never got
better around here" (138).

It is through Sofi's actions to combat this seemingly inevitable process
and the attitudes sustaining it that the novel textualizes further a narrative
of persistence and a cosmopolitan ethos. Though prominently associated
with the domestic sphere of the home, Sofi successfully undertakes a cam-
paign to be mayor. This effort not only collapses the domestic and political
spheres, but also allows Sofi to work toward the persistence of her community and culture. The linchpin of this effort is the cooperative Sofi forms,
an effort that, like Loca's death, engages her entire community.

> There were many community-based meetings in which
> debates [occurred] as to what ideas would lend themselves
> best toward some form of economic self-sufficiency for their
> area before some people came up with a plan that eventu-

ally mobilized everyone into action. It would take YEARS
of diligence and determination beyond this telling to meet
their goals, but Sofi's vecinos finally embarked on an ambi-
tious project, which was to start a sheep-grazing wool-weaving
enterprise, "Los Ganados y Lana Cooperative" (146)

The narrator here clearly emphasizes the effort of Tome's inhabitants—
particularly its women—to achieve self-sufficiency and, through that, to
persist. And here is where Castillo's novel veers sharply from the fate of
Véa's Buckeye Road. In Véa's novel, its community and the conglomeration of cultural differences it contained faded from its imagined world.
Not so with Castillo's Tome. The narrator explicitly states that it would take
years of work beyond the time of the novel for Sofi and her neighbors to
achieve their goals, but implicit within this statement is the fact that they
do. In this, then, we know that Tome persists within its storyworld not only
spatially but temporally as well. It has a future beyond the events the novel
itself contains; it avoids being relegated nostalgically to the past.

Sofi undertakes a further political action, the formation of M.O.M.A.S.,
which stands for "Mothers of Martyrs and Saints," that crystallizes the
power of a cosmopolitan ethos. Through this organization, Sofi and her
larger community of Tome will push themselves beyond any marginal
status into the political and economic centers of their world. As the narrator describes, the annual M.O.M.A.S. conference evolves into "a world
event each year, taking the cake over the World Series and even the Olym-
pics" (249). It thus becomes its own spectacle, though not one of violence
and exploitation, and partakes then in the general spectacularization witnessed in the novel's world, though again for very different ends. Likewise,
M.O.M.A.S. becomes a marketing juggernaut and consequently participates in the novel's world's capitalism.

Every year the number of vendors of basically more useless
products and souvenirs than what a tourist could find on a
given day at Disney World grew. For example, there were
your T-shirts with such predictable stenciled phrases as "The
Twenty-Third Annual Convention of M.O.M.A.S. Flushing,
NY" or "Perros Bravos, Nuevo Leon," or "Las Islas Canarias,"
or "My Mother Is a Member of Mothers of Martyrs and
Saints—Genuflect, Please!", the usual posters, stationery,
forever-burning votive candles with your favorite saint's or
martyr's picture stuck on (or an instant photo of your own

> kid, if you preferred), "automatic writing" pens, and, then, of
> course, the all-time favorite—La Loca Santa and her Sisters
> Tarot Deck drawn by a lovely and talented artist in Sardinia,
> Italy. (249–250)

Again, this is a temporal expansion of Sofi's effort, as the first shirt mentioned references at least twenty-three years of M.O.M.A.S. conferences. Too, this organization and its members participate in their world's capitalism. They produce what even the narrator describes as effectively useless junk, similar to (and surpassing) the souvenirs of Disney. In this, the novel is casting U.S. and even worldwide capitalism and its spectacles not as a wholly separate, distant, and exploitative force to be avoided, but rather as something that Sofi and her organization can themselves exploit. In this reciprocal exploitation, they are implicitly viewing themselves, and thus the cultures and values they embody, as a part of their imagined world. Far from being doomed to nonexistence as seemed initially inevitable, Sofi, Tome, and its inhabitants persist and perhaps even flourish within the novel's imagined United States and world. And a concomitant part of this persistence is her/their cosmopolitan ethos, through which they see the hegemonic society and world not as a force to be avoided for its exploitation, but rather as something she/they too can exploit and thus, within which, participate.

Furthermore, their interjection and intervention into their capitalist/spectacularist world is cast not as some kind of betrayal, but rather playfully. Though useless, their products are not dangerous in the way others have been. The one-upmanship with Disney, the t-shirt mottos, the parenthetical interjection and even the description of the tarot deck as "the all-time favorite": all of these give the novel's narrator a barker-esque bombast and enthusiasm that invites if not cajoles the reader into sharing the novel's light-hearted view of this effort. The end result is that the expansion of Sofi and her community into her/their world is not presented as threatening. And this is something that the narrator's cajoling, playful, and even cross voice achieves throughout the novel. In the same way that the narrator herself is personalized and subjectified, so too is what she talks about. The voice in the novel treats highly gendered and raced differences not through an objectifying, epistemological lens but rather views it/them in ontological terms, as subjects. They are not a product to be consumed within an already-established and centered subjectivity, but something that interacts equally with that subjective understanding, attempting to seduce it into sympathy. This further transformative effort, one that acts on the reader as much as it exists in the world of *So Far from God,* presages the effort in the novels in Part Two of this project that, through their spatial/temporal representations and innovations, similarly challenge and thus transform their readers' understandings and ethical positionings.

## FOUR

*Changing Minds in Ana Castillo's*
Sapogonia *and Arturo Islas's*
La Mollie and the King of Tears


T he preceding texts by Rechy, Viramontes, Véa, and Cas-
tillo, with their respective spatial and textual constructions of persistence,
represent a first step toward answering Anzaldúa's earlier-mentioned call.
These works dramatically embody the need to "leave the opposite bank,
the split between the two mortal combatants somehow healed" (Anzaldúa
100). Cultural identities—male and female, Anglo and Chicano, gay and
straight—represented spatially and separately, belong to the same national
space rather than to disparate ones. However, they do not, to again borrow
from Anzaldúa, fully stand on the same "shore." That is, there remains a
perceptible distinction between these cultures. Though a space like Véa's
Buckeye Road may be represented as persisting within the U.S. nation-
space alongside U.S. Anglo society, it and the cultural differences it comprises remain a distinct and separate entity within that space. Thus, though
the physical divide may be ameliorated in the worlds of these texts, a cultural divide remains within both these worlds and their readers' minds. In
particular, lagging behind in these representations of persistence is a pervasive change in the characters' and thus the readers' consciousness that
results from their recognition of this new cultural disposition. Though the
preceding texts may gesture toward such a consciousness, such efforts are
limited and contingent. Rechy's Amalia, for example, can be said to reach
the point at which her understanding of her world alters—and the novel
ends. In Viramontes, such a consciousness is precisely what the story laments as a failed possibility. Véa's Beto and Castillo's Sofi come closest to
embodying such a transformed state; however, Beto's is best seen in his
adult form, which only briefly enters the narrative, and Sofi's is abstracted
into the group effort of M.O.M.A.S. In the end, what the preceding works
accomplish lacks a further-reaching representation of the mindset—what
Anzaldúa terms, in admittedly highly gendered terms, the "mestiza con-

sciousness"—that coincides with the changed cultural conditions they depict.

A fuller representation of such a new mindset begins with the novels by Ana Castillo and Arturo Islas, *Sapogonia: An Anti-Romance in 3/8 Meters* (1994) and *La Mollie and the King of Tears* (1996). They resonate with Anzaldúa in valuing "divergent thinking" that gestures "toward a more whole perspective, one that includes rather than excludes" (Anzaldúa 101), but do not circumscribe this thought to a single gender. In representing such, these two works—and those by Véa in the next chapter—instantiate a second narrative paradigm, what I term "transformation." Where the texts in the preceding chapters mapped resistance and persistence in their characters' interactions with and movements within their respective storyworlds, these texts map a coming to a new consciousness toward differences and thus a transformation of their Chicana and Chicano protagonists and/or larger storyworlds. Specifically, these works challenge and frustrate efforts to understand and so reduce differences to static, reified, epistemological categories. In their place, these novels depict peoples and cultures of difference as dynamic, subjective, and living entities or beings and so argue for conceiving of them in ontological terms. What they share with the texts preceding them in this discussion is their communication of this transformation through a poetics of space that uses their protagonists' relationship to particular and national spaces, as well as the represented nature of those same spaces.

Such an interaction between space and consciousness has been largely muted in discussions of fictional or narrativized consciousness. This absence can be seen as a consequence of the more general neglect of space in narrative lamented earlier by Wesley A. Kort. He writes, for example, that "narrative theory, rather than doing justice to the full potential of spatial language in narrative discourse, subordinates it," specifically to "temporal language, that is, the language of action and events" (10). Narrative theory thus neglects or obscures the "force and meaning" space and place in fictionalized narratives possess, how they are "related to human values and beliefs" and a "part of the larger human world" (11). As should be obvious from the previous chapters, I too see fictional space as functioning within how a text communicates its "beliefs" or ethics. Here, though, I assert this function of space within not only these works' characters' own fictionalized ethical consciousnesses, but also within the space of the text itself, its narrative constructions, working to alter or affect a reader's own ethical positionings.

This emphasis has been largely absent from some of the seminal works on fictional consciousness, including Dorrit Cohn's *Transparent Minds* and Alan Palmer's *Fictional Minds*. Both Cohn and Palmer assert the primacy of consciousness in fictional texts. As Cohn explains, "fictional consciousness is the special preserve of narrative fiction" as such fiction is the only place "in which the unspoken thoughts, feelings, [and] perceptions of a person other than the speaker can be portrayed" (vi, 7). Palmer echoes Cohn in his description and definition of narrative fiction as "the presentation of mental functioning" (5). Their analyses of such mental portrayals, however, obviate the role fictional space and place can have in communicating narrative consciousness. Cohn's admitted predilection "for novels with thoughtful characters and scenes of self-communion" consequently removes such minds from their textual worlds (v). The focus is on isolated and self-communing personas, an emphasis that has translated across narrative theory in general, as shown by its clear attachment to such devices as stream of consciousness writing and such frequent examples as the "Penelope" chapter of James Joyce's *Ulysses*. Palmer, in fact, eschews just such an emphasis, noting that "the strangeness of the device of direct access [to fictional minds] should not allow us to forget that the reader's experience of the minds of characters in novels does not depend solely on that device" (11). Instead, Palmer highlights how such knowledge comes through the actions, behaviors, and speech that derive from and thus indicate a character's mental state: "Just as in real life the individual constructs the minds of others from their behavior and speech, so the reader infers the workings of fictional minds and sees these minds in action from observation of characters' behavior and speech" (11). Like Palmer, Lisa Zunshine, in *Why We Read Fiction*, advocates a social or behavioral approach to assessing fictional minds. She writes of how writers "have been using descriptions of their characters' behaviors to inform us about their feelings since time immemorial" and, further, how we as readers have learned that "the default interpretation of behavior reflects a character's mind" (4).

But though both Palmer and Zunshine privilege what we can call the "social mind," they downplay the role of where such society occurs in fictional narratives: the spaces and places of the storyworld. In Zunshine, descriptive passages of that world become something the reader tolerates (if not skips) as an interruption to the "real" activity of having their mind-reading capabilities stimulated. As spatial descriptions fail to as immediately gratify a reader's "mind-reading adaptations," they may be easily ignored (26). As with cognitive mapping in general, this strategy results from an (over)emphasis on what the reader's mind is doing in relation to fictional consciousness. It neglects the ways in which the text generates a sense of a character's mind, which does not solely depend on how the text parallels how our minds are presumed to function in reality. Palmer goes even further. He describes the fictional text not "as the representation of an objective storyworld, but as the interconnection of all the subjective embedded narratives of all the characters who inhabit that fictional work" (141). In other words, a storyworld only exists as it does from a/the character's/characters' perspective(s). It has no objective reality within a text.

Though one can imagine texts where this claim holds true, I would argue that it is not true for all novels as Palmer claims. Again, this position seems a product of privileging the reader over the text. As he says, "fictional minds do not exist except by the semiotic operation of reading texts . . . . [I]t is only the reader who can have an awareness of a fictional mind" (141). But to say that fictional minds do not exist until the reading act is to ignore the objective reality of the words on the page and the text itself. In contrast, I would argue that fictional minds exist through the interaction of reader and text. Recall, for example, the passage from Rechy detailing Amalia's environment. There are objective realities to her storyworld that do not just exist in her mind: the weeds and dirt, broken-down cars, iron bars, the homeless and the graffiti. The hardening and decay of the novel's storyworld is not just in Amalia's mind; it is an objective aspect of the world around her. Amalia's dismaying perspective suffuses the passage, yes, but it is her assessment of the objective world around her that produces such dismay and thus her consciousness. The reader's sense of her mind results, then, from how the passage conveys her reality, but its doing so does not make that reality just a product of her mind. There is both a storyworld and a storyworld as produced by Amalia's mind, and both contribute to a reader's apprehension of her fictional mind.

It is, then, this relation between storyworld spaces and places and fictional consciousness that underlies this chapter's discussion of Castillo's *Sapogonia* and Islas's *La Mollie and the King of Tears*. That is, I want to examine how these authors construct their protagonists' minds in relation to their worlds to indicate how both those minds and their worlds need to change. Both Castillo and Islas target, on one level, the blinkered understanding within Chicano culture produced by its Aztlán mythology and patriarchal, masculinist ideology. Additionally, both authors parallel this problematic and reifying mindset to that of mainstream U.S. Anglo society, implicating and indicting both for their similar effects. In *Sapogonia*, Castillo criticizes a resulting reification of gender differences with her Chicano protagonist Máximo Madrigal that contradicts the nature of the novel's titular Chicano/a homeland, which is more aptly embodied by the novel's Chicana protagonist, Pastora Velasquez Aké. In Islas's posthumous novel, Louie Mendoza must navigate a culturally heterogeneous San Franciscan landscape that not only contradicts but also transforms the heteronormative and masculinist consciousness he similarly embodies. In both works, space and place are not simply constructs of fictional consciousness. Rather, they contest and challenge characters' minds, an effort paralleled by these texts' own challenge to their readers' minds. Kort contends that the "spatial theory" implicit within narrative fiction in general needs to be "released" (18–19). So too do I seek to "release" and express the spatial understanding of consciousness that Castillo's and Islas's novels generate, an understanding that seeks to transform previously resistant and divisive ones.

## NEGATIVE AND POSITIVE TRANSFORMATION IN ANA CASTILLO'S *SAPOGONIA*

*Sapogonia: An Anti-Romance in 3/8 Meter*, Castillo's second novel, centers on the experiences of two migrant characters from its titular country: Máximo Madrigal and Pastora Velasquez Aké. These two characters' lives (and bodies) progressively intersect as they move to, from, and within the United States. The novel does not move linearly through their adventures. It opens with a surreal and dream-like depiction of Máximo's murder of Pastora and, from there, turns back to Máximo's youth and eventual journeys to find, first, his biological father and, later, success and acclaim in the United States. Alongside Máximo's efforts and conquests, the text details the experiences of Pastora, who develops a greater presence in the novel as its narrative develops. She engages in both heterosexual and lesbian affairs, political activism (at no small risk to herself ), and encounters Máximo at various points in her life. The novel eventually returns its reader to just before Máximo's murderous act, but preempts its completion with a shift to an epilogue depicting a very much alive Pastora gardening with husband and son.

Behind both characters' experiences stands the novel's imagined Latin American country of Sapogonia. Not only is it the country of origin for both protagonists, but it is also an alternative Chicano/a homeland. Sapogonia stands as a space of ontological ambiguity similar to that featured in Anzaldúa's mestiza consciousness.[1] Too, it is represented as an ur-space from which all people of mixed descent originate, but whose fullness and inclusion have been co-opted and betrayed by the heteronormative patriarchy of the Aztlán-based mythology behind the Chicano Movement. The novel critiques these masculinist attitudes not only for how they seek to reify and flatten feminine identity and being into epistemological categories, but also for how these efforts and effects parallel, if not ally, with U.S. racism and sexism.

The relationship each of the main characters has with Sapogonia and the consciousness it represents facilitates the novel's textualization of transformation. Máximo falls well short of the inclusiveness Sapogonia symbolizes. He remains, instead, an egotistical, monadic, and dominating male figure who imposes his views and categories on the world around him, expecting it to fit into those structures. He thus fails to transform and, as a result, suffers psychic alienation and existential angst when something or someone, notably Pastora, disrupts his categories. Pastora, on the other hand, does transform and so fulfills the promise symbolized in the novel's imagined homeland. She eventually demonstrates a compassion for others and othered beings and becomes herself a complex, dynamic character in spite of Máximo's efforts. Reinforcing the contrast is the novel's third-person narrator. She moves between these distinct consciousnesses and comes to identify and sympathize not only with Pastora but also with other women facing similar male domination and reification. Too, the presence of narrative shifts and gaps creates a textual ambiguity in *Sapogonia* that prevents the reader from developing a Máximo-like facile understanding of the text. Such textual ambiguity parallels that of the novel's titular country and thus presents to its reader a similar challenge as that space does to the novel's two protagonists.

The ambiguous presence of Sapogonia hovers over the entirety of Castillo's novel. It stands counter to what Castillo presents as the patriarchal and exclusionary space of Aztlán promulgated by the Chicano Movement. Wilson Neate describes the "reductive precedent" for understandings of Chicano/a identity and community that are the consequence of the nationalist movement's adoption of this mythology and past:

> Given that ethnic identity was considered . . . to be linked to
> the Aztec heritage and given that, much like its patriarchal
> pre-Columbian model, it was constructed largely as a male-
> oriented identity, a crucial aspect of the ideal and idealized

> Aztec society represented and valorized in culturalist criti-
> cism — and similarly reconstituted and propagated in nation-
> alist narratives of Chicano/a identity — was the domination of
> women. (17–18)

What Neate describes here is precisely what Rechy imagined in *The Miraculous Day of Amalia Gómez* when Amalia encountered the mural celebrating the Chicano's Aztec past (see Rechy 145). Amalia's wondering about the status of women in this image points out women's absence from that past due to its male-centeredness. Amalia's own experiences in the present confirm the lingering effects of this ideology, as she herself suffers from the male domination that is its consequence. Similarly, Castillo seeks to undermine this absenting of women by reforming her Chicano/a home-land as an inclusive space. Unlike Aztlán, Sapogonia is *"a distinct place in the Americas where all mestizos reside, regardless of nationality, individual racial composition, or legal residential status — or, perhaps, because of all of these* (Castillo, *Sapogonia* 1, original italics). Sapogonia's status as the ori-gin of all peoples of mestizo descent necessarily includes men and women, providing within the novel's world a corrective. Castillo substitutes this in-clusive space within her storyworld for the exclusionary one of Aztlán and the Aztec past and identity that privileges male identity and community.

As a result of its inclusive nature, Sapogonia becomes a space of ambi-guity within the storyworld it inhabits. As a mestizo space, it features a conglomeration of not only genders, but also races and ethnicities, na-tional identifications, and residency statuses, as listed in its opening de-scription. The novel's Prologue further creates a sense of this space's pro-found ambiguity, most prominently in its nature as a country. Sapogonia is a specific place, yet it cannot be "identified by modern boundaries" (2). It lies somewhere to the south of the United States; as the origin of all mes-tizo peoples, the temptation might be to equate it with all of the extant Latin America. The text, however, prevents such an identification. Mexico is explicitly mentioned as separate from Sapogonia, Máximo and all others having to travel through Mexico City from Sapogonia on the way to the United States. Later in the novel, Máximo sends his sculptures to Brazil for a showing, marking it and by extension South America as likewise dis-tinct. Even Sapogonia's very nature as a homeland creates ambiguities. As Maya Socolovsky relates, "[T]he borderland mestizo no longer originates from more than one place, but instead has a single and pure place of ori-gin: Sapogonia. But that pure origin . . . is itself based in hybridity, so that hybridity becomes the origin of one's race" (76). Thus, it is both pure and mixed, a racial origin but also racially hybrid.

Further reinforcing Sapogonia's ambiguity is its magically real nature. As Máximo somewhat realizes when he returns home late in the novel, Sapogonia is a place where the real and the supernatural coexist and even blur. He visits his strife-torn country and, upon learning about the uncertain fate of his grandparents, leaves the relative safety of his mother's home for theirs. There, he has a ghostly encounter with his Mamá Grande's spirit. Even as her and her husband's bodies rot in their bedroom, this spirit prepares a meal for Máximo and asks him to make arrangements for the pair's burial (Castillo, *Sapogonia* 249–250). Sapogonia's ontological status, then, is profoundly ambiguous in how it elides a variety of distinctions, from those of racial and national identity to those between the real and the magic or supernatural, the living and the dead.

The ambiguous nature of this imaginary homeland has not been fully recognized in preceding critical efforts to appraise its significance to the novel. Monika Kaup, for example, renders it in wholly abstract terms, casting Sapogonia as a "country of the mind, geographically vague, and . . . located at an elevated mythical level in time and space to contrast the rest of the narrative" (239). Though in fact "geographically vague," Sapogonia is not only a mental space; it is also a physical space within the novel's world that, though it may foster a particular consciousness, cannot be reduced to only a psychological reality. Similarly, Sapogonia is not so distinct in time from the rest of the novel's world. It is subject to the passage of time and history, and the effects of such, as made clear upon Máximo's return home. He explicitly states that "something changed" (Castillo, *Sapogonia* 246). The country's idyllic and even Edenic natural features—"the aroma of guayaba trees" and "the sun pouring onto the streets"—find themselves "replaced by the smell of gunpowder" and "mourning filtered through the air." The people themselves are changed: "Men and women passed each other on the street without a greeting, the tipping of a hat, the tickling of a baby's chin. Beggars were more humble than ever" (247). Such changes root Sapogonia in history and time. Socolovsky similarly relegates Sapogonia to mythology. Even as she highlights how Sapogonia attempts to "demythologize the distant Aztlán that remains fixed in a specific historical heritage and cultural past," she simultaneously mythologizes Sapogonia as a "Borderland Aztlán, a mythical country" that gives "rise to an active political nation that functions like any other through its own myths and imagined communities" (77). Such a move seems counter to both the material realities of exploitation, domination, and threat to Chicanas within which Anzaldúa grounds the borderlands concept and the reality of Sapogonia within the novel's storyworld. Socolovsky distinguishes it from an "active, political nation." Sapogonia gives rise to this, but is not it itself. Instead, the country is both mythological and political. It is a national borderlands, but it still exists and acts within the present of the novel's world.

Sapogonia is perhaps better described as a heterotopic site within Castillo's storyworld. It exists as a space of ambiguity—specifically, an ontological ambiguity born of how it collapses distinctions. It is a "real" site, a "real" country within its world that fosters a particular awareness or consciousness. As Castillo rewrites it, then, Aztlán becomes a reduction of Sapogonia, which encompasses Aztlán but is not wholly congruent with it. It is, in a sense, "larger." The novel writes a new history including the Sapogón and the Sapogóna, that, out of which, both enter the world. Too, the politics of this revision are oriented differently from those of the Aztlán-based Movement. Instead of reaching back from the present to recover a lost, mythic past and cultural heritage, Castillo associates Sapogonia with a movement and politics coming out of a past into the present. The country's capital, Puerto Sapogonia, crystallizes such a shift. It serves as a way station or doorway into the larger world of the text and the United States in particular.

However, what gets described as the actual history of Sapogonia does not follow through on the country's promise. Rather, it reflects the male dominance within Chicano/a culture. In its initial description, Sapogonia's history is tied to the male Sapogón. It describes him as "of a certain wealth and class status," speaking "fluent French in addition to his native Spanish"; he will "also attain fluency in English" as "achievement now weighs almost exclusively on recognition by the United States of America" (Castillo, *Sapogonia* 1–2). It is the Sapogón as so described that the country's "history of slavery, genocide, immigration, and civil uprisings" has given birth to (1). Notably absent from this recitation, of course, is the Sapogóna; she is, in fact, only referenced once in this passage: "Sapogonia (like the Sapogón/a) is not identified by modern boundaries" (2). There are, in essence, two Sapogonias: the idealized mythic space of mestizo origin and the historical reality that has been male-centered and -dominated.

Castillo positions Máximo as the embodiment of the patriarchal reality that exists within the novel's imagined world. Castillo, through the novel's narrator, inscribes Máximo within a legacy or pattern of such exclusion and domination that is not only a part of his own consciousness but also that of the Chicano in general within the novel's world. What defines Máximo's consciousness is a narrow-minded treatment of women. They are, in a sense, absent from Máximo's consciousness. Specifically, their desires and feelings, often if not always the opposite of Máximo's, are repeatedly nullified. An early example of this absenting occurs when Máximo retells his adolescent rape of a girl. He explains, "In all honesty, I hardly know why I took that girl by force. It wasn't as if I couldn't have had any other girl that I wanted without a struggle, but somehow it occurred to me to choose this one and once I realized that she didn't love me, that she didn't even like me, it was too late. I was committed to having her" (12). The girl herself merited little consideration at the time of her rape, and still does. He can think of nothing about her that drove his actions, in essence failing to recognize or remember her as an individual. She remains only "a girl" or "that girl." Similarly, his amorphous desire wins out over her explicit dislike.

Furthermore, Máximo generalizes the nullification of this particular girl to all women: he knew and knows he could have had, like he did her, any girl without a struggle. This recollection is only the earliest example of what becomes a pattern in Máximo's behavior. While living in Paris with his college friend, El Tinto, Máximo seduces Catherine, the virginal daughter of his friend's lover. He only ponders the implications of his actions afterward: "Why, in the process of loving women, did man have to nullify something so profound that it was no longer physical?" (32). After relocating to the United States, Máximo begins an affair with another woman, Laura Jefferson, which ends up the same. As he angrily confronts her, Máximo demands, "And why are you wearing that ugly rag? Haven't I asked you a hundred times to get something else?" Here, Máximo references his demand that she "wear sexier things at home" to excite him, an effort to fetishize Laura, to make her, as the novel's narrator describes, "the mere object of his sexual arousement" (174). In Máximo's mind, women only exist in such flattened or reified forms. Their individuality, identity, and desires disappear when Máximo imposes his will and body upon them. They are, in other words, precluded within and excluded from his consciousness.

Máximo is not alone in this representation. Castillo very quickly extends his treatment of women to Chicano men in general. The mindset Máximo displays is one he inherits as part of a fraternal and paternal legacy. Máximo elucidates the fraternal legacy as he continues his recollection of his first rape by describing the reaction of his victim's brothers: "Her brothers were like mad dogs when they caught up to me. If it wasn't for my grandfather, who had approached and shot his gun in the air, they would have killed me" (12). However, neither the brothers' outrage nor Máximo's deserved retribution last long. In fact, Castillo has Máximo go on to voice his and the brothers' reconciliation: "It was all part of the ritual. I never resented that they tried to drown me. I expected something of that sort to come after I'd left the girl by the side of the road. Afterwards, we became good friends, her brothers and I, probably because of mutual compassion, forgot about the deflowered sister, and gave ourselves up to fraternal esteem for each other" (12). Máximo's own words indict the brothers as complicit in their sister's rape. The identification of their retaliation as part of a "ritual" implies that their actions are a part of the rape. Their vengeance becomes only a rote part of this transaction between men. What we learn of the brothers' subsequent actions does little to counter this impression. How else to explain their eventual friendliness with Máximo? That their friendship derives from a "mutual compassion" signals a lack of the same for Máximo's victim. In the end, the brothers' filial responsibility and connection lies with Máximo, their fellow man, not his anonymous and negated prey, their sister. They share in a mindset with Máximo that excludes and wholly absents her from consideration.

Complementing this fraternal legacy of women's negation is a paternal one passed down to Máximo from both his itinerant father, Pío de la Costura, and the grandfather who rescued Máximo from those same brothers. Pío, for example, looks at his tryst with Máximo's mother as merely "an adventure of his youth" (55). Such a description of her objectifies and fetishizes Máximo's mother just as Máximo will Laura Jefferson. Though Pío seeks to make amends for his absence—by teaching Máximo flamenco guitar and outfitting him for his journey to the United States—no such amends are made to, or even thought of for, Máximo's mother. We further learn, through the admiring voice of Máximo, how his grandfather thinks similarly of women. "The one my grandfather had tried to run, but seeing she was done for, submitted without a whimper or complaint. It was afterward, when he was about to leave, that he heard her sob. 'Don't cry,' he told her. 'It happens to everyone sooner or later. It wasn't that bad was it?'" (100). Here again, the woman is unable to affect her situation: not only is she "done for," but she is also already "had" when Máximo begins his description. For his effort to "console" her and decision to marry her, Máximo further lionizes his grandfather: "It would have undoubtedly made my grandfather, in my perspective, even more noble than I already thought him. It was hard enough to know that he was one of those men on which great novels are based" (98). In Máximo's mind, this rape becomes a heroic narrative displaying his grandfather's generous and even gentlemanly nature. Such hero worship chafes against his actual treatment of Mamá Grande, here and after their marriage. Once married, Máximo's grandfather did not allow his wife "to wear her native costumes, except, of course, when she went home on visits." She likewise "was not allowed to pray to her row of clay statues. He made certain his diminutive wife was a God-fearing Roman Catholic, and built a shrine in the garden for a life-size statue of the Virgen de los Remedios." According to Máximo, this "privilege meant a great deal to Mamá Grande," and his grandfather's deigning to grant it only adds to his nobility (10). However, it simultaneously exposes the grandfather's own dominating desires, ironizing Máximo's effort to heroicize him and locating within him the origin of that patriarchal legacy, which implicates him in the narrow consciousness the novel as a whole critiques.

The implications of this male consciousness extend beyond Chicano culture and identity, as Castillo further parallels these attitudes to the racism and exploitation within U.S. society. The novel draws this parallel in two specific scenes where Máximo runs up against U.S. immigration officials, the first having an immediately chilling effect on him: "He stood frozen, watching the men watch others, and for the present forgot the women who went on their way. He reminded himself that he looked Caucasian. He was dressed in denim pants and his sheepskin coat. There was nothing about him that could give him away" (76). At the root of Máximo's fear is an anxiety over his ability to "pass," an ability that signals his membership in another "brotherhood." These officials calling out to Máximo, "Hey buddy, I think you dropped this," further indicates such belonging. As a result of this call, Máximo feels a "curious sense of freedom" and acceptance by U.S. society (76). But Máximo is likewise being welcomed into the fraternal embrace of another exploitative and oppressive entity: U.S. society.

In a second scene between Máximo and immigration officials, Castillo more explicitly establishes a link between U.S. racism and Chicano dominance of women. When the restaurant he works at is raided by U.S. immigration, Máximo's still-present Sapogonian accent gives him away and he is "thrown against the wall and searched" (174). He sublimates his rage over this humiliation into a rape of Laura Jefferson. She becomes "the despising symbol of all he aspired but had to work for, beg, steal." Máximo once again fetishizes Laura, this time into the embodiment of U.S. society's racism, and he assaults her, "excited by her humiliation" (175). In this instance, racist humiliation sublimates into the sexual domination and exploitation of women. The two feed into each other and women are the victim of both forces. Overall, Máximo becomes a twisted image of the Chicano male promulgated by that Aztec mythology. Neate observed about the Chicano Movement that its assertion of an Aztec mythology and identity in response to U.S. racism brought with it the domination and absenting of female identity and desire. In Máximo, a similar confrontation with U.S. racism brought about his domination of Laura, showing an extreme consequence of this male consciousness.

One dimension of Máximo's representation, then, sets him up as the embodiment of this chauvinistic and dominating mindset. The other dimension is the novel's critique of such a blinkered consciousness, particularly for its reification of women, through its effect on Máximo. Máximo deteriorates over the course of the text, degenerating into an "alienated and fragmented psyche" (Walter 90). But his descent can also be seen as a product of how he falls short of the inclusion represented by his homeland. Máximo's journey in *Sapogonia* is "a journey away from communion into solitude" and "the core of this journey lies [in] his inability to see women, especially Pastora, as individuals with whom communion is achieved not only through sexual intercourse but also through human intercourse" (Gómez-Vega 244). Máximo's limited interaction with women indicates his limited view of them: he sees them only as sexual objects and not as beings. As a result, he fails to achieve a more human communion with them, the kind of communion the ideal Sapogonian establishes within the novel's world.

The alienation and isolation Máximo ultimately suffers is the ironic consequence of his mindset. Máximo's own objectifying, reifying perspective, in the end, objectifies and reifies him. In this, Máximo negatively embodies the transformation of consciousness this novel textualizes. He fails to move beyond the narrow strictures of his male-oriented, heterosexist, and implicitly "American" point of view. The text most clearly points to the limitations of this consciousness when it is frustrated by peoples and experiences that defy it. Such moments cluster particularly around the figure of Pastora, who not only helps to undermine this consciousness but also to suggest its alternative.

One way that Castillo presents Máximo as reified is how, from the very start of *Sapogonia*, she reduces him to a cliché. Prefacing the novel proper is a parodic definition of the "anti-hero" that clearly attaches to Máximo: "1. In mythology and legend, a man who celebrates his own strength and bold exploits. 2. Any man who notes his special achievements. 3. The principal male character in a novel, poem, or dramatic work" (iii). The combination of elements in this definition casts the principal male character in this and any novel as an egoist who celebrates himself and his own doings. And Máximo clearly follows through on this prescribed role. For example, he celebrates his effort to find his estranged father Pío as a "dramatic search" (43). The novel's narrator reveals it to be anything but "dramatic": "Máximo lived in Barcelona for three months before he decided to look for his father. It wasn't an original idea. It came to him one night when he was watching a film on television" (16). The narrator continues, "As it turned out, that sappy piece of entertainment was the top that sent him spinning into one situation, and then the next, which in the end became his destiny" (16). Contrasting Máximo's heroic narrative, this description emphasizes the banality and randomness of his "quest." The movie inspiring his search is an overly sentimental one. The "top" metaphor reduces Máximo's newly born effort to find his father to a product of random gyrations and impacts. The conclusion of Máximo's search reinforces its random aspects: instead of reaching his goal and heroically overcoming the obstacles to finding his father, Máximo and Pío reunite when the two happen to be locked in the same jail cell (52).

The narrator similarly flattens what to Máximo are perhaps his most prominent accomplishments, his sexual conquests. When he attempts to seduce Pastora's younger sister Ruthie, he resorts to the clichéd role of seductive artist. As Ruthie explains to her sister, "He took me to his studio to show me his work, you know, his sculpture and stuff" (237). Like the artist who invites his target to view his sketches, Máximo here lures the naïve Ruthie and then stereotypically asks her to model for him. As Pastora scornfully mocks, Máximo is "a wolf without enough imagination to use a ploy other than the oldest in modern history" (237). His efforts become even more laughable as Ruthie describes how Máximo tried to have sex with her but "couldn't get it in!" (237). Máximo's engorged member parallels his own inflated ego; he fancies himself one of "the greatest cocks in Western civilization," but like his ego, his penis is similarly over-enlarged and frustrates his effort (237). Máximo becomes in these scenes and elsewhere a comic figure for our ridicule and thus a far cry from the heroic figure as which he celebrates himself.

Besides serving to undermine Máximo's bloviated sense of himself, the above examples also position Pastora in contrast to Máximo. There, she derisively mocks his effort to seduce Ruthie; the text likewise identifies her as the source of its redefinition of the anti-hero. But beyond these discrete instances, Pastora counters Máximo with a contrasting attitude and mindset that more clearly reflect that Sapogonian ideal of inclusiveness. She demonstrates a compassion for others, that capacity for "human intercourse" referenced by Ibis Gómez-Vega, wholly lacking in her male counterpart. Furthermore, she disturbs both Máximo's life and the world of the novel with an ontological ambiguity that parallels that of the novel's Chicano/a homeland.

Pastora's contrast with Máximo is immediately apparent upon her first significant appearance. Her compassion for others combines with a disregard for herself that directly opposes Máximo's rampant egoism. We first encounter Pastora at her lowest point: depressed, not eating, and smoking heavily, she mourns her recently aborted fetus. However, Pastora is not wholly consumed by her problems. When she encounters Perla, a fellow artist, she immediately feels "Perla's humiliation and the rude disregard for her pain" as her affair becomes a subject of gossip (109). When Perla reveals her humiliation—"There's just no code of honor among women!"—Pastora befriends her, a move that demonstrates precisely the alliance and sympathy Perla disavowed (110). Such feelings sharply differ from those of Máximo who, for instance, betrays his friend El Tinto without pause when he sleeps with the latter's lover's daughter. Pastora has two further immediate effects. Her compassion for others leads to her own recovery, it being inconsistent with her self-neglect and self-destruction. But her compassion is also transformative. Diego Cañas, likely the father of Pastora's aborted child, is changed by her suffering. Not the first woman he impregnated, Pastora, unlike those others, does not inspire the same anger and resentment: "Pastora's mourning touched him. He remembered each occasion when he had almost become a father. He felt a tug at an absent womb in his lower abdomen and he cried with her" (106). The sight of the mourning Pastora inspires a compassion toward women that Diego, like Máximo, has previously lacked. Not only then does the novel establish Pastora as a person possessing compassion, but also as someone able to kindle the same within, and thus transform, others.

However, Pastora's compassion inhabits a storyworld where such feeling is not the norm. As the novel's narrator explains, "Dominant society was closing again. The youth was interested in individual achievement, financial success. No one wanted to hear about their neighbor's starvation, rape and pillage in American cities. No one joined hands and together raised them up like chains of fists" (186). This passage describes a world governed by self-interest and competition. It is a world of Máximos: those guided by self-focus, materialist desire, and a willed blindness to the sufferings of others. Pastora even observes this tendency in herself: "And she was no different, susceptible to the same illusive temptations invented by those few who had power. She allowed herself to be persuaded by the finer things in life. She frequented elegant restaurants as she had never done before. Her closets now held expensive clothes" (186). But Pastora is aware of her temptation, and thus self-aware, in a way Máximo is not. She knows this about herself and thus can also work to resist and counteract it within herself and her world. In doing so, she runs up against her world's narrow-mindedness. When she attempts "greater efforts to make the real difference for all Sapogóns" by transporting immigrants into the United States illegally, she is arrested and imprisoned (200). While in prison, her compassion for her fellow inmate Mary Lou runs her afoul of Mary Lou's bull-dyke tormentor, and Pastora is punished for her selfless involvement: "It is the committee's assessment that you could have avoided the whole incident had you not insisted on advising Mary Lou when you knew what the possible consequences were" (219). For her compassion, Pastora is punished. For her failure to be self-involved, she is castigated. Such moments dramatically demonstrate how Pastora exists in this novel to contrast not only Máximo's narrow-mindedness, but also that of the larger U.S. society and world. Such experiences as these indicate the extent of the change or transformation that world requires.

In addition to her compassion, Pastora's ambiguity further proves an exception within her world and especially to Máximo and his psyche. Gómez-Vega points out how there are two Pastoras in the novel: the one seen "through Máximo's eyes," a "woman who accepts him, unquestioningly, physically and emotionally, without making demands on him," and the Pastora we see outside of Máximo's view, a "vibrant, fully-committed individual who risks her own life to help others" (246). Implicit within Gómez-Vega's characterization is how Máximo's perspective proves its own undoing. It creates one of the two Pastoras and in doing so frustrates his effort to essentialize and contain her. This irony most prominently occurs in his labeling her a "witch." Pastora's supernatural appellation stems from rumors about her that pervade the social circle she and Máximo inhabit, but he quickly latches on to the label in order to explain those aspects of her being that defy his expectations. She possesses an "incapacity to surrender herself" and a "character of infinity," that, to him, make her an "enigma" and constant bother (Castillo, *Sapogonia* 134–135). He consequently grasps this label in an attempt to explain her power (at least for himself) and thus contain it. "Pastora was a witch, an unequivocal bruja who'd undoubtedly used her wicked power to hex him; a drop of spitballed wax on the back of his neck, one night, his hairs left on her pillow, pulled from his chest the moment he'd drifted into a heavy sleep after coming. Somehow she'd managed to take something so vital and potent from his being" (192).

But though this passage exhibits Máximo's need to define and thus reify Pastora's being, it simultaneously ironizes and unsettles that effort. The term "witch" itself admits Pastora's own supernatural and so uncategorizable nature. Furthermore, this classification gives Pastora a power over Máximo, a power he still gropes to explain. Consequently, its use makes explicit the unexplainable control she has over him rather than allowing him to define and contain her. Such irony, of course, critiques not only that term but also the consciousness from which it emanates. As Gómez-Vega observes, Pastora "is only a mystery to the man who does not care to know her, the man who acknowledges women only through his own vision" (249). The end result of Máximo's effort, of his mania for certainty, is the alienation and psychic fragmentation mentioned earlier. It is importantly a torment created by his own mind. It results from his inability to move beyond the reductive consciousness the novel associates not only with his gender but also with the larger U.S. society within which he seeks acceptance.

But it is not only Máximo's understanding and mindset that the novel seeks to challenge. It simultaneously frustrates a parallel mindset in its reader. Paralleling Pastora's ambiguities are the uncertainties that gather around her within the novel's narrative, disrupting the latter. These epistemological gaps present a challenge not only to Máximo but also to the novel's reader. The text of *Sapogonia* frustrates a narrative certainty and closure that creates a dissonance between that reader and Máximo. Whereas he is further undermined by how his reality eludes his epistemological grasp, the novel and its narrator coax its reader to simply accept—to tolerate, to use Anzaldúa's term—such ambiguities rather than reduce them to something "known." In this effect, the novel's text strives to engender in its reader that very transformation Máximo so patently fails to achieve.

The most prominent of these gaps manifests around Máximo and Pastora's sexual relationship. From Máximo's perspective, there is uncertainty as to whether such a relationship exists. Their first encounter occurs "off-screen": Chapter 21 ends with Máximo coaxing a ride home from Pastora; Chapter 22 begins as he awakens, disoriented, not knowing where he is or if he had sex the previous night, largely owing to his drunkenness (Castillo, *Sapogonia* 147–148). Pastora's appearance in this scene only reinforces these doubts: when Pastora appears, her face is painted red and yellow, marking her as Xalaquia, *"a temporary personification of Coatlicue who danced and pirouetted, hair loose and flung about."* Upon witnessing this surreal image, Máximo passes out from a pain in his chest; when he wakes, he finds himself in his own bed and home (149, original italics). In this series of events, Máximo's mind cannot account for Pastora's magical presence, and he is ejected from her reality back to his narrow one. Pastora possesses a magically real presence not dissimilar to that of Mamá Grande when her spirit encountered Máximo, further cementing Pastora's resonance with her homeland.

Pastora's presence is similarly ambiguous at a New Year's Eve party Máximo attends with his then-paramour, Maritza. Leaving the dance floor, Máximo enters the kitchen to find Pastora. Máximo subsequently maneuvers Pastora into a broom closet and prepares to have sex with her. Only he suddenly finds himself being slapped awake by Maritza amidst a crowd of partygoers, all of whom discovered him in the closet alone with his fly open (296–297). This time, it is Pastora who disappears, but the effect is the same. Máximo is once again a figure of derision, but, moreover, what he saw and experienced is replete with epistemological uncertainty.

Castillo further undermines Máximo's mind and perspective through how the power to know belongs to Pastora. Two chapters after Máximo's surreal ejection from her apartment, Pastora confirms their sexual encounter: "The night before, on that bed she had made love. The essence of that lovemaking remained, not only in the odor left on the sheets. The presence of Máximo Madrigal was heavy, a substance more disturbing than blood" (151). She similarly confirms the unreality of the encounter in the broom closet. Máximo calls Pastora in a clear attempt to prove she was at the party. But she tells him she was in California over the holiday and thus definitively not at the party (299). Not only then does the novel undermine Máximo's perspective, but it also privileges Pastora's in the same way that it privileges her compassion and selflessness over his selfishness and egocentrism.

The creation of these gaps in Máximo's perspective likewise undermines the masculinist mindset that the novel makes him embody. This mindset cannot encompass wholly the imagined reality of the novel's storyworld. The text's narrative structure also undermines the validity of this male consciousness. As this consciousness dominates the novel's storyworld, Máximo and his perspective initially dominate the novel. Part One of *Sapogonia* revolves around Máximo, and he provides one of its two narrational voices. The other belongs to a third-person narrator who is both distinct from and tied to Máximo's voice. This third-person voice often provides biting commentary about Máximo, particularly pointing to his ignorance and disengagement. For example, this narrator marks his obliviousness to the political reality of Sapogonia. Though he sees the military and the terror it produces as new, this narrator observes, "There was nothing new about that" (87). Too, when Máximo looks back nostalgically on how reporters were often disappeared during his youth, the other narrator castigates such talk as "casual, like an afternoon hobby" to point out even further Máximo's lack of engagement and awareness (87). Furthermore, this narrator does not slip into indirect free discourse with Máximo, but rather always functions in thought report: "Máximo had thought of the French girls"; "He envisioned himself in costume"; "He decided to go outside" (19, 114, 177). At the same time, however, the third-person narrator appears narratively dependent on Máximo, never veering from the events surrounding him in Part One of the novel. Also, Máximo in his narration at least once refers to events the third-person narrator voiced. Máximo references "that ridiculous movie that I mentioned before," but that mention was given by the novel's other narrator (41, 16). At the end of Part One, both speak directly to the novel's reader: Máximo, recalling part of a song written for the loss of one of Mamá Grande's sons, says, "That's all that I remember of it, but you get the idea," while the novel's other narrator, immediately subsequent to this statement, states, "Máximo put down his guitar and waited for you to turn the page" (101). The curious metafictional synchronicity of the pair hints at their linkage at this point in the novel, setting up a consonance between not only the two narrators, but also between them both and the novel's reader.

This changes, however, in Parts Two and Three, which coincide with the introduction of Pastora. Her arrival frees both the narrator and reader of Máximo. This shift occurs with the first sentence of Part Two: "It wasn't that he had fallen in love with her" (105). Castillo tricks the reader into thinking the "he" refers to Máximo, the only male referent the pronoun has at this point in the novel. This assumption proves wrong. The "he" actually refers to Diego Cañas, and the novel here leads us to find Pastora at her post-abortion nadir. In fact, Máximo, who so dominated Part One of *Sapogonia*, is entirely absent from the first several chapters of Part Two and will become even more so as of Part Three. The first five chapters of this later section focus almost solely on Pastora's efforts with undocumented immigrants; the chapter that does not focuses on Dora, the undocumented woman for whom Pastora goes to jail. Additionally, the third-person narrator's sympathies come to lie with Pastora and women in general. Castillo creates this consonance between the third-person narrator and the novel's women, most often through the employment of free indirect discourse. The narrator, at one point, sarcastically refers to Máximo as "the Cortes of every vagina he crossed," a description rooted in both Pastora's feelings toward him and her idiom (160). As Máximo assaults Laura, the third-person narrator describes her reaction: "He held her firmly but without need as she didn't fight. She bit into the satin quilt, it would be over soon" (175). The final statement—"it would be over soon"—reads as Laura's thoughts as she bites into the quilt, she and the novel's third-person narrator hoping for a speedy resolution, the latter again showing sympathy for the woman through its infusion by her consciousness.

Such statements also position the novel's reader in consonance with Castillo's women. We come to accept more and more their critical view of Máximo and the kind of male he represents. This effort to align the reader's sympathies with the novel's women, and Pastora in particular, reaches its culmination in Chapter 38, which deals with Pastora's time in prison. With this chapter, the narration shifts to the second person and present tense: "You wake on your own in the morning, gather your things at the foot of the bed the night before, and make your way to the bathroom at the far end of the long room" (213). The "you" here is Pastora, but the chapter's use of "you" is simultaneously another direct address to the novel's reader. Its presentness likewise puts the reader and Pastora at a similar time, not in the past tense as is the rest of the novel, but "now." The reader coincides with Pastora in this chapter, his or her sympathy fashioned into a direct correspondence. We are here at this point in the narrative, and its structure as a whole coaxes us to be Pastora, or like Pastora.

The ultimate test of the reader's similarity to Pastora and the consciousness she represents comes at the novel's end, which subverts any kind of narrative closure. The closing chapter of the novel proper leads us to literally just before Máximo's murder of Pastora. He spills Pastora's sewing basket, which holds the shears he will use as a weapon; he picks them up and runs his fingers over them, "stepping lightly toward her" before the chapter ends. As Pastora ostensibly slips away, Máximo is attacked by a cat and "screams, falling on the floor that is no longer the carpeted one of her bedroom but a cobblestone street" (7–8). The reader does not see the murder occur. Nor can the reader be entirely certain that it did occur when narrated to start the novel. The surrealism here of course parallels that apparent in Máximo's other intimate encounters with Pastora. Did he actually murder her at either point? The novel's reader is left unsure. Further disrupting the closure is the novel's Epilogue, which depicts Pastora daydreaming while working in her garden, surrounded by her husband Eduardo (Dora's former husband) and son. What has happened here? Does Pastora live? Does she somehow inhabit the body of Dora? Does this scene somehow precede the murder, even though it fits nowhere within the novel's continuity?

*Sapogonia* offers no answers, rendering the text itself contradictory and ambiguous, much like the country for which it is named and that Pastora represents. In a sense, the end of the novel brings its reader to the point of that alternative consciousness that Máximo, and men like him, fail to reach. We face the same challenges presented by the ambiguity of Pastora and Sapogonia both. The reader can dismiss the Epilogue, hardening into certainty, then, Pastora's demise, but such a move seems a violation of the whole text. One could alternatively render wholly abstract the novel as Elsa Saeta does when she reduces it to "a giant literary Rorschach—a text that reveals more about the reader and the interpretative process than about the text itself" (72). But doing so circles us back to those treatments of fictional consciousness that opened this discussion and their privileging of reader over texts and textual spaces. Rather, I would argue that Castillo's *Sapogonia* attempts to embody in its protagonist Pastora—and in the failures of Máximo—something like Anzaldúa's new mestiza consciousness in its urge toward inclusiveness. But also, the novel, in its text, creates a space to foster such a mindset in the reader, just as such a mestizo space inhabits, ambiguously and uncertainly, the novel's world.

## CONTAINING MULTITUDES: THE ORAL GEOGRAPHY OF ARTURO ISLAS'S *LA MOLLIE AND THE KING OF TEARS*

Similar ambiguity pervades the world and narrative of Arturo Islas's posthumously published novel *La Mollie and the King of Tears*. Set in 1973 in San Francisco, as the comet Kahoutek threatens to strike Earth, the novel opens with protagonist and full-time narrator Louie Mendoza waiting in the hospital for word on his lover, La Mollie, after her suicide attempt. A self-described "Mex-Tex Chicano" from El Chuco "in South El Paso near the old Santa Fe Bridge" (Islas, *La Mollie* 4–5), Louie tells his tale to a stranger with a tape recorder. He recounts the events of both his day and his life that have led to this point, collapsing the past and the present into each other. As Paul Skenazy describes, "[E]ach movement across San Francisco catapults Louie across time [and space], so every step forward in space is a leap backwards in time" (204). Too, the San Francisco that Louie gives voice to in his tale is culturally and socially confluent. Louie narrates and navigates a multitudinous social and cultural geography that includes the upper-class Anglo society of La Mollie and the Chicano/a culture associated with his estranged girlfriend Sonia; Shakespeare and Walt Whitman (both of whom preface the novel in epigraphs from *Romeo and Juliet* and "Song of Myself"), as well as *Gone with the Wind* and *The Wizard of Oz*; and Louie's own abundant machismo and heterosexuality along with the homosexuality of his brother Tomás. He narrates and inhabits a storyworld that is replete with differences; as Frederick Aldama explains in *Brown on Brown*, Louie's world is "palimpsestic" in how it "enfold[s] race, sexuality, class, and gender," making again the divisions between them ambiguous (74). Throughout his tale, Louie narrates himself moving between and within these various sociocultural forces and their attendant spaces.

Louie, then, mirrors Castillo's Máximo in how he too inhabits a multitudinous world. However, Louie starkly differs from Máximo in both his relationship to that world and the effect it has on him. Máximo was progressively tormented by how that world failed to fit into the narrow-minded categories of his male-identified consciousness. Louie shares some of the same objectionable qualities of this mindset—homophobia, sexism, machismo—but where Máximo ultimately remains trapped within the narrow confines of his heterosexist consciousness, Louie evolves in his view of the world. Louie's development, as a result, crystallizes both a narrative of persistence and one of transformation. Demonstrating the former is how Louie moves between and within different ontologically defined spaces that try to essentialize Louie and the difference he represents. Louie's ability to circumvent these efforts asserts such difference as a persistent and participatory part of U.S. culture. Beyond this, *La Mollie and the King of Tears* textualizes a transformation of Louie's own ontological status and consciousness. Louie becomes a "plural personality" that partakes, consciously and unconsciously, of the competing and contradictory influences that make up the novel's imagined San Francisco (Anzaldúa 101).

Through Louie's narration, the storyworld of the novel becomes what Brian McHale identifies as an "ontology," or "eclectic and anarchic landscape of worlds in the plural" (*Postmodernist Fiction* 10). Louie explicitly identifies the novel's San Francisco as being just so, composed of varying and different "worlds." In first describing his lover La Mollie, Louie tells us that she "comes from another world, man," that of an elite Anglo intelligentsia (Islas, *La Mollie* 4). Like La Mollie, Shakespeare too "comes from another world," one repeatedly emphasized as wholly separate from Louie and others like him in high school English with Miss Leila P. Harper. The movies, references to which pervade both Louie's tale and his consciousness, present yet another world. He states, "I love those old movies, man, 'cause they make me feel like I'm a Martian watching a world I can't live in no matter how much I try" (19–20). In comprising these and, as will be seen, other worlds, the storyworld of *La Mollie and the King of Tears* becomes a conglomerate of different ontological spaces, different spaces and definitions of being. To such a space, McHale associates a series of typical questions: "What is a world?; What kinds of worlds are there, and how are they constituted, and how do they differ?; What happens when different kinds of worlds are placed in confrontation, or when boundaries between worlds are violated?" (*Postmodernist Fiction* 10). For McHale, then, such a conglomerate landscape raises questions concerning the nature of those worlds themselves and their relationship to each other.

But questions can also be raised about the subjects inhabiting such spaces and their relationship to the sociocultural worlds that compose them. Louie's narrative raises precisely such questions about himself and the difference he represents in relation to these spheres: In what way(s) does Louie himself inhabit this world and its inset worlds? Can Louie inhabit them, and on what terms? And, perhaps most importantly, how does Louie negotiate these spaces and their terms? In the case of the worlds mentioned above, each attempts to define Louie and the difference he represents in essentialist terms and/or itself as separate from him. However, Louie repeatedly circumvents and destabilizes these efforts, often through a strategic deployment of essentialized identity, which allows him and such difference to persist within these worlds and the larger one that comprises them.

The first such world is that of La Mollie and an Anglo intellectual and liberal elite; however, their view of Louie exposes the limits of their liberalism. Both La Mollie and her fellows see Louie in essentialized terms. He confirms for them "how tolerant they are," letting him into their circle. But the conditions they place on Louie's entrance—that he's "not like the other Mexicans" they hypocritically complain about as having ruined Texas—reveal the paucity of their tolerance (Islas, *La Mollie* 22–23). The same limits impinge upon La Mollie's view of Louie. To her, Louie embodies what she assumes is the impoverished cultural experience of Chicanos/as along the Texas/Mexico border: "Well, she decided that I, Louie Mendoza, was gonna give her the inside dope on what people were really like in the towns by the Rio Grande, especially El Paso" (29). To La Mollie, Louie stands as "a real example of ethnic and racial poverty, resulting in cultural deprivation" (30). Both La Mollie and her circle, then, impose an essentialized identity and position upon Louie that signals how they view him and what he represents. Further demonstrating his consciousness of how they view him, Louie momentarily rails against the same in the form of his listener: "But you don't wanna hear about how much I can cry, do you? You want us Chicanos to be tough little Mexicans that got calluses on our scars and come outta the barrio with steel knuckles thinking the world's a prize fight" (155). In this statement, Louie voices the ironic distancing effect of a flattened, essentialized understanding of cultural differences that even the "sympathetic" elements of Anglo society exhibit. U.S. Anglo society only goes so far in its acknowledgment of cultural difference and so maintains a distance between itself and those different from it.

Another, similarly narrow-minded world is the U.S. Anglo society represented by Louie's high school. In relating his high school experiences, Louie prefaces them by making clear this institution's nature and effect: "[W]hat they was teaching us at la High was how to be good little obedient Messicans and stay in our place" (9). Here, Louie's high school becomes an arm of dominant U.S. society, teaching Louie and his friends "their place" in relation to that society, a place they must, in dominant society's view, accept and keep. Louie further identifies this effort to define cultural boundaries as he expands upon Miss Harper's teaching, specifically of Shakespeare, whose works become an apparatus in the maintenance of this distance and relationship. In her approach to Shakespeare, Miss Harper privileges her understanding and knowledge over that of her students, in particular those like Louie. As Louie explains, Miss Harper "gets them ready" to understand Shakespearean tragedy, implicitly assuming that their own experiences and culture(s) have not done so and cannot do so (9). Louie goes on to make this assumption explicit, when he tries to draw a parallel between his lived experiences and those told in Shakespeare: "I raised my hand and said, 'You mean like in the projects, Miss Harper?' Everybody else laughed, but she don't say nothing and just looks at me the way them old-maid teachers do and goes right on talking about Hamlet and Macbeth and them other court dudes like they know something we don't" (9). For Miss Harper, Shakespeare represents a knowledge and way of being wholly foreign to her students; furthermore, Louie and his fellow students have to understand Shakespeare's world on its own terms. Louie has her reiterate just such a point when she commands her class "to imagine what Macbeth must be feeling when he says those lines [in the 'tomorrow and tomorrow and tomorrow' speech] right after the poor loser gets told that his old lady is no longer among the living" (11). Again, they must understand the imagined experiences of Macbeth and Hamlet within their worlds—both story and ontological—and based only on those worlds. Her students have to understand what Macbeth feels, how *Hamlet* defines itself as tragic. And such an insistence creates not only a distance but also a hierarchy between the Anglo society of Miss Harper and the Chicano/a world and experience of Louie and his classmates.

What Louie and his classmates must not do is precisely what he does in putting his original question to Miss Harper: attempt to relate to or understand the plays in terms of his *own* experience and thus ameliorate that distance and hierarchy. Louie's effort to connect *Hamlet* to the projects is met with scorn, as likely would his further ruminations that Laertes "reminded me too much of Lencho Gonzalez, one of the guys I couldn't stand in the Fatherless Gang," or on Ophelia as "the first wetback in the history of the English language," or that Lady Macbeth committed suicide "'cause she couldn't wash her hands" (10, 11). In such statements, he implicitly refuses to sublimate his world and being to those Shakespeare defines. In doing so, Louie is clearly not being the "obedient Messican" the school insists he be. He instead presumes to equate if not privilege his experiences with those in Shakespeare, thus subverting the distanced, privileged position Miss Harper, and the U.S. Anglo society she represents, wish to assert for themselves.

Corollary to this leveling effect is the end result of Louie's efforts to understand Shakespeare's *Hamlet* in his own terms. They lead to many of the critical commonplaces associated with Shakespeare's most famous tragedy. Louie's lengthiest pondering of the play and its protagonist's quest for revenge evidences this fact:

> I never knew no guy out for revenge who talked as much as
> Hamlet. He's the prince, right? And he can have it all just
> by killing the jerk who murdered his old man and is now
> making it with his old lady. She's something else, man, and I
> won't even get started on her, though right now I'm thinking
> that's maybe why the guy talks so much — to keep from think-
> ing about her. Anyways, stead of killing the dude everybody
> knows is guilty, poor pitiful Hamlet puts it off and puts it off,
> boring everybody but Miss Harper to death, driving his girl-
> friend bananas — what she saw in the guy, I'll never know —
> and accidentally killing *her* old man *and* his own mother be-
> fore he gets to the creep that started it all. Then he dies in the
> arms of his best friend, who just sorta hangs around the castle
> with nothing to do til the end. (10, original italics)

Couched in Louie's particular idiom, this passage gestures toward what critics themselves have interrogated about the play: Hamlet's inexplicable delay and its resulting unnecessarily large body count, Gertrude's possible culpability in King Hamlet's murder and the Freudian relationship between her and her son, and the odd presence of Horatio throughout and particularly at the end of the play. This passage places Louie's interpretations on par with those of more "traditional" readers. Louie casts his ultimate critical judgment upon *Hamlet:* it does not make sense. Hamlet takes too long in his vengeance, Ophelia's love for him is anomalous, and the less said about Hamlet and his mother the better. In his comments, not only is Louie able to enter into and understand the world of Shakespeare's *Hamlet*, but he also operates toward and within it on his own terms, making the play subject to his experience and understanding rather than the other way around. In doing so, he further unsettles the hierarchical distance Miss Harper strives to assert between the ontological world of Shakespeare and her students and thus that same distance between Louie's culture and that of U.S. Anglo society.

Louie similarly circumvents the essentialized, ethnographic understandings of La Mollie and her elite circle, this time through a strategic essentialism. When they treat him "like a dumb Mexican" because of his accent, he simply plays the part. "That lets em all stay all smug, and I can laugh at em for being so stupid." Similarly, when Bruce, a "vampire-lawyer" Louie finds particularly annoying, talks about how minorities have ruined Texas, Louie responds to "his holier-than-thou look" with his "dumb Mexican look" (22, 23). When La Mollie objects to Louie's belief that "people are pretty much alike anywhere if they're poor and ignored by the rich," calling him on what she labels his neglect of "the racial and ethnic dimensions of the process," Louie responds: "Jes, baby, joor rye. We're poor *and* Messican up and down the Tex-Mex border" (29, original italics). Though La Mollie responds as if Louie has proven precisely her point, he has instead strategically deployed her essentialized view of him to undermine it to his audience, both the man with the tape recorder as well as the reader. He knows how to appear "Mexican" as defined by an Anglo perspective, and in being so calls attention to the artificiality and reifying properties of that society's essentialized understanding of cultural differences.

While Louie's interactions, past and present, with dominant U.S. society undermine the processes by which it essentializes and reifies him, his narrative elsewhere metaphorizes the impoverishing effect of these processes. This effect manifests in how Louie speaks of the movies and the ways both they and the moviegoing experience have been homogenized and thus drained. For Louie, movies were, and in many ways still are, a powerful, often sexually charged experience. He tells his listener of a "foreign flick" he saw as a kid, "about a little boy and his dad and how poor they are and how the dad finally has to steal a bicycle to make ends meet" and how it made Louie cry "for years just thinking about that one." Similarly as a kid, Louie relates how he "almost went blind sitting in the dark for hours watching the Hollywood stars and some of the Mexican ones, too, like María Felix. They had magic, man, and they made magic" (20–21). In both these examples, Louie evidences a clearly and powerfully emotional reaction to film. In a similar vein, he urges his listener, as an example of movies' sexual charge: "Imagine touching Betty Grable's legs or Ava Gardner's hair. I get turned on just thinking about it" (20). A similar such power and magic was to be found in the movie theaters that Louie frequented, such as "the old Plaza Theater—it looked like this grand Moorish castle with stars blinking on the ceiling" (21). But such power and magic as the movies formerly possessed is no longer to be found. Louie explains: "Nowadays, the movies aren't for shit. You walk out dazed, stand outside the theater and ask yourself 'What happened?'" The foreign movies La Mollie drags Louie to are "nothing but pure caca far as [he] could tell—boring isn't a good enough word" (20). And the theaters themselves have deteriorated: "you wind up in one of them little cubbyholes and pay an arm and a leg" (21). The power and pleasure Louie formerly experienced has been impoverished by discomfort, disorientation, and boredom.

Louie's narration connects his world's problematic cultural forces to a process of homogenization and impoverishment similar to that which the movies metaphorize. Expanding upon the disorientation he feels coming out of modern films, Louie says, "Half the time it's like being in a hospital—you just don't know how you got there and can't figure out why you stayed" (20). Perhaps not surprisingly, the films Louie finds so disorienting and unpleasant, La Mollie's elite circle lauds: "La Mollie thought the clothes were 'gorgeous' and everybody in her crowd couldn't stop talking about how 'brilliant'" they were (20). Louie here establishes an affinity between the disorienting sameness of the waiting room and the aesthetically homogenous films praised by Anglo elites. Earlier, he asks his listener about the similarity of hospital waiting rooms, as his occupancy of one in the present recalls to Louie the one in which he spent time after his daughter Evelina was born: "Why do you think they make em all like this, with the same ugly linoleum and pukey green color on the walls?" (14). He elsewhere remarks upon a similar urge toward sameness in Anglo society in general, and Miss Harper in particular: "Now, whenever I hear anyone ask 'Why can't they learn to speak English?' specially if they say it with a Texas accent, I think about Macbeth and Miss Harper and wonder how come some accents are okay and some ain't" (12). All Louie's experiences with these sociocultural forces reinforce the drift toward homogenization and sameness furthered by both U.S. institutions and its elite. And, of course, Louie stands as a difference that must too be eliminated in the same way the magic of the movies has been obliterated or a comforting variety to hospital waiting rooms.

Yet, even as these homogenizing forces work to essentialize and thus contain Louie and his difference, they fail. He circumvents Miss Harper's effort to privilege and distance Shakespeare from him by interpreting the Bard in his own words and through his own experience. He strategically deploys the essentialized image La Mollie and her circle have of him, and that deployment both evidences and undermines that view.

More fully, the metaphorical difference embodied by the movies Louie himself loves, even if their presence wanes in the novel's storyworld, still exists, persists within Louie's consciousness. Louie's narrative evidences their palpable presence as he clearly and often renders his own experiences in terms of such films, even if he cannot physically or really enter into the heightened movie-world. In one of the novel's earliest passages, for example, Louie casts his morning sexual encounter with La Mollie in a metaphor drawn from *Gone with the Wind*: "Right in the middle of my giving it to her the way Rhett gives it to Scarlett the night he lugs her up them red velvet stairs after almost crushing her skull between his hands, La Mollie says 'It's the end of the world!' And I'm saying, 'Oh yeah, baby,' and she says, 'Not this, stupid,' ruining my concentration and turning me into that pansy Ashley Wilkes. I hate it when she does that, man" (3). Here, Louie draws contrasting metaphors from his movies to describe his sexual prowess and masculinity. He begins as manly, strong Rhett Butler, "giving it" to La Mollie, but ends weak and soft and limp as the less masculine Wilkes. Similarly, upon discovering La Mollie after her suicide attempt, Louie "figured it was time for Errol Flynn, so I peeled around them two cars in my way, flipped em off, and started speeding towards Portero" (154). *The Wizard of Oz* serves as another filmic lens through which Louie renders his experience. He uses it, for example, in a description and characterization of the women in his life, both past and present: "Cause like every woman I've ever known who was a real woman, La Mollie is a witch—a Glenda-the-Good-witch, not a Margaret Hamilton 'you-and-your-little-dog-too' witch. Teresa was like that a little bit, and Evelina was" (33). *The Wizard of Oz* in particular appears throughout the narrative, as in, for example, near the end as Louie speeds La Mollie to the hospital. He sees a vision of Evelina "wearing a summery dress with lotsa bright flowers all over it and she looks all shiny and healthy like she never lived or died. She seems about as far away from pain as Oz is from Kansas" (154). Though, according to Louie, the presence and access to the heightened world these films represent is fading from his world, their presence persists, in spite of this, within Louie's own mind and consciousness.

And the same is true of Louie's consciousness. It persists, as evidenced by his being the one telling this story, in its fullness and in spite of those efforts that seek to essentialize and contain it. We see Louie's persistence in any number of subtle ways throughout his narrative: the fact that he moves between and within these various institutions and circles and seems neither to compromise himself nor to draw their ire, and his sly comments to not only La Mollie and her circle, but also with a wink to his audience within and outside his textual world, clearly point to how he strategically circumvents such efforts. Louie's very narrative, and the fact that what we read is not his audience's transcription of his voice, but Louie's voice and its expression of his consciousness, preserves both. They, and he, then, persist within the U.S. nation-space this text imagines, in spite of how it too imagines similar forces of homogenization and essentialization as found in the earlier works by Rechy, Viramontes, Véa, and Castillo.

Unlike those earlier works, however, *La Mollie and the King of Tears* additionally textualizes a narrative and ethics of transformation. The narrated Louie persists within his storyworld, moving within and between its cultural forces and spaces and circumventing their efforts to codify and contain his difference. As before with the persistence narrative, there still functions an opposition and distance between U.S. Anglo society and Chicanos/as. It is, however, in the Louie who narrates the story, his narrating self or consciousness, that we see this distance and opposition ameliorated. We see in the narrating Louie that he does not simply persist amongst his various cultural and social forces, but is rather changed by them. In spite of the lingering maintenance of that spatial distance and opposition, those forces permeate Louie's consciousness. This includes not only those forces, such as those outlined above, that are uncomfortable with and opposed to Louie's presence, but also those from which Louie himself experiences discomfort, most prominently homosexuality, crystallized in the form of his brother Tomás. The narrated Louie demonstrates a clear discomfort with and even fear of his brother's and gay men's lifestyle, but the narrating Louie expresses instead compassion and understanding toward them. Thus we witness between Louie's narrated past and his narrating present a transformation of his consciousness toward sexual difference.

The narrating Louie's borrowings from his various cultural forces is conscious. Louie himself explains: "I'm an eclectic, man. Since I learned I can't control nothing, not even myself sometimes, I take from here and from there whatever works" (45). Louie's previously discussed use of films as metaphors for his experience is a clear example of his conscious eclecticism. But Louie's borrowings go beyond the cultural experiences he enjoys. They also include the ones that Louie disdains. We might be surprised, for example, to find that he draws from even those films that he earlier criticized as "pure caca." But that is exactly what he does to convey a sense of his previous night to his audience: "The rest of last night was like one of them foreign flicks La Mollie and Bela [Bruce, the vampire-lawyer] like so much, man, all fuzzy at the edges and just a buncha little cutouts of scenes here and there that you figure go together but you ain't got a clue how" (109).

Louie will similarly borrow from Shakespeare in his narration. For example, he uses what he learned of Shakespearean tragedy from Miss Harper to describe his life early on in the novel:

> You know, while I been letting you in on my life, I just been
> thinking how so far it's sorta like a two-act play. The first act's
> a tragedy, sadder than *Hamlet* cause I weren't no prince, and
> the second is a real crazy shoot-em-up comedy with a big
> black hole in the middle of it. Both acts are a lot more inter-
> esting than anything old Shakespeare ever put into words,
> words, and more words, man, I can tell you. (13)

In spite of his earlier disdain for Shakespeare's representation of experience, Louie finds the Bard's work to be a suitable metaphor for the course of his life, dividing his past and present along the lines of tragedy and comedy. Too, *Hamlet* itself serves as a standard for comparison: Louie's life has been sadder, crazier, and ultimately more interesting. Finally, we can even see the lingering presence of Louie's forced memorization of Macbeth's soliloquy, as Louie's "words, words, and more words" resonates with Macbeth's "tomorrow, tomorrow, and tomorrow" line.

Louie's use of Shakespeare as a framing device for aspects of his narration resonates with Islas's own. Already mentioned is how Shakespeare serves as one of two epigraphs to the novel, but his extra-textual presence reaches further. For example, it is evident in the novel's title. After reaching the hospital with La Mollie, Louie again thinks back to his high school experience with Miss Harper and Shakespeare and draws this connection:

> Old Leila P. used to tell us that King Lear dies thinking that his good daughter is still alive and so he dies happy. But I knew better, man. Cordelia's too good to live on in any play Shakespeare'd write. I liked her cause she don't say too much and just goes around doing for others. I kinda like the Fool, too, cause he don't pretend to make sense when he talks and of course makes the most sense of all. That dumb old man Lear? He was the King of Tears, man. Me, Chakespeare Louie from the projects, I know almost from the beginning of the story, even if him and Miss Harper don't, that the old king's daughter is as dead as a doornail at the end. (155)

Lear is the King of Tears, but so too will Louie be should La Mollie die from her attempted suicide: "Then that old man Lear's gonna have to defend his throne cause I'm gonna cry so much that all the people'll be wanting to anoint *me*" (155). The apparent granting of this title to Louie—for the only "King of Tears" La Mollie would be associated with would be Louie—at least suggests the likelihood of La Mollie's suicide attempt having been successful. Similarly, Louie's claimed foreknowledge of Cordelia's death, that he knew she was "dead as a doornail" from the start, perhaps further implies an unconscious knowledge on Louie's part of La Mollie's death from the very start of his story. The fact that this final chapter is titled "Just Like Romeo and Juliet," and how it clearly asks us to see Louie and La Mollie's relationship, particularly at this point in the narrative present, in parallel with these tragically star-crossed lovers, further hints at La Mollie's death at least, if not her Romeo's.

We can see then two levels of transformation here. There is, of course, Louie's in how his imbrication within varying cultural spheres and influences has left its mark on his consciousness. Even those negative influences pervade his narration, often as framing metaphors, and thus his consciousness. But too, there is a way in which we might say Islas attempts the same transformation in the novel's reader through how his construction resonates with Louie's transformation. Louie can be said to draw, consciously and unconsciously, from dominant and often oppressive cultural influences in constructing his narrative, thus demonstrating how he himself is not so distant from but in fact connected to, if not a part of, those cultural forces. In the same way, Islas's construction, and in particular extranarrative use of Shakespeare to frame his narrative of Louie's experience, perhaps suggests to the reader that we too should not see Louie as wholly distant and separate from dominant Anglo culture and its devices. Islas thus encourages the reader's own transformation from the distant and opposed understandings underpinning, though to different extents, both resistance and persistence.

Louie's cultural borrowings, both conscious and unconscious, speak to a state of ambiguity paralleling that of Pastora. Louie, in his self-described eclecticism, takes from "here and there" amongst his cultural influences "whatever works" as a frame to help convey his experiences to both his audiences. He is, in essence, a conglomerate persona. The upshot of this inclusiveness is to present to the reader a Louie who is not distanced, not opposed to U.S. society but rather permeated by and drawing from it. He is not passive but active in his borrowings, not static but dynamic, not epistemologically categorized but rather simply being.

The flip side to this in *La Mollie and the King of Tears* is Islas's representation of Louie's relationship to differences he himself essentializes and/or finds uncomfortable and threatening. As Aldama notes, "Louie Mendoza coexists with other sociosexually emplaced subjects while physically traveling *across* a 1973 San Francisco metroplex" (Aldama, *Critical Mappings* 301, original italics). But though Louie may occupy the same imagined storyworld with differently sexed and differently sexually oriented people from himself, he does not do so unproblematically or comfortably. His discomfort, then, parallels that of U.S. Anglo society toward him. And, just as Louie transforms in his relationship to the dominant society, so too does he transform toward that difference that he himself initially fears. Though Louie may not explicitly "experience the sort of epiphany that traditionally identifies a character's dialectical synthesis of the encountered other" (301), that epiphany is implicit within the disjunction between Louie's past/narrated self and his present/narrating one.

Louie's own "sociosexual emplacement" is almost too emphatically heterosexual. His opening page Rhett Butler/Ashley Wilkes metaphor for masculinity is but one of the means by which Louie repeatedly emphasizes his heterosexuality. When La Mollie asserts to him the homosexuality of football, Louie refuses to see the symbolism: "Well, I look, man, and I don't see nothing, but what La Mollie sees is a buncha men in tight pants bending over a ball, asses in the air, waiting for a signal so they can go after the true object of the game" (Islas, *La Mollie* 60). Louie's macho identity does not allow him to acknowledge the symbolism La Mollie asserts—at least

not consciously; his own descriptions of the game's events, that a "wide re-
ceiver has just been creamed" and has a "hard time getting up," however,
speak for La Mollie's interpretation (60). Louie elsewhere will assert that
he "can't have sex without pussy," "loves the taste of women," and, upon
leaving a gay bar, he insists to the inquisitive and interested bouncer "I
got a woman waiting for me" (77, 138, 143). In such statements as these
and others peppered throughout his narrative, Louie asserts not only his
own heterosexuality but also a distance between himself and homosexual
others.

Concomitant with Louie's over-abundant heterosexuality is the expression of a discriminatory attitude toward not only gays but also women that is
reminiscent of Castillo's Máximo. Louie will repeatedly refer to gay men as
"pansies," "pussies," "fairies," and "fruits." He very often compares women,
including La Mollie, to whores; cheats on his then-girlfriend Sonia to be
with La Mollie; and sexually objectifies women, as when he first encounters Sonia: "To me, she was pure Chicana in that low-cut black dress, black
spiked heels with ankle straps—I love ankle straps, man, they give me real
dirty thoughts—and no bra or panties." He goes on to describe how she
would "pull up her dress just enough to tease everyone," and "let her bright
red fingernails linger above her cleavage just long enough to make the
angels notice" (47). La Mollie, too, is similarly objectified, in a passage
just before the description of Sonia: Louie compares sex with La Mollie
to "getting to make love to the whole United States of America, man. Not
only that, it was letting me teach it stuff it hadn't dreamed up yet and letting me hurt it a little bit for being so mean in the past. I ain't never had
anything like that" (46–47). The near juxtaposition of these two passages
emphasizes Louie's objectifying, discriminatory gaze toward women. They
are objects, sexual or metaphorical. Their individuality and subjectivity is
neglected or compromised. Sonia only exists in Louie's description to affect others; there is no sense of her self in her actions, just that she functions
to titillate the watching men. La Mollie, too, is essentialized. She becomes
a symbol for dominant U.S. society and very quickly becomes objectified
as "it" and "that" which Louie now "has." Louie's attitudes toward women
and gays thus parallel the essentialized, reified view that Castillo's Máximo
had toward the same, but also the view U.S. Anglo society has of Louie.

But unlike Máximo, Louie does not remain static in these attitudes and
succumb to their ironic effects. As regards women, the narrating Louie
appears to have had just such an epiphany about them, as well as men.
He tells his listener about men, for example, that "we're too stuck to the
ground punching it out all the time" and "we guys can be fuckers. And we

wanna conquer everything" (33, 34). Here, Louie explicitly recognizes men as conquerors, as colonizers, and implicitly indicts his own sexual objectification that stands as an instance of this pattern. More to the point, the speaking Louie differs from his narrated self in how he speaks of the women in his life. That earlier self replicates the same problematic attitudes. But in his narrating present, speaking particularly of La Mollie, Louie's statements are suffused with guilt over the role he gives himself in La Mollie's suicide attempt, a guilt that makes explicit how he is no longer viewing her as simply a symbolic and sexual object. The opening sentence of the novel is one such statement: "I shoulda told La Mollie I'd be back to her place right after the gig." Similarly, Louie wonders "if I'm ever gonna feel her fingers on me again" (3). Notice that he is no longer talking about "doing it" to the passive La Mollie, but rather she is the one acting on him, touching and stimulating him with her fingers. A parallel moment ends the first chapter. Louie again laments: "So it's my fault what happened cause I didn't believe La Mollie. I let her go, man, like I was dropping a tissue, grabbed my jacket and sax, and as cool as cool can be" (35–36). Again, he indicts himself for not believing La Mollie, but further he indicts the objectification of La Mollie that caused him to not believe her in the first place. More so, his description of his departure is another moment that evokes Louie's filmic sense, but here he almost seems to regret living up to the image of the retiring, scorned hero he then played.

There is a more pronounced but also ironically subtle shift indicated in Louie's attitudes toward gays. For one, the novel again seeks to ameliorate the distance Louie established between himself and homosexual men. Louie's initial encounter with Sonia takes place in a "unisex bar" and her effect is not just limited to him: "She was burning the place up, and everybody knew it, even the two fairies behind me arguing about where she came from." One of those two men even admits to his companion, "God, I think she's turning me on" (47). And just as the two men replicate Louie's reaction to Sonia, so too does he seem to replicate theirs, paying attention, for example, to the "cute little waiter" carrying drinks (48). For another, additional to these affinities, Louie's borrowings from gay culture demonstrate that it, like U.S. Anglo society, permeates his consciousness. The two men at one point identify Sonia as a "fag hag," and when Sonia finally kicks Louie out for his philandering, he insults her by calling her the same (48, 57). In stemming from the same past instance, these affinities and borrowings show how the boundaries Louie attempts to assert between himself and homosexuality are always already destabilized and undermined by how he comes into contact with gay individuals and spaces.

Two specific gay men play a prominent role in furthering Louie's transformation regarding homosexuality. The first is Virgil Spears, whose "boy-
hood friendship" with Louie "stands in as an alternate possibility of desiring
in the world." He challenges Louie's "heteronormative mindset" that assumes that Virgil's desire is a pathology resulting from childhood abuse,
an essentializing assumption that he directly confronts (Aldama, *Critical
Mappings*, 307–308). Virgil demands that Louie "tell me exactly when
you decided to be straight. I wanna know the moment you looked down
at your crotch and your brain told your dick it was only gonna be interested in pussy for the rest of its life" (Islas, *La Mollie* 75–76). In interro-
gating Louie, Virgil both interrogates the idea of homosexuality as a choice
and, simultaneously, Louie's ignorance that assumes homosexuality to be
pathological in origin and nature. Virgil's challenge leaves Louie founder-
ing. As he explains, "Back then, all I could say to Virgil was something lame
like, 'Well, what did you learn from your old man and how come you're
still calling the old fucker "daddy"?'" (77). Even though Louie admits to a
continued cluelessness, his statement that "back then" all he could do was
interrogate Virgil about the continued influence of his abusive father at
least implicitly indicates how the present/narrating Louie recognizes that
this was the wrong thing to ask, and he would ask, if not say, something
different. But even with Louie's continued incredulousness evident, this
exchange opens up in him a compassion toward Virgil. The pair hug, and
when Virgil's father later kills himself, Louie "stayed with him [Virgil] at his
place, day and night, for a week. I didn't even care what any of the brothers
in the gang thought about it" (77).

More telling of Louie's transformation are the moments he narrates
concerning his gay younger brother Tomás. Again, and more markedly,
Louie's narration of these moments exposes a disjunction between his narrating and narrated self. Louie's past attitude appears late in the novel, as
he hobbles his way across San Francisco's Castro District after leaving the
hospital with his leg in a cast, his ride having abandoned him. He spies his
brother's car outside the colorfully named Mind Shaft and, approaching
what he knows to be a gay bar, Louie once again feels compelled to reassert his heterosexuality: "Like I told you, man, I can't even think about
sex without tits around. Real soft ones" (138). His entrance into this space,
and subsequent characterization of it, again evokes Louie's fear and feeling
of threat: "I do one of them Wild Bill Hickoks and go for a corner where
my back's covered. I figure I'm pretty safe where the bar meets one wall
and nobody can get behind me unless they force it" (140).

Louie's fear is explicit: he suffuses his invocation and mimicry of Wild

Bill and the masculine figure of the American cowboy with a sense of threat. As he leaves, Louie is further consternated by the doorman's amorous advances, which Louie spurns by asserting his heterosexuality; the doorman responds: "That's what they all say when they look in the mirror, baby" (143). This statement lingers in Louie's mind, as he tells his listener how he has "been thinking about what he said about looking in the mirror and I can't come up with what he meant" (143). In this scene and its lingering presence in Louie's mind, we again see exposed his lack of understanding and palpable fear of what he sees as wholly different from himself. Along with this exposure, though, Louie's statement also makes clear how this experience has, in fact, permeated his consciousness.

But when Louie tells of an earlier encounter with his brother, we see an entirely different attitude and compassion toward and even identification with gay culture. Far from the judgment, disdain, and fear evidenced in the Mind Shaft, Louie expresses understanding and sympathy for not only his brother but also those like him. As he states, "It's none of my business what Tomás does with his dick, man. He's my brother. My business is to love him, right?" But Louie's love and sympathy is not limited to his fraternal relation: "I'm telling you, man, these sissies have a hard life. I'm serious" (71). Furthermore, Louie's fear of gay men has instead been transformed to not only an effort at acceptance but, too, solidarity:

> On the way, I try not to pay attention to the way guys walking
> up to Castro Street keep looking first at my crotch and then
> at my face the way straight dudes look at girls' asses and legs
> behind their backs. I don't understand guys making it with
> other guys but as long as they don't mess with me that way
> they're okay, man. It's mostly the straight dudes who go
> around raping people. They're the ones I'm scared of when
> I see em coming towards me in a pack. (72)

In many ways, this passage sums up not only Louie's realizations about gay men, but also about himself toward women. Implicit in his comment about the similarities between how gay men look at him and how straight men look at women is how he has done the latter himself, as his introduction to Sonia makes clear. Louie is consciously trying not to be bothered by the looks of gay men, trying to overcome the fear that manifests when he later recalls the scene at the Mind Shaft. In fact, that fear has now been shifted to "straight dudes," a source of fear and reprisal not only for Louie but for women and gays as well.

There is both an attitudinal and temporal disjunction between these events. The earlier-occurring one, when Louie and Tomás separate for the evening, seems more understanding and compassionate than the later-occurring one at the Mind Shaft. The explanation for this inconsistency though lies in the attitudinal disjunction. When he narrates the Mind Shaft scene, Louie speaks in the present tense, as his narration seems to enter this moment and thus the attitude he possessed and expressed then. However, when talking about the earlier moment, Louie speaks directly to his listener about what he understands (and still does not) and feels toward gay men like his brother, and it is here, then, that we start to see the transformation in Louie effected by his direct encounters with gay culture. He demonstrates a previously lacking compassion toward gay men and culture, one that results from their not being so physically and psychologically distanced from him through processes of discriminatory essentialization and reification. As was the case with Pastora in Castillo's novel, such compassion as Louie here demonstrates indicates the growing inclusiveness of his perspective and consciousness.

In his Galarza Lecture, delivered at Stanford in 1990 and titled "On the Bridge, At the Border: Migrants and Immigrants," Islas describes in himself much of what he depicts in Louie Mendoza. He cites, for example, how he and his family "slide with ease from one language to another . . . sometimes stopping to create new worlds and expressions that are part of a border culture with an atmosphere all its own." He finds himself and locates his characters "on the bridge between cultures, between languages, between sexes, between nations, between religions, . . . between two different and equally compelling ways of looking agape at the world" (Islas, *Uncollected Works* 231, 232). Perhaps not surprisingly, Islas has Louie born next to a bridge, his birth place signaling his own later positioning between cultures, negotiating with and amongst them. But Louie's ability to "bridge" these differences does not extend solely to himself; he too acts as a bridge toward a similar compassion and understanding in his novel's reader. As Islas elsewhere writes, "[T]he act of writing and reading fiction is that through it we can be disciplined and seduced into imagining other peoples' lives with understanding and compassion, even if we do not 'identify' with them" (236). Louie telling his story dramatically depicts how he himself is "seduced" into identifying with those from whom he formerly distanced himself and excluded. Not unlike Castillo's narrator in *So Far from God*, Louie's lively and exuberant tale seeks to do the same to its readers, seducing them into compassion and understanding toward those differently sexed, gendered, raced, and ethnic from themselves.

## FIVE

*The Transformative Spaces of Alfredo Véa's* The Silver Cloud Café *and* Gods Go Begging

Alfredo Véa's second and third novels—*The Silver Cloud Café* (1996) and *Gods Go Begging* (1999)—complete the "narrative trilogy" initiated by the previously discussed *La Maravilla* (Cantú 210). The three novels interlock and overlap through how the lives of their protagonists resonate with each other. For example, Beto's childhood in *La Maravilla* terminates with his journey to a migrant worker's camp called French Camp. This same camp plays a pivotal role in *The Silver Cloud Café*: Zeferino del Campo, the novel's protagonist, eventually recovers the memories of his own arrival and experiences at French Camp, thus picking up where Beto's narrative life left off. Both Beto and Zeferino serve as soldiers in the Vietnam War, but their traumatic experiences remain untold. *Gods Go Begging*, on the other hand, extensively depicts the wartime experiences of its protagonist, Jesse Pasadoble, who, like Zeferino, works in his present as a defense attorney. As Roberto Cantú explains, "Alberto, Zeferino, and Jesse Pasadoble [are] three names of the same 'fictional' character" (240). The overlaps and resonances among their respective stories and plots allow the novels to function not only as a trilogy, but also as an interlocking narrative.

Unlike their plot-based unity, these texts' ethics differ or, perhaps better, evolve. *La Maravilla* was shown earlier to encode a narrative paradigm of persistence: differences—racial, ethnic, cultural, sexual, gender, class—existed and participated within the novel's imagined U.S. nation-space. The latter two novels of the trilogy, however, textualize a narrative of transformation within their storyworlds. That is, they, like the works of Castillo and Islas in the previous chapter, assert the need to conceive of difference in something other than the flattened, epistemological terms that reify such peoples and cultures. Véa's latter two novels extend the critique Castillo and Islas make about Chicano culture in particular to the contemporary

world in general. Both *The Silver Cloud Café* and *Gods Go Begging* represent a 1990s U.S. nation-space marked by the heterogeneity and difference
of the postmodern age. However, these storyworlds far from exhibit what
David Harvey asserts as "essential" to postmodernism, the "idea that all
groups have a right to speak for themselves in their own voice, and have that
voice accepted as authentic and legitimate" (48). Instead, what the reader
encounters in these worlds is what Davis describes in *City of Quartz* as the
"bad edge of postmodernity": "The old liberal paradigm of social control,
attempting to balance repression with reform, has long been superseded by
a rhetoric of social warfare. . . . In cities like Los Angeles . . . one observes an
unprecedented tendency to merge urban design, architecture and police
apparatus into a single comprehensive security effort" (224). This same war
is being waged by the dominant U.S. Anglo society in the San Franciscan
storyworlds of Véa's novels; that society's weapons are the flattened, reified
conceptions of difference that seek to reduce and thus contain differences
within epistemological categories: all this in the name of a desire for what
Davis terms "security" and Véa calls "comfort."

Both novels further represent this desire for comfort, this "search for
secure moorings in a shifting world," as progressively complicit with the
homogenizing force of capitalism (Harvey 302). Per Mary Pat Brady, capitalism needs to "regularize the meanings and uses of spaces . . . to naturalize violent racial, gender, sexual, and class ideologies." The result is what
she terms "evacuated space," a consequence of "space's abstraction into
geometric homogeneities, its reconceptualization as quantitative, [and]
its immersion in exchange relations" (4, 6). This regularization of space
into measured—and thus secure or comfortable—homogeneities of and
ideologies toward difference operates both spatially and temporally in the
two texts. As Harvey again describes, "[T]he history of capitalism has been
characterized by speed-up in the pace of life, while so overcoming spatial barriers that the world sometimes seems to collapse inward upon us"
(240). A similar kind of "time-space compression" exists in Véa's imagined
worlds. Capitalism collapses time and space in its global operations, and
so too do the forces of homogeneity concomitant with it function globally
and transtemporally.

In the face of these efforts, though, are the spaces of uncodifiable and
uncontainable difference that permeate both storyworlds. Similar to Buckeye Road, spaces like the titular Silver Cloud or the Amazon Luncheonette
in *Gods Go Begging* stand as embodiments of (at least potentially) uncodifiable, uncontainable, and thus persistent difference. But such spaces also

have a further effect through which the texts encode their narrative of transformation. These and similar spaces make these worlds ontologies, the "anarchic landscape of worlds in the plural" described by McHale (*Postmodernist Fiction*, 10). Additionally, they signal within the novels' storyworlds, and more so than in previous texts, the presence of Foucauldian heterotopias, those spaces found "in every culture, in every civilization" that exist as "something like counter-sites . . . in which the real sites, all the other real sites that can be found within the culture, are simultaneously represented, contested, and inverted" (Foucault 24). Like McHale's ontologies, Foucauldian heterotopias are "capable of juxtaposing in a single real space several spaces, several sites that are in themselves incompatible" (25). They thus become spaces and sources of discomforting variety, heterogeneity, and difference that contrast the homogenizing, reifying force of both global capitalism and dominant U.S. Anglo society.

And like the forces that they subvert, these imagined spaces in Véa's novels compress or intertwine time and space in the service of such transformation. In *The Silver Cloud Café*, Véa nests his various temporal/spatial locations—early twentieth-century Mexico and the Philippines; Stockton, California in the late 1950s; and its present of 1993 San Francisco—within each other to indicate how both the homogenizing and contrasting forces develop over time and space, reaching their apotheosis in the novel's present. On the other hand, Véa's interlacing of time and space in *Gods Go Begging* indicates stasis: that, despite differing temporal/spatial locations (Chihuahua, Mexico; Vietnam War-era Laos; present-day San Francisco) the same desire for homogeneity operates, concentrated at various heterotopic sites where these forces become transparent and thus contested. These texts' desired transformations first occur within their respective protagonists: Zeferino del Campo in *The Silver Cloud Café* and both Jesse Pasadoble and Calvin "Biscuit Boy" Thibault in *Gods Go Begging*. They transform from how the blinkered desires of dominant U.S. society condition them to view both themselves and their worlds. Their respective transformations parallel how Véa means his readers to view their extant worlds, the ethical position within which he seeks to encourage and emplace his readers, which his texts' generic and narrative constructions likewise foster.

## COMFORT AND JOY: EPISTEMOLOGICAL CERTAINTY AND ONTOLOGICAL POSSIBILITY IN *THE SILVER CLOUD CAFÉ*

Of the three texts in Véa's trilogy, *The Silver Cloud Café* is, as Cantú sums up, "arguably the most difficult" (210). The novel an also be said to have received the harshest reception and has gone out of print. This lack of critical and commercial success likely arises, at least in part, from its narrative complexity. The novel opens in San Francisco in spring 1993, the day after the mysterious murder of Bambino Reyes, an albino Filipino and former seminary student. Teodoro Cabiri, a Filipino hunch-backed dwarf, who goes by the moniker "Ted for Short," repeatedly confesses to the murder. The mystery behind the killing also includes a third Filipino, the homosexual Faustino, who is in love with the spirit of deceased poet Constantine Cavafy; King Pete Claver, a former boxer and current hot dog cart proprietor; his estranged wife, the prostitute Queenie who, the same night as the murder, finds her virginity restored; and Father Humberto, a Mexican priest, who, though executed during the Christero War, is still alive (in spite of repeated suicide attempts) for an unknown purpose. Ted for Short becomes the client of Chicano lawyer Zeferino del Campo, the novel's central protagonist, whose interactions with his client reveal the lawyer's connections to and/or repressed past with these figures, all of whom also bear some connection to the novel's titular café. Adding to the convolutions of its plot are "narrative juxtapositions, temporal and spatial displacements, and the hermetic or obscure nature of the novel's allusions," all of which contribute to the overall complexity and irreducibility of *The Silver Cloud Café* (211).

Of course, the troublesome challenge the text presents to its reader parallels the similar challenge to limited understandings occurring within its storyworld. There, we find how Véa "questions minimalist tendencies in the United States that reduce persons to a racial or ethnic identity" (211). *The Silver Cloud Café* subverts those reductive tendencies, which derive from an implicit desire for epistemological certainty, through its representation of heterogeneous and kaleidoscopic spaces of what I term "ontological possibility." Through the creation and effect of such spaces within its imagined U.S. nation-space, the novel asserts peoples and cultures of difference not as objects to be epistemologically categorized and thus reified, but instead as subjective beings, from which stems a transformative possibility.

Crucial to the textualization of such transformation is the novel's interlacing and (con)fusion of time and space. *The Silver Cloud Café* does not unfold linearly, even in its narrative present of San Francisco in 1993, between May 9 and May 24. It opens on May 15, then jumps to May 22, while it is only toward the end of the novel that the events preceding the murder on the night of the 14th become known. Between these present-day scenes are flashbacks to earlier times and spaces. The most significant of these temporal/spatial locations is Stockton, California, during 1958 and 1959, specifically the site of French Camp. Located at the literal center of the novel, this narrative insert proceeds achronologically, the later-occurring events being presented first and the earlier ones last. Further flashbacks return us to the Mexican state of Michoacán in 1927, and Father Humberto's involvement in the Christero War, as well as, through the reminiscences of both Ted for Short and Faustino, to the later time and place of the Philippines and the pair's childhood meeting. There are, then, in the novel a total of four temporal/spatial locations nested within each other, like a set of Russian dolls.

And, in the same way that opening each of the dolls reveals another within it, the various temporal/spatial locations, when arranged chronologically, build on each other palimpsestically. Through the novel's narrative present, the traces of its various pasts can be perceived. In the same way, then, that the novel "articulate[s] a splintered world—the Philippines, the United States, Spain, and Mexico—into a unified geopolitical totality" (213), it also temporally and spatially totalizes the operation of a desire for epistemological certainty and comfort as a network of homogenization, exclusion, and violence. The novel's narrator explicitly gestures toward just such a network when it frames the representation of the earlier Christero War as a conflict that resonates with the novel's present:

> But, even now, the conflict persists in full force in the feeble hearts of men. The proof is there in clandestine gatherings of cross-burning buffoons who, in the name of God, demonize others who are different in language or in color. The proof is there in the legion of hairsprayed and bewigged televangelists who insist through perfect teeth that personal wealth and a full head of hair are a true measure of heaven's favor. The proof is in the constantly recurring fall of man's wisdom, from far-reaching vision and personal enlightenment down to institutionalized teachings, and from there downward to close-minded dogma. (Véa, *Silver Cloud* 62)

Here, the narrator declares how the forces at play in this early-twentieth century conflict find new expression in voices and figures from the subsequent years of this same century. Racist and/or exploitative groups like the Ku Klux Klan and TV evangelists are cut from the same cloth, as are, more generally, any dogmatic beliefs that circumscribe man's full wisdom, vision, and potential. But it is not only these forces of homogenization, exclusion, and violence that persist. Véa consistently locates within all of his temporal/spatial localities heterotopic spaces that are likewise ontological (in McHale's sense) in how they conglomerate seemingly incompatible differences together, and through this contest—however, albeit, briefly—the reductive, narrow-minded consciousness of dominant U.S. society and global capitalism.

Mexico's Christero War is chronologically the earliest of the flashbacks, "one small but deadly military engagement" of the conflicts that continue to the novel's present (62). As summarized by the novel's narrator, the Christero War was a conflict between the church priests in Mexico and the teachers who, with the government's help, usurped the priests' position as educators. It began "in minor backwater skirmishes over the souls of peasant children. The church conspired to blame every sickness, every miscarriage, every drought on the new teachers, while the teachers exposed and publicly condemned nuns who had taken secret spouses and priests who had sired illegitimate children" (64). It is a conflict between the sacred and the secular, both of which retaliate against the other.

But further entwined with this conflict are wealth and, thus, a nascent capitalism. The narrator points out, for instance, that prior to the conflict, "the Mexican Catholic Church owned more pesos than the Mexican government, half the arable land, and one of every three buildings in the country" (64). The government's subsequent nationalization of the Catholic Church was an effort to take that wealth and land for itself, and reduce the church's officials to "the lowly status of tenants at suffrage" (64). Here, we see the first instance of a capitalist desire insinuating itself into a clash over difference, providing perhaps the truer and also baser desire motivating the conflict. As a result of the war, Father Humberto and his brother Miguel Augustine are executed, the latter later being beatified as a saint, the former inexplicably surviving throughout the century, to carry his scars from this conflict into the novel's present.

Similarly nascent in this earliest of temporal/spatial localities is the symbolic presence of the irreducible, heterotopic spaces that permeate all the novel's localities. The narrator describes this earliest example as "the one small landmark to that war and to its countless dead," in the same way that Father Humberto and Miguel's martyred corpses serve as the Christero War's "solitary formal monument" (63, 66). But this landmark is only "a room, not a dignified chamber or silent cloister or reverent alcove. It is simply a room lined with shelves and coat hooks that is not a part of the church, nor is it part of the secular world outside. It is, in all truth, a way station on the frontier between the two" (63). Being "found in each and every cathedral, church and chapel in Mexico," this room exists as a real site within the storyworld of *The Silver Cloud Café* (63). In this, it parallels how a Foucauldian heterotopia exists as an actual site in the extant world.

Likewise similar is its nature as a site where incompatible spaces come together. This room exists at the confluence of the sacred and the secular, but does not belong solely to either. It marks where these literally conflicting spiritual and cultural forces come together. It is of them, and yet belongs to neither, an inherently contradictory notion that, consequently, makes this space uncodifiable. It makes transparent the binary logic of secular and sacred and simultaneously transcends what in the novel is a destructive logic.[1] Though such spaces are everywhere in Mexico at this time, their effect remains only symbolic. They stand as a symbol of what is (potentially) to come within the novel's storyworld, as the ur-space of what in the present will be transformative spaces like the Silver Cloud.

Between that present and the Christero flashback stands, first, the time and space of the Philippines and, in particular, the meeting of Ted for Short and Faustino. That meeting, and thus the room in which it occurs, offers another heterotopic space of conglomerated and, furthermore, allied differences. Ted for Short is a hunchback from the age of seven; as he explains to Zeferino, "That was the year my left shoulder began to twist upward and this hump was in its infancy" (219). Ted for Short suffers the smallminded bigotry and fears of not only others but also his own parents. His father tries to abort his birth. His mother enters him into a competition to play the baby Jesus in the Passion of the Christ in hopes that he will be, as Ted describes, "miraculously cured of my small size while up there on the cross" (220). In both the mother's and father's reactions and efforts, Ted for Short's tale dramatically demonstrates that backlash against discomforting differences. Faustino suffers similarly for his homosexuality. The two meet during Ted for Short's return visit to the psychic doctor originally paid to abort his birth; like Ted for Short, Faustino has been brought here in hopes of a cure. As he tells Ted for Short, "Hello, I am Faustino. My family brought me up here to Baguio because they think I am a *bakla*" (230, original italics). This desperate effort comes only after Faustino's father hires a series of prostitutes, all of whom fail in their attempts to "cure" his son. It is, ultimately, the same fear that drives both sets of parents to their similar measures, a fear implicitly identified within their larger society. When Faustino asks Ted for Short what his father fears, the answer is "everyone's opinion" (231). That a similar fear of public scorn lies behind Faustino's treatment as well makes sense, given how the two characters are twinned with each other in the novel. Both characters function in this earlier moment to indict those fears as they manifest then and as they will in the novel's narrative present.

Ironically, what results from the efforts to eliminate both Ted for Short's and Faustino's respective differences is not their destruction but rather their alliance. Ted for Short and Faustino, upon encountering each other, recognize themselves in each other: Ted for Short describes how he found "a mirror of another kind" in Faustino. Faustino similarly declares that "when our eyes met, our lives were grafted together. His grief reached out and joined with my own. His sorrow felt and understood mine, and we had not even spoken a single word to each other" (230, 268). The novel gives their alliance a physical reality when Ted for Short climbs on Faustino's shoulders to pull the angel mobiles down from the room's ceiling: "a jubilant Faustino danced from one end of the operating room to another as his new friend liberated first Michael, then Gabriel, then over a dozen others, clutching them all to his breast" (231).

Thus, just as the Christero War gave birth to its landmark room, the parents' discomfort gives birth to the bond between their outcast sons. And the novel presents this moment as a literally transformative one. The older Ted for Short's remembrances include how he "was overwhelmed by the feeling that something momentous had happened in that room so long ago; some inexplicable thing had transpired to change both of their destinies" (231). Burgeoning here is the kind of momentous transformation that the novel imagines not only as necessary in its narrative present of 1993 San Francisco, but also in the present of its readers.

It is in the flashbacks to Stockton, California, in 1958 and 1959 that this fear, its accompanying desire for safety/comfort, and the divisiveness of global capitalism initially come together. As before, the novel likewise gestures toward sites of ontological difference and possibility that exist in contrast to these forces, though again their effect is, at best, compromised. Of all the flashbacks, those to Stockton have the most direct impact on the novel's present, beginning with the fact that they reveal Zeferino's repressed experiences in French Camp with Ted for Short and Faustino. Furthermore, they set the stage for the cultural condition of the novel's present, as the text links the two time periods by leapfrogging the thirty-plus years in between. The novel's narrator frames this leap backward with an admonishment of both Zeferino and the novel's reader for a kind of cultural amnesia:

> You must seek remembrance, for ours is a land of amnesiacs
> who pretend that there is no past; that America is a multicul-
> tural land when, in truth, it is an anticultural place that has
> ever been blessed with persistent and enduring cultures that
> have survived never-ending efforts to drag them out of sight;
> push them out of mind; to imprison them in the past. (125)

The amnesia critiqued here by the novel's narrator echoes Alaimo's criticism of U.S. multiculturalism for its reification of cultural differences and Hogue's complaint about nostalgia's relegation of peoples and cultures of color to an anachronistic past. Cultural differences, as real presences within the U.S. nation-space, as something to be dealt with in their specificity and context, become, according to the narrator, forgotten or imperceivable, and unthinkable. To paraphrase the end of the passage, they are rendered out of sight and out of mind. Or, that is what U.S. culture desires: to be able to forget about cultural differences even while paying lip service to the same through an evacuated multiculturalism.

The flashbacks to Stockton, then, dramatically represent the violence and exploitation that result from this willed amnesia. This effort begins in the litany of legal actions taken against a variety of peoples and cultures in not only Stockton, but also all of California:

> In 1932 a state law prohibiting "Mongolians" from marrying
> within the state was challenged. In the case of Roldan v. Los
> Angeles County it was held that Filipinos were not Mongoli-
> ans. The state law was promptly changed to include "Malays."
> In 1934 the Supreme Court limited most constitutional rights
> to whites only . . . the right to own property, the right to apply
> for citizenship. The ruling specifically excluded Filipinos.
> (133, original ellipsis)

In this passage, Véa's narrator explains a process by which Filipinos became a legal category of exclusion. Ironically, this exclusion emanates from an initial victory. The success of the Roldan case was to exempt Filipinos from the category of "Mongolian." The ultimate effect, though, was to create "Malay" and "Filipino" as new categories of exclusion, categories that reverberate through later decisions such as the Supreme Court ruling in 1934. The narrator continues:

> In Stockton as well as in many other places in California, antimiscegenation laws were translated into hundreds of local ordinances that prohibited everything from mixed marriages to interracial dancing. Filipinos, Mexicans, and Chinese were prohibited from using public parks and recreational facilities as well as public toilets. Though the antimiscegenation laws were struck down in 1948 by the State Supreme Court in the case of Perez v. Sharp, the local ordinance—now based on color rather than national origin—lived on, both on paper and in the hearts of landowners and the police. (133–134)

These local ordinances proliferate these legal efforts to contain cultural differences. The failed general effort gives way to targeted ones that exclude now specifically categorized groups from the U.S. public. Crucial is the final statement: the spirit behind these laws lingers "in the hearts" of men even after the laws themselves were struck down, not only in the Stockton-based time periods but also on into the novel's present.

The owners of French Camp, the setting of the 1959 flashback, explicitly manifest this spirit and likewise tie it to a capitalist motivation. As the novel's narrator explains, the owners of the migrant workers' camp and similar sites reap a financial benefit from fomenting conflict between these groups: "By using isolation and scab workers, the landowners had managed to keep the various racial groups angry at one another and alienated from American society. This tactic guaranteed low wages and a ready supply of laborers" (134). Here, we see the ironic counterpoint to Ted for Short and Faustino's alliance. The similarly excluded and similarly exploited groups turn against each other, all to the financial benefit of those who exclude and exploit them all. Most insidious, the workers themselves, such as Tacquio, a Pinoy worker in French Camp, come to see their fellows as the problem: "Tacquio shook his head at the very thought of brown men dancing in downtown Stockton. Why couldn't they be satisfied with the Chinese dance halls?" (134). Tacquio clearly objects to his fellow workers wanting more than their owners allow; their lack of satisfaction with their lot is, to him, the problem, not the capitalist enterprise that imposes these limits. And, in both 1958 and 1959, the owners and other white men of the camp strike out at their Mexican and Filipino workers for their alleged transgressions: in the 1958 flashback, their excuse is an ordinance against public dancing, which the workers break by going to the Rose Room dance hall; in 1959, Faustino's homosexuality, seen as deviant, provides their rationale, voiced by Tacquio: "He is a she and she wants to love a man. He is against children and every natural thing. Since she has been at this camp, the weather has gone bad and the shoots of grass are coming up small" (189). Tacquio's screed echoes those fears of Faustino's parents. He uses the same derogatory term — "*bakla*" — as they did. He castigates Faustino as unnatural and his presence as a bad omen, images that recall both Faustino's father's reaction to his homosexuality and Ted for Short's parents' fear at their son's birth. The narrator describes his/their rationale as the "twisted rationalizations of brutish persecution, still living in mortal mouths, five hundred years after the Inquisition," a time frame that extends to, if not beyond, the novel's narrative present (189). In the end, this violence is all-consuming: the mob in 1958 vandalizes the Rose Room beyond repair, and French Camp implodes when Faustino kills Pietro Ditto, one of its owners and the leader of the mob confronting Faustino (and, as will be revealed later, the father of Bambino Reyes).

But prior to their destruction, the Rose Room and French Camp serve another of the novel's purposes. They are their respective time periods' heterotopic spaces. Both sites' initial descriptions emphasize their nature. The Rose Room is "an elegant taxi-dance hall famous for the beauty of its dancing girls," whose proprietor, the resurrected Father Humberto, "cherished both gentility and good manners." Above it is the Flip-Flop, "a filthy hotel" where Father Humberto runs "a whorehouse that caters mainly to migrants and field hands" (161). The building housing these operations thus juxtaposes two seemingly incompatible spaces and values: a brothel and a dance hall, the carnal and the romantic, the whore and the virgin. Such juxtaposition proves perplexing even to those who work there; as one of them explains, "I just can't help but wonder why he has a house of pleasure and a dance hall full of stuck-up virgins, all in the same building" (165). That building likewise features a temporal conglomeration: it is "a warm Victorian charmer, with brass pineapple sconces, gas lamps, and floral carpet motifs" and boasts both a "textured wallpaper handmade in Persia and an intercom system taken from the innards of a wrecked Portuguese passenger ship that had been salvaged off Macao" (163). This site retains the traces of a variety of historical periods and places: ancient Persia, the Victorian era, the Great Depression, Portugal, and even Mexico's Christero War through Father Humberto's ownership. Thus, physically and qualitatively, the Flip-Flop/Rose Room building, as a real site within this storyworld, is heterotopic in its juxtaposition of differing and conflicting elements or qualities. It symbolizes the same sort of global, historical, and geopolitical connections that the text as a whole attempts to symbolize and fashion within its storyworld.

And, importantly, the novel establishes a, for lack of a better term, power to this space and its heterotopic nature. As with the earlier such spaces, it proves discomforting, whether we locate that discomfort in the perplexity of the women who work there or the violent retaliation of the mob. Additionally, it signals the ability of people of color to circumvent the various legal limitations to their presence in U.S. society. "When the Great Depression came, the hotel had been sold at public auction to the present owner, who bought the building through a white purchasing agent who had created a lucrative niche for himself by buying property for 'ghosts,' people who could not legally own property in America" (163). Father Humberto successfully circumvents and so frustrates that society's effort to render such peoples as him as "ghosts," as non-presences within the United States. Further establishing its power is another comment by Father Humberto's perplexed employee: "I think he needs them all. Somehow I think he needs both halves of it, whatever those halves are" (165). Father Humberto's need, of course, parallels the need the novel imagines for its imagined U.S. nation-space as well, the need to include "it all" rather than only "some."

French Camp, too, first appears as a similarly powerful heterotopic space. The power of this space is evident upon Zeferino's first remembrance of his time there. When the young Zeferino arrived at French Camp, the first sounds he heard were "music and laughter coming from the bunk-houses," sounds that indicated the humanity housed within its confines (127). Such powerful humanity continued to wash over Zeferino; it "rolled over him in waves":

> Once inside the rounded hut, he felt suddenly uneasy about the smiles he witnessed there. It seemed to him that the laughter from those brown faces was somehow tinged with pain, that their smiles were just shadows of real happiness to be found elsewhere under the sun.
>
> He had sensed their feelings as he walked past the screen door and into the long room: our laughter is an imitation of joy; we will all be somewhere else next month and next year, perhaps even back home where we belong. But for now, this food will do, this bed will do. (128)

Like the Flip-Flop/Rose Room building, French Camp encompasses opposite and even competing feelings: laughter and sadness, smiles and pain,
fleeting community and prolonged isolation, joy and weary resignation.
Such feelings not only communicate a common humanity with Zeferino,
but also amongst the Mexican and Filipino laborers in general. Later events
put such common feeling into action. For example, the narrator goes on
to describe the culinary exchange that occurred once a week between the
Mexican and Filipino workers, where each group cooked a culturally traditional meal of their own for the other (141–142). Another such instance
comes when all the men in the camp attend Father's Day at Zeferino's
school in place of his absent and never-identified father (123–124). Such
moments exemplify a bond of similarity establishing itself across differences, like that of Ted for Short and Faustino. It furthermore contrasts the
efforts of the landowners to foment conflict between these groups, which,
though ultimately successful, are clearly not the direction Véa desires for
his storyworld and the one it represents. However, for now, the novel's
world continues in this direction in spite of the existence of these hetero-
topic/ontological spaces. Their violent destruction forestalls the potential
and clearly wished-for transformation represented by such even more concrete spaces like the Flip-Flop/Rose Room building and French Camp.

As mentioned previously, the novel establishes a direct line of descent
between the events of Stockton in these flashbacks and its present. The
former feeds directly into the latter. By leaping from the time and space of
late 1950s Stockton to early 1990s San Francisco, the novel creates a continuity between these two temporal/spatial localities. The absence of the
thirty years between them is significant. Set in 1958 and 1959, the Stockton flashbacks are poised at the cusp of the 1960s and thus just prior to
the counterculture and civil rights movements of that period. A hint of
such appears in the efforts of Cesar Chavez to organize French Camp, but
these are of course frustrated by the camp's destruction. Absent such energies, what remains instead is the general pattern of the 1970s and 1980s: a
growing, global dominance of capitalism; catastrophically violent events
(in particular to this and Véa's texts in general, the Vietnam War); and
continued race-, ethnicity-, sex-, class-, and gender-based inequities and
exclusion. In essence, by leaving out the time period and energies of the
1960s and its various revolutions, the novel likewise indicates the absence
of what those could have led to, implicitly something other than what it
represents as the cultural condition of the 1990s, in which those divisive
and destructive forces reach their apotheosis.

The novel's vision is thus consistent with what José David Saldívar characterizes in *Border Matters* as "the continuing desire of the United States for 'pure' national and cultural spaces" through a re-establishment of a cultural "border patrol [that] once kept the barbarians out and safeguarded the culture within" (20–21). This desire establishes a continuity between the novel's present and its other temporal/spatial localities: various characters give explicit evidence of that same problematic fear and resulting desire for containment. For example, a white paramedic tending to the newly virginal Queenie on the night of Bambino Reyes's murder exclaims, "Where in God's name do these people come from? Where the hell do they come from? Why can't we close the borders and keep them out? What we need is a fifty-foot fence clear around this country" (Véa, *Silver Cloud* 80). The immigrant cabdriver Anatoly demonstrates his experience of this desire's impact, noting how Americans "were constantly calling for a census of immigrants and their families, and for identification cards. Now they were restricting languages, closing schools, and sealing borders." He further parallels these actions to those carried out against his fellow Romani in Bulgaria that drove his departure: "Anatoly had left his native land when the campaigns of assimilation had begun, when the Romani tongue was prohibited in the schools and Gypsies were not allowed to travel about. The government had called for a census of Romani and for identification cards to be carried by all legal citizens of Bulgaria" (120). In addition to demonstrating the global operation of these forces, these efforts lamented by Anatoly more locally recall the exclusionary ordinances from the Stockton flashbacks. Both find another corollary in the efforts of Lex Dedwood, San Francisco's city attorney:

> In his latest memo to the Mayor, the attorney presented a new statute that had incorporated whole paragraphs from Henry VIII's act for the punishment of vagabonds, rogues, and beggars. In his footnotes, he had included specific references to Elizabeth's act of 1562 against Gypsies, nomads, and counterfeit Egyptians, and the 1666 edict by Louis XIV providing for the punishment of Bohemians and wanderers. (17–18)

Dedwood similarly cites the *Fremdrasse*, which stems from the 1935 Nuremberg Laws passed under Hitler, a lineage that fits nicely with the other exclusionary acts from throughout history, once again highlighting their global and temporal transcendence and so that of their motivating desire (18).

Furthermore, the litany of legal precursors exemplifies again how such efforts to contain cultural differences simply redeploy in changing conditions. Far from being invalidated by contemporary cultural heterogeneity, these efforts instead adapt to those circumstances. The anonymous white Inspector investigating Reyes's murder provides further evidence of such continuation and adaptation:

> He was a veteran officer who hated the computerized, talk-show world into which he would soon retire. He hated the new categories of crimes that had come into existence in the last few years: child abductors, disgruntled employees, and twelve-year-olds with machine guns. In the old days the world had been so much simpler. There had been real cops and real criminals, the good and the bad, and a hazy but visible line in between.
>
> Now there were amateurs and civilians involved; stalkers, postal clerks, and kids who killed for designer shoes. The police force itself looked different now. There were female cops with degrees in sociology and gay cops who patrolled the Castro District and Noe Valley. The world even looked different. Now there were Guatemalans and Russian Jews everywhere you looked. Nowadays you needed an interpreter at every crime scene. (4)

The Inspector's nostalgic longing for the "good old days"—days when cops were cops, and criminals were criminals—displays dominant society's discomfort with contemporary cultural complexity. He and those he represents have seen their old epistemological categories exploded by differences. All sorts of new crimes and new criminals, and thus categories of the same, have arisen, from stalkers and child kidnappers to disgruntled postal workers and thrill killers. Such an explosion necessitates the creation of new epistemological categories to account for such developments. This necessity even infects the police force itself, which now includes women and gays. The Inspector's obvious dissatisfaction with this state of affairs makes transparent his discomfort.

That dissatisfaction also points to how such epistemological efforts may have reached their limits. Those categories are being stretched to the point of uselessness, as the awkward category "twelve-year-olds with machine guns who kill for designer shoes" exemplifies. In *Magical Urbanism*, Mike Davis decries this "stubbornly binary discourse of American public culture" for how it "has yet to register the historical significance of [the] ethnic transformation of its landscape." Like Véa, he identifies how categories like "Hispanic/Latino" and "Asian-American" that derive from this discourse are "artificial, racialized box[es] . . . invented by the majority society to uncomfortably contain individuals of the most emphatically disparate national origins" (15). Véa reveals (and so destabilizes) precisely this epistemological discourse. Dominant U.S. society wants to (needs to?) feel that U.S. culture is "known." Hence, the anxiety when dealing with those cultures that are different and thus "unknown." However tenuous, the discourse underlying the Inspector's comments, and indeed much of dominant society's actions toward peoples and cultures of difference throughout this novel, speak to the continued prevalence of this desire for epistemological certainty.

The present-day of the novel, then, casts its San Francisco as a restrictive and more and more homogenous space/time, once again echoing Rechy's *The Miraculous Day of Amalia Gómez*. There, Rechy symbolized this cultural "hardening" in the literal hardening of Amalia's physical environment. In Véa, the hardening is more metaphorical.

> The city had grown hard since the days when Hunter's Point was a shipyard bustling with workers and the long docks were dotted with lunch boxes. A mortal rigor had set in slowly, imperceptibly, as the number of office workers doubled and redoubled on the myth of a service economy. Workers had been replaced by investors, insurers, and market prognosticators. Men and women had come to town and sealed themselves into towering glass closets. Their disciples had followed closely behind, doing lunch and monotonously chanting the bottom line. (Véa, *Silver Cloud* 24)

The narrator further details how the "city ossified as the corporations exported their jobs under the new rationalization of a 'global economy,' the old 'free-trade' characterization having run its expedient course" (24). With terms such as "hard," "rigor," "sealed," and "ossified," San Francisco metaphorically "hardens," just as Amalia's home did with its iron bars and concrete houses. Furthermore, the novel implicates capitalism in this state of affairs. It is the "myth of a service economy" perpetuated by U.S. capitalism that induces the "mortal rigor" of its office workers. They become alienated automatons, locking themselves in their closets, and monotonously going through the motions at work. The city becomes homogenous at the hands of capitalism. It stiffens, corpse-like, as jobs are exported in the name of the "global economy," just the latest buzzword replacing preceding justifications. Implicit within this description is an indictment for how U.S. society facilitates its fate. There is a desperation here, U.S. workers throwing themselves off the cliff of capitalism like lemmings in the name of a myth they so desperately want to believe in.

The narrator sounds a similar note when describing how the above "investors, insurers, and market prognosticators" hide in their towering offices, "wagering on work as if somewhere steel would still be smelted, as if somewhere in America dies were being cut and oxyacetylene was still being lit. As if human hands still spot-welded fenders. As if someone in America was still bending to cut the cauliflower, to caress the asparagus" (24). The nostalgia here echoes that of the Inspector. U.S. society too yearns for the "good old days" of human labor (though much of the French Camp scenes put the lie to this image) and tells itself these activities still go on, while remaining ignorant of both how they do not and the consequences of this loss: "San Francisco was full of insubstantial things: a metal-and-glass canopy sheltering imaginary labor; lease futures; productivity options; insurance-policy buyouts. Buildings that no one sleeps in, they are filled with manila files and actuarial charts, the mere shadows of lives" (26). What is more and more missing from the novel's storyworld is precisely what first washed over Zeferino when he came to French Camp, what Ted for Short recognized in his bond with Faustino: life and humanity.

Véa uses Ted for Short to similarly indict contemporary America for its capitalist shortcomings. Ted for Short is the foremost spokesman for the novel's vision of how and what dominant U.S. culture and society have deprived themselves. In one of his conversations with the young Zeferino at French Camp, Ted for Short echoes *La Maravilla*'s "Prólogo," specifically its criticism of people's narrow minds. "When you are critical of humans . . . and these days you have to be . . . you must say that they can't see their horizons. It is a terrible sin, my boy, to have a little mind" (137, original ellipses). Where the deceased voice of the *curandera* grandmother Josephina lamented the limitations people impose upon their own minds, Ted for Short more fully castigates that narrow-mindedness, labeling it a sin. And, again, that sin ultimately originates with capitalism, as he elsewhere explains:

> I wonder about this country sometimes. You don't trust
> people here; you can only trust their motives, their invest-
> ments. It is the morality of the marketplace. Yet, beneath the
> store window, it is so beautiful and there is such a diversity of
> people. But, in the end, the very things that should be posi-
> tive are perverted here. If people in this country see a beauti-
> ful landscape, they immediately want to sell it. They rush to
> put a hotel on it. Then they get angry if someone else puts a
> hotel in front of theirs. If they see a beautiful heritage, they
> exclude it until it's watered down enough to be acceptable.
> (146)

What Ted for Short enumerates here parallels the capitalist evacuation of space Brady theorizes. The capitalist mindset sees everything—be it land or cultures—only in terms of their acceptability or, perhaps better, market-ability. For them to be marketed, their acceptability must be maximized, which requires them to be, in Ted for Short's terms, "watered down" or homogenized. The capitalist mindset shown to dominate this novel's story-world also proves destructive to how the world should, and perhaps still could, be. As Ted for Short further notes, "It is the myth of sameness that diminishes us all in the world. The myth of sameness deprives us of our pride and our shame" (324). The diminishment Ted for Short identifies is borne of a loss of humanity. In losing both pride and shame, the people in the novel's imagined U.S. nation-space lose the full gamut of human emo-tion, becoming, as was seen before, lifeless automatons. As Ted for Short goes on to summarize, "our failure to see the many worlds in our world has left us all heartless and homeless" (324). These many worlds, many cultural worlds or spaces in particular, are what capitalism's ascendancy has sought to homogenize and so eliminate.

But they are also what *The Silver Cloud Café* speaks to as a solution. It echoes Davis in advocating a "cultural syncretism" as "a transformative template for the whole society" (*Magical Urbanism* 15), a transformation textualized around the novel's present-day heterotopic space, the Silver Cloud Café itself. If Ted for Short laments his world's failure to see the many worlds within it, the novel concretely locates their presence in the heterotopic spaces throughout its many temporal and spatial locales. These spaces find their contemporary embodiment in the Silver Cloud. Not only is the café a space of ontological juxtaposition like those preceding it, but, in representing it so, Véa further ascribes to it a transformative effect that subverts and unsettles that dominant, epistemological desire.

The café's heterotopic and ontological nature manifests upon its first mention. Beatrice, the café's transsexual bouncer, attempts to describe "this beautiful little bar in the Mission District" to Zeferino: "It's not a gay bar, but it's not straight either. I guess it's a Mexican bar and café. It's not like any place I've ever seen" (Véa, *Silver Cloud* 37–38). Beatrice's description is the reader's first indication that this space contrasts the storyworld it inhabits. It is neither gay nor straight, and its clientele similarly bridges these two categories. To put it another way, the Silver Cloud cannot be categorized by either of those groups, cannot be known through them. The best term Beatrice can come up with, "Mexican," reinforces the café's singular nature. It parallels those terms used by the novel's anonymous Inspector to categorize his world's new crimes and criminals. In that earlier case, the tenuousness of those categories underlined the Inspector's society's unease with their world's explosion of differences. Beatrice's unease is different. It is not that "Mexican" serves as an epistemological term, reducing the Silver Cloud to some known category. In fact, this term remains ambiguous in its application. Beatrice's unease is more ontological, in that she appears uncertain whether this term adequately conveys the full nature of this powerful and significant space. As she goes on to tell Zeferino about the Silver Cloud, "Just working there these past few months has restored my hope for us all" (37). Here, the text signals a double transformation, one actual and one potential. Beatrice has had her hope restored. But also, the Silver Cloud and what it represents clearly stands as hope for the novel's imagined San Francisco and, indeed, U.S. nation-space.

Like Beatrice, the café's owner Raphael muses on the Silver Cloud's heterotopic nature. From his hotel room overlooking the café, he watches Zeferino approach the building and thinks, "It was like an ark, like a *communidad de culturas*, a rest stop from all the selfishness and cruelty out there" (103, original italics). Raphael underlines his café's uniqueness, specifically by noting its community and thus conglomeration of cultures. Not only does the Silver Cloud serve as a place of cultural community, but it also preserves that community in a world losing any communal feeling. Raphael's Biblical metaphor expresses this point. He is Noah, constructing his "ark" to save all cultures not from a God-created flood, but rather from a flood of capitalist homogenization. The café accomplishes this goal literally in "preserving" the lives of the novel's migrant and ethnic characters. Raphael rattles off a list of the novel's major characters—Ted for Short, Humberto, King Pete, Queenie, Anatoly, Miguel Govea—all of whom find solace at the Silver Cloud (108). But, too, these characters all carry with them or embody their storyworld's ethnic and cultural differences: immigrants, ethnics, the physically disabled, women, gays. In preserving their lives, the Silver Cloud preserves their diverse cultural heritages by bringing them all together into a single space.

In this way, then, the Silver Cloud fulfills in the novel's present the legacy of those past heterotopic spaces. Like them, the café is a concrete, real space within the storyworld. Also like them, it juxtaposes diverse cultural differences. But the Silver Cloud surpasses its predecessors in the effect this heterotopia has within its contemporary time and space. In addition to the nature of such spaces, Foucault further explicated the function of heterotopias, how such spaces "counter" the dominant "sites of culture," by likening them to a mirror:

> In the mirror, I see myself there where I am not, in an unreal virtual space that opens up behind the surface; I am over there, where I am not, a sort of shadow that gives my own visibility to myself, that enables me to see myself there where I am absent; such is the utopia of the mirror. *But it is also a heterotopia in so far as the mirror does exist in reality, where it exerts a sort of counteraction on the position that I occupy.* From the standpoint of the mirror I discover my absence from the place where I am since I see myself over there. (24, italics added)

What Foucault defines here is a counteracting effect heterotopias exert on the reality in which they exist. Such an effect emanates from their own dual nature as both "real" sites within their world, but also "unreal" and "virtual" in their utopian nature. The heterotopic mirror allows the viewer to be absent from the place where they are. But also, the viewer would see how where they are, their reality, is not the utopia the mirror contains. The mirroring heterotopia not only makes the viewer visible to himself or herself, but also makes visible the worlds where they are and are not, making transparent the difference between the two. Here would seem to be its counteraction: by making visible somewhere the reality is not, the heterotopia manifests the differences between the world it projects and the world it inhabits to its viewer. Precisely such a counteractive effect is what the Silver Cloud Café exerts on Zeferino del Campo. Exposure to this heterotopic space transforms Zeferino's understanding of his storyworld. It is, then, in Zeferino that the novel most clearly textualizes its narrative of transformation and new consciousness toward differences.

When first introduced in the novel, Zeferino exists in a state congruent with the homogenization and alienation of its anonymous hordes. He appears cynical and bitter, which he directs toward the city's homeless. "Do you think somebody places ads in the rest of the country? 'Wanted: shadow boxers and toothless women, openings at the San Francisco Civic Center.' There must be sixty people talking to themselves within forty feet of this bench. Would you look at that, even a deaf-mute signing to himself! Christ Almighty!" (Véa, *Silver Cloud* 19). Tellingly, Zeferino's exclamation here echoes that of the white paramedics tending to Queenie and bewailing the proliferation of immigrants. Zeferino likewise initially possesses an attitude about Ted for Short similar to that of dominant U.S. society. To Zeferino, he is "some strange old guy" with a similarly strange "Greek" or "Gypsy" name (20, 22).

But perhaps most clearly indicating Zeferino's blinkered state is the fact that the Silver Cloud Café has been up to this point invisible to him.

> Zeferino drove down Folsom Street wondering why he had never noticed Raphael's Silver Cloud Café and Bar. He had driven down Folsom Street, down Seventeenth, and even down Shotwell on hundreds of occasions, investigating scores of cases. He conjured up a mental picture of the area as he waited at a stoplight—the Rite Spot restaurant was there, a transmission repair shop, and an empty field surrounded by Cyclone fencing. (88)

Here is literally a moment of cognitive mapping within this novel's story-world. But Zeferino's mental representation of the street on which the Silver Cloud sits fails to include this space. Despite having been down these streets "hundreds" of times, Zeferino has never "conjured" the café as part of what exists here. By extension, Zeferino's understanding of his larger culture and world absents the cultural worlds embodied by the café. He, like the anonymous drones of his society, has simply accepted a homogenized, watered-down, and thus incomplete picture of his world. As Zeferino himself will soon realize, "he, like so many others, had succumbed to the smug belief that his own cynical view of the world was accurate" (115). On the contrary, his view, and the view of this world's others like him, is proven radically and sadly inaccurate.

Zeferino's transformation from this narrow-minded perspective begins immediately upon his arrival at the Silver Cloud. And as suddenly: "The instant he saw it he pulled over. He slammed one wheel into the curb, killed the engine, and slumped back violently in his seat like a man who has just had a fatal seizure" (88). The Silver Cloud's effect is instant and violently intense. It has Zeferino slamming his brakes and killing the car's engine. Most significantly, it creates in Zeferino intense discomfort. His lungs heave, his eyes bulge, his hands quake. The literal discomfort Zeferino feels at this moment signals that he is being shaken out of his comfortable, cynical, narrow-minded perspective. This change begins with the return of his repressed past, a "locked door of a room that had been sealed shut for over thirty years." As he remembers the "reincarnated lines of brown men laboring in their prime," as he reinhabits a "Quonset hut full of farmworkers somewhere in the Central Valley," Zeferino reconnects to a community and communal history (88). All that he has repressed, or more accurately that his world repressed and he simply accepted, returns to him through the intervening function of this heterotopic space. It clearly counteracts the position he has occupied for the past thirty years since his flight, after the murder of Pietro Ditto, from the disintegrating French Camp with Ted for Short. Zeferino now sees himself within this past, this culture, which effectively absents him from the one he has occupied since his childhood.

And with this counteraction comes relief. What the Silver Cloud offers to him is "irresistible." He feels "joyful because memories to the contrary were now sprouting in his soul" (88, 115). Zeferino is no longer, like so many in the novel's storyworld, searching for "secure moorings in a shifting world," no longer looking for an epistemological certainty that necessitates imposing reductive categories on a diverse world. He is instead "taking advantage of all of the divergent possibilities" this pluralistic, eclectic, anarchic space offers (Harvey 302). Near the close of the novel, Ted for Short asks Zeferino a single question: "after all your education, after all this time, after all that you've seen and remembered, do you really believe in angels?" (Véa, *Silver Cloud* 338). Zeferino's answer to this question, and thus the hope it gestures toward, remains unknown. But the fact that Zeferino can now be asked if he has hope signals the change in him from how he first appeared in the novel. This transformation is toward a new understanding and thus consciousness of his world, one that acknowledges cultural difference as the condition of the contemporary United States, not an anomaly or even an outcast presence within it.

The same challenge the storyworld puts forth to Zeferino, the novel puts forth to its reader. There is another heterotopic space inherent within *The Silver Cloud Café*, and that is the space of the novel itself. This discussion of Véa's second novel began by noting the irreducibility of its plot. The same could be said about the novel's generic identification. Véa's *The Sil-*

*ver Cloud Café* juxtaposes various "incompatible" or "irreconcilable" generic "worlds." Cantú, for example, characterizes it as a "Chicano historical novel," "a narrative . . . account of the farm worker," a "murder mystery, Gothic tale, and interpolated historical essay" (210). Additionally, there is a variety of specific authorial/textual resonances juxtaposed within the text: the magical realism of Gabriel García Márquez, the modernism/naturalism of John Steinbeck and *The Grapes of Wrath* in particular, and the California noir of Raymond Chandler. The text of *The Silver Cloud Café* is then as eclectic, as plural, as anarchic as the storyworld it creates and just as resistant to epistemological categorization. Thus, I suggest that the novel functions for its reader just as the Silver Cloud functions for Zeferino. The physical book is a real site within our culture and society. And the world it imagines counteracts its/our own, unsettling our comfortable positionings and flattened understandings of cultural differences within the U.S. nation-space, challenging us to transform into a larger, more inclusive perspective than that which generally prevails.

## SUPPOSING THINGS COULD BE DIFFERENT: *GODS GO BEGGING*

Véa's third novel, *Gods Go Begging*, shares much with its immediate predecessor. As in *The Silver Cloud Café*, Véa makes a palimpsest of disparate temporal and spatial localities. In each, we find in force those dominant forces of exclusion, epistemological containment, and destruction. Likewise, heterotopic spaces persist in each time to contrast and combat these forces, speaking to a world, or at least an understanding of a world, different from the homogenous and alienated one created by global capitalism. And, at the heart of this story, stand a lawyer and his defendant: Chicano public defender Jesse Pasadoble and Calvin "Biscuit Boy" Thibault, an accused double murderer.

In spite of their obvious similarities, *Gods Go Begging* textualizes its narrative of transformation quite differently from that of *The Silver Cloud Café*. For one, the relationship among this novel's times/spaces of Chihuahua, Mexico, Vietnam War-era Laos, and present-day San Francisco is static. The same processes of exclusion, epistemological containment, and destruction that evolve between times and spaces in *The Silver Cloud Café* translate across the times and spaces in *Gods Go Begging*. Furthermore, the heterotopic spaces in this novel form less from a confluence of cultural differences than from the concentration of dominant society's destructive desire for "comfort." Erupting at these sites in all of the novel's times and spaces are "transtemporal hills" that are that desire's comeuppance. Specifically, they rob that desire of its transparency and collapse it into itself. In this temporal/spatial collapse, *Gods Go Begging* signals that birth of a new world and consciousness for its primary characters and their storyworld, and by extension fosters the same for its readers.

In *Gods Go Begging*, Véa interlaces three temporal/spatial localities: Chihuahua, Mexico, at an undisclosed point in the twentieth century; occupied Laos during the Vietnam War; and the present day of San Francisco, California. However, the relationship among these times and spaces is distinct from that in *The Silver Cloud Café*. San Francisco served as the previous novel's primary setting, with the other localities nested within that time and space through flashbacks. *Gods Go Begging* instead juxtaposes its present with the Vietnam era. The novel's suggestion of stasis, then, stems from how these two distinct eras are not only paired but also linked by various characters' experiences in each, particularly Jesse as well as the chaplain of his platoon. Both furthermore duplicate each other in how they depict the treatment of cultural differences by dominant U.S. society.

The novel initially establishes this resonance between its two primary times/spaces through the character of Jesse Pasadoble. The novel's narrator repeatedly draws parallels between Jesse's wartime experiences and his present as a public defender. For example, when Jesse and his fellow lawyers gather in the cafeteria at the Hall of Justice to swap tales of their legal experiences, their resulting laughter is "foxhole laughter," the stories themselves "war stories" (Véa, *Gods* 28, 29). Jesse's own thoughts, reported by the narrator, about himself and his compatriot lawyers explicitly further this metaphor. "Grunts of the law, he thought, field medics performing triage in the crowded jails and holding cells behind the staid courtrooms. We tend the wounded, he thought, those who were wounded by life, by testosterone, by poverty" (37). Here, Jesse and his fellows are both soldiers ("grunts") and field medics; the literal bullets he once faced find their corollary in the present "ordnance" of testosterone and poverty. Though locations may have shifted, conditions remain the same. Jesse is as much figuratively "at war" in his present as he literally was in the past. Explicit events in the two localities likewise resonate with each other. For instance, as Jesse and his friends laugh at their various stories, the narrator describes how that laughter "rolled from the dining room and out into the hallways, where it splashed onto the steel doors of four elevators and onto the swollen racks of the evidence room at the end of the hallway" (42). This moment echoes one of Jesse's formative experiences during the Vietnam War. He befriends Hong Trac, a Vietnamese POW who is eventually murdered by U.S. soldiers, but not before Jesse and Trac's own simultaneous laughter "turned heads from one head of the compound to the other" (80). Like the war metaphor used to describe Jesse's present existence, such common occurrences between the two localities suggest their essential similarity and thus stasis.

Both time and spaces share another important quality as well: a dominant lack of human feeling to which those moments of laughter prove the merest exception. The description of a Russian soldier's death during the war emphasizes the institutional and anonymous nature of how his body will be treated. His remaining body parts are categorized and inventoried, forms filled out in duplicate and triplicate, and a "boilerplate notice of death and letter of condolence were cut by a clerk-typist" (92). The soldier's body is swiftly cataloged, his life reduced to paperwork. The autopsies of the bodies of Mai Adrong and Persephone Flyer, for whose murders Calvin stands accused in the novel's present, are similarly institutional and anonymous. The coroner verbally partitions Mai's body, cataloging and inventorying it just as with the soldier's corpse:

> *Jane Doe 37 is a small Asian woman in her mid- to late forties. I can see no adipose tissue. Her breasts are soft but not pendulous. She is well muscled and unremarkable except for the fact that I can detect no remote scarring or injuries on the epidermis. She has beautiful skin. Delete last sentence from written text. There is significant bruising to all fingers, the palms, and the side of the hands opposite the thumb.* (13, original italics)

The language is formal, institutional. Even the tiniest bit of human feeling that slips in, the remark about Mai's beautiful skin, must be excised from the official report. Both locations, then, possess similar qualities of anonymity and inhumanity, which add to the similarity and stasis between them. These qualities furthermore signal in both the presence of the processes of homogeneity, violence, and exclusion. The inhumanity metaphorized above is that directed toward the peoples and cultures of difference inhabiting the novel's storyworld.

However, inset between the novel's primary locales is a third—early twentieth-century Chihuahua, Mexico—which is, chronologically, the novel's earliest exhibitor of these forces. This flashback centers on the youth of Jesse's platoon's chaplain, born Guillermo Calavera, later named William Calvert, still later named Vô Dahn (meaning "no one"), and finally Mr. Homeless. The chaplain is the only character to exist in all three localities; thus, his past serves as an origin point for the novel's later times and spaces, as well as for the forces at play within them. The novel details the chaplain's Chihuahuan past as he floats down the Mekong River, having just abandoned his platoon/flock for the second and final time. "Slowly, the trembling and tenuous mind of the floating man was wholly transformed from the high grasses that lined the banks of the Mekong River into the grasses of his youth in Mexico" (198). There, his family was the target of their village's material greed and dehumanization. As the narrator explains, the Chaplain's family was "reputed to be *ermitaños y avaros muy famosos*, famous hermit-misers that pretended to be suffering abject poverty but who in reality possessed wealth beyond Midas" (202). The villagers further resent the family as "niggardly, peso-pinching" farmers (202). They manufacture that resentment into rumors that the chaplain's father and grandfather "were not even human at all. If the truth be told, the two men had begun life as lowly *insectos*, as burrowing spiders, *arañas* who had been magically transformed into fully grown human men only after having made an unbreakable pact with Satanás, the devil himself" (204, original italics). Adding to these beliefs are the sounds the townspeople hear emanating from the house: "There had been ear-splitting sounds like the ones that sprang from the legs of giant crickets and the mandibles of the largest butterflies" (205). It is the greed of the townspeople that leads to these dehumanizing rumors, a greed that, as with *The Silver Cloud Café*, gestures toward capitalism's implication in these processes. Like the conflict of the Christero War before, this conflict is, at its heart, a conflict and jealousy over wealth, making its resulting dehumanization a result of a materialism that will only grow as the novel moves toward its present of global capitalism.

Similarly implicated here are racial and ethnic hatreds. One can already see in the rumors crafted about them the discomfort with the family's differences. What is "different" or "odd" about them underpins their rumored insect past. The family's (alleged) wealth is a product of a Satanic deal. What proves most troubling to the village becomes the fodder for their discriminatory imaginings. Such discrimination becomes even more pointed when the chaplain reveals his family's ethnic heritage. Three years after deserting the war, and now living with Mai Adrong (who goes by the name Cassandra), the chaplain finally understands "what that buzzing in his childhood cellar had been."

> It had been the soaring and driving intonations of his father's
> voice. It had been the resin and the horse hairs of the ancient
> fiddle. There had been secret services in that basement for
> spider families. There had been weddings and bar mitzvahs
> and silent seders. Now he remembered those slaps to his face
> whenever the family was in the midst of strangers and an odd,
> foreign word inadvertently leapt from his mouth. (214)

Revealed here is the family's Jewish identity, stereotypes of which retro-
actively feed into the family's perceived miserliness. Like their supposed
wealth, the family must obscure their Jewish faith and practice it only in
secret. "Spider," consequently, becomes a derogatory term for "Jew." Nor is
all of this confined to just this one family, as all such "spider families" must
go to great lengths to hide this heritage, apparently for fear of how the rest
of the village would react. Though this revelation resolves a mystery in the
chaplain's own past, it more importantly reveals a secret motivation behind
the family's exclusion and dehumanization, the discomfort their larger society feels as a result of the family's cultural identity and difference.

Such discomfort and its consequences are not long confined to just the
chaplain's Mexican past. He laments what his native country has, in his
and the novel's mind, done to itself. Mexico is "a land whose primary sensibility is that of profound loss. Everyone in Mexico felt it. The sense of loss
had its roots in the time of the conquest: the loss of a hundred native religions, the loss of an entire race of peoples" (196). But, too, he criticizes his
adopted country of America for much the same: "His world back home in
America was a land obsessed with comfort; with the avoidance of pain . . .
at any cost. America was the chaplain's adopted country. There, everyone
who could afford it dashes headlong into comfort, into barricades and behind walls for a life without disease and agony—hiding from both risk and
passion alike" (196, original ellipsis). Invoking the gated communities of
the wealthy, the narrator echoes what Davis describes about the contemporary rich Los Angelinos who barricade themselves from perceived racial
and class threats. Too, this is not just an epidemic of the novel's present-
day America. It is imagined as the country's historical legacy. Elsewhere,
Jesse identifies the Puritans as another instance of this desire's operation,
citing their revulsion at "the carefree spirit and nakedness of the Indians"
(113). This revulsion serves as the impetus behind the Puritans making "it
a capital crime to have sex with them" (113). And he goes on to make explicit the lines of descent that connect the present to this past. "This simple
idea of cultural difference as blasphemy is the very foundation of American

racism. It wasn't much of a leap from the Puritans to the Aryan Nation. It wasn't much of a leap from their laws against consorting with the Indians to the Jim Crow laws in the South and the antimiscegenation laws in the west" (114).

The historical legacy of American racist exclusion traces back from its present to its very origins, and so too does the suffering of those peoples forced to bear the burden of that racism. The Vietnam War serves as another instance of this fact: "In Vietnam, there was no comfort, nor would there ever be. The Creole sergeant had been right. Those boys, like the slaves from Africa, like the hopeless Indians, like true artists and the poor, had been chosen to bear the discomfort of their country, to bear the loss" (196). As in *The Silver Cloud Café*, the operation of this desire breaks across temporal, national, and historical borders to inflict itself upon all peoples and cultures of difference, a fact that the novel's palimpsest of its three temporal and spatial localities makes apparent.

But along with the pervasiveness of these homogenizing forces comes the ubiquity of those heterotopic spaces that contrast and undermine them, the "transtemporal hills" that appear in all three times/spaces. The Chihuahuan hill on which the chaplain's family lived and within which they hid their "treasure" is one example. The hill is, in one dimension, where the family and their heritage are relegated by that dominant desire. Simultaneously, that relegation robs that desire of its transparency, making explicit its operation and thus destabilizing it. However, the Chihuahuan hill is but the initial instance of these hills' dual appearance and significance. Later versions of this space more fully express both the spatial manifestation of that desire and its disruption. As the novel more fully explicates through the hills that exist in the central paired times/spaces, such hills are the continuing effect of dominant America's desire for comfort—"It had always been built on a hill" (197)—but also that desire's potential undoing.

Upon resuming the telling of Jesse's Vietnam War experiences subsequent to the murder of Hong Trac, the novel's narrator first establishes a focus on the hill on which the platoon will be stationed. Its birth is an apotheosis of that dominant desire:

> In the first light of day and far into the descending heat of
> evening, the small hill remained stunned, shivering, and
> confused. Somehow the age-old laws of geological time had
> been reversed in an unnatural, confounding instant. Molten
> magma had poured from the sky and splashed down onto a
> perplexed earth, fiery calderas had cracked open everywhere,

cinder cones and vents had erupted not with pressure from
below. Above its ruptured topsoils, the hill was spiteful and
suffering beneath its freshly wounded crust. The crest was
smoke-enshrouded and down below, in its deepest bedrock,
the hill had been rudely torn away from the ancient comfort
of tectonic, subterranean rhythms. (88)

The images combine to emphasize the unnaturalness of this birth. At first,
this hill is cast as a newly born infant, stunned and shivering in its nakedness, confusion, and isolation. But this hill did not erupt up from the earth;
it rather poured, unnaturally, down upon it. It happened quickly, suddenly,
not after eons of geological time. The earth does not recognize what has
been imposed upon it, being "confounded," "perplexed." There is a sense of
violation, as the creation of this hill cracked open the earth's crust, unnaturally creating plumes of smoke and fire from above, not below. In its own
way, the hill too suffers. It is "spiteful" and disconnected from the earth,
not a part of its powerful and comforting rhythms.

Furthermore, the hill is a space of war, and it is in being such a space
that the novel more directly connects it to that dominant desire. The paragraphs that follow the description of the hill's birth detail not only the conflict taking place upon it, but also that conflict's effect. "Two groups of men
had met on one face of this hill and their savage intentions had left every
tree limb and tree disfigured. Unwatered since the last monsoon rains, the
small hill of dry land and cracked earth had been sickened to nausea by this
forced feeding of burned sulfur and human fluids" (88). Instead of flowers
and plants, "scores of red seeds had erupted from human bodies, bursting
violently through the drabness of cloth and skin—seed of stomach, seed
of lung, hopeless grains set onto the wind" (88). This grisly picture paints
again the unnaturalness of this space, as nature itself is replaced by death
and destruction. Human bodies are now scattered like, and instead of,
seeds, and so too are their memories and lives: "On a stem of wild lemon
grass hung a taste for grape soda and shepherd's pie, the memory of her
goodbye, even the newborn baby's impulse to cry when the world was up-
side down. On a leaf of wild lemon grass specks of sense were stranded and
fading—three digits of a phone number, a single syllable from the second
verse of a cherished song, and half a glimpse of a woman's entire face" (88).
War becomes not just the destruction but also the perversion of humanity.
As Amos Flyer, Persephone's husband and Jesse's sergeant, explains to the
chaplain as they claim these bodies, "all this fucking war adds up to" is "*un
ballet bleu infame*" (96). He identifies that as "a French phrase that means

lewd acts with underage boys" (96). Jesse will later tell his on-again, off-again girlfriend Carolina something similar. "And when desire is stripped of humanity," he said as his final words, "all that remains is war" (291). Both statements link the war and its destruction to an inhuman and prurient desire.

What ultimately establishes this desire as the same dominant one are those "boys" themselves, the "colored boys, the Okies, and the spics," not to mention Native American and immigrant soldiers "still fighting Vietnam and America at the same time" (197). That is, the people fighting and being destroyed here are precisely those peoples of difference dominant society fears. And the hill, then, becomes the embodiment of that common desire. It functions as another "heterotopia of deviation." Foucault identifies asylums and even retirement homes as examples of such heterotopias, but the Vietnam War and its hill is one within the storyworld of this novel. It is where peoples of difference—be it racial, as in the case of the African-American, Chicano, Native American, and immigrant soldiers, or class, as with the so-called Okies—are located for their "deviance" from a "required norm" (Foucault 25). For this difference, they are relegated to this hill, this war, in the same way the chaplain's family was relegated to their small hill for their perceived and real differences. In this relegation, the hill becomes not unlike *La Maravilla*'s Buckeye Road. Both are spaces of conglomerated, outcast differences born of a desire to contain and eliminate them from the U.S. nation-space.

Also similar to Buckeye Road is this space's transformative effect: the relegation of these cultural differences to the same space has the effect of breaking down the divisions between them that function in the "normative world." In *La Maravilla*, the novel's narrator describes how exposure to the different cultures within Buckeye Road ameliorates the divisions between its inhabitants. Here, Amos Flyer makes essentially the same point: he speaks of how for "most of these black kids," this is "the first time they have ever been allowed to sit and eat with whites"; how back "in the world," you "never see" what you see here: "Mexican kids talking with blacks." Too, "these boys from the reservation ain't never seen a white man except on television" and now fight for and, more importantly, beside them (Véa, *Gods* 96). The hill itself is a product of the imposed divisions that are, ironically, unsettled by how that hill conglomerates those differences together. A similar transformation can be seen taking place in Jesse's previous interaction with the POW Hong Trac. These two combatants find a way to communicate, interact, and even establish a rapport, to the point that Jesse is outraged when he discovers Hong Trac's body and figures out the cause of his death. In both these instances and in this particular space/ time, then, the lines between enemy and ally, black and white, Mexican and black, Native American and white, lose their divisive power, if only for a time.

But while this specific transformation may appear limited by its location, an additional one echoes *The Silver Cloud Café* in how such heterotopic spaces counteract normative positioning. Again, this transformation lies in the "mirroring" function of heterotopias and how they allow the subject to see not only themselves where they are not (the utopia of the mirror) but also how their worlds are not the one their reflection inhabits. Amos Flyer uses the metaphor of a car's speedometer to explain just this effect. Their "old life was a car with a nice big speedometer on the dashboard. When you was happy, you would be cruising along at sixty. Top speed was around seventy miles an hour. When you was sad, your life would be po-kin' along at ten miles an hour or sometimes even slower." (93). The range ascribed to their former experience defines its "comfortable" limits. From zero to sixty is as much as society wants to experience, in effect cutting themselves off from what lies beyond both sides of that range. The effect of the war, however, has been to erase those limits for those like Flyer, the chaplain, and Jesse, as Flyer goes on to explain: "Now you understand that there's happiness far beyond sixty miles an hour, and there's sadness and grief way, way down below zero." In how most of society remains within those limits, Flyer further casts it and their former selves as simply "idling" or "asleep" (94). More to the point, the rest of the world not only remains comfortably ensconced within those blinkered limits, but also chooses and acts to remain within them.

That same choice was taken from these men. By relegating them to this space, dominant society robbed them of that same comfort. It is a violent, painful process, paralleling yet exceeding the violent spasms felt by Zeferino when he discovered the Silver Cloud for the first (conscious) time. The men here have been exposed to intense horror, sadness, and even happiness such as that experienced by the chaplain after he survives the previous night's attack. But, as Flyer describes "there is one benefit to having your brains and stomach slow-cooked by hatred and fear" (97).

> The padre watched as amber strands from the sunset seemed to dive down from the sky, coalesce into a small aurora bore-alis, then flow into the sergeant's mouth and down into his lungs. The whites of the Creole soldier's eyes began to glow with the inner light.

> "Once you been here, padre," whispered the sergeant as he held his breath, "you can taste a sunset." (98)

This magically real moment of Amos Flyer literally ingesting the sunset symbolizes the greater experiences of which he has now become capable of partaking. It is a possibility outside of what normative society imagines, outside of what it epistemologically deems or categorizes as "possible." In this sense, then, we see Flyer, and by extension all the men in the platoon, as existing outside the epistemological borders normative society imposes on reality and, by necessity, through which it also limits it. To the rest of the world, what these men have become will be marked as "crazy," but that designation results simply because they no longer can be contained within normative epistemological categories. The transformation that occurs with these soldiers opens them up to what the novel posits as a "truer," greater range of experience. It further indicts as impoverished that dominant desire and the world it creates where and whenever it operates, the fullest point of this being the novel's present.

*Gods Go Begging*'s present-day of San Francisco, California, perfectly replicates the conflicting forces and potential transformations represented within the flashbacks to Laos and the Vietnam War. This replication further underlines the essential stasis between these eras and spaces; how, in spite of decades' passage, the same cycle of cultural conflict and strife continues. Symbolizing this vicious cycle is the novel's opening chapter and its juxtaposition of the morgue, where Mai's and Persephone's bodies are autopsied, with the restaurant where they lived and died. The two places are qualitatively different. The morgue stands as an institution of U.S. society and thus reflects that society's ever-increasing deficit of humanity. The morgue is "lonely," "airless," "dispassionate," "bloodless," "devoid of cushions or warmth," "numbing," "empty," "heartless," "silent," "sanitized," and, perhaps most telling of all its descriptors, "lifeless" (2). In this space where human bodies are treated dispassionately, there is a concomitant lack of passion, feeling, and ultimately life.

Intercut with the activities in the morgue are flashbacks to Mai's and Persephone's kitchen/soon-to-be restaurant, the Amazon Luncheonette. As Persephone cooks, the narrator makes clear how this space not only possesses but also emanates the passion, blood, warmth, and life lacking in the morgue and the society that space represents. "Outside her makeshift kitchen the glorious scent of her handiwork commingled with a breeze and was prying at her neighbor's windows, pushing in over the usual smells of Potrero Hill and the housing projects and overwhelming everything with the combined perfume of Palermo, Baton Rouge, and Saigon" (6). Contrasting the stultifying environment of the morgue is their kitchen's warm aroma. It is far from "sanitized," rather carrying with it the scent of combined cultural influences. The scent and their kitchen are alive: their work is "glorious" and pushes into and overwhelms their surroundings. This overwhelming power manifests itself in an even greater effect. The scent momentarily pauses games of streetball and dice, gang warfare, and drug trade, alleviating the competition, conflict, and even fear that is customary to the hill: "For a moment no one on the south side of the hill looked warily over his shoulder, then checked his waistband for the comforting bulge of a gun" (6). If these activities are the modern equivalent of the violence on that Laotian hill, then the scent from Mai's and Persephone's kitchen, in its ability to disrupt and assuage this conflict, marks that space as qualitatively different from the society that creates such conflict. Not insignificantly, the kitchen/restaurant is another place like Buckeye Road and the Silver Cloud where opposed cultural differences exist comfortably together. Mai and Persephone themselves represent one such crossing, Mai being married to Trin Adrong, a Vietnamese soldier, and Persephone being wedded to Amos Flyer. The two men themselves, at least in one form or another, simultaneously exist here. Their photographs stand next to each other on a shelf, and the women's cooking fuses each man's cultural influences. In this nature and this power, then, the Amazon Luncheonette stands as another of the heterotopic spaces that exist within Véa's linked storyworlds.

However, as such a space, the Amazon Luncheonette most fully parallels spaces like the Flip-Flop/Rose Room and French Camp. Its juxtaposition with the morgue inherently inscribes this space's destruction. The chapter begins in the morgue, with Mai's and Persephone's bodies on the table, framing the kitchen with their, and thus its own, destruction before it even appears. Likewise, the cuts to the Amazon Luncheonette and the women's efforts build up to the day and even the very hours prior to their murders at the hands of local street thug Little Reggie Harp and his unwitting accomplice, Calvin "Biscuit Boy" Thibault. Upon reaching the events of their death near the end of the chapter, the flashback circles back to the morgue with Mai's and Persephone's bodies lying cold on a slab. Structurally, then, the opening chapter evokes the historical cycle of destruction, for, even as it proffers an alternative space and perhaps history, if not future, it precludes both by inevitably invoking that space's destruction.

Potrero Hill, which serves as the site of the Amazon Luncheonette's downfall, is the transtemporal hill created in this time and space by the continuing desire for comfort of dominant society. It is the climax of not only this historical cycle but also a recognizable U.S. capitalism that preys upon America's youth.

> An oligarchy of sports and movie celebrities ruled over a new consumer peasantry. Like poor soldier serfs, these children built their lives around the imaginary castles of athletes and actors. In this land of functional illiteracy, there were icons everywhere, sports icons, icons of status, icons on the computer screen. There were icons on every television urging children to buy denim icons for their legs and canvas icons for their feet. As a new medieval era dawned, iconography, cryptography, and feudal impotence merged and now held sway. (169)

Ironically, capitalism's ascendancy fosters a new feudalism to rival its medieval predecessor. But an even more pronounced effect is the absence of a substantive culture. In its place are the icons of mass culture promulgated through and by sports and entertainment celebrities. These icons are nothing more than Baudrillardian simulacra that "substitute signs of the real for the real itself" and furthermore "mask the absence of a basic reality" (Baudrillard 343, 347). The net effect of this substitution is to render those "poor soldier serfs," the children of the present-day United States, impotent in how they enslave themselves to such iconography and consumption. Calvin/"Biscuit Boy" initially exemplifies this deprived ontological state, as Jesse's first impression of him is as "semiliterate, bookless, wordless, and thoughtless," his mind awash only in the icons of mass consumer culture (Véa, *Gods* 46).

Adding to the novel's point about contemporary mass culture and its depredatory effects is the miasma surrounding Potrero, effects that earn it the nickname Tourette's Hill. This hill's effects are "the result of radon gases from all this concrete mixing with hamburger wrappers and the tons of cocaine residue that have fallen onto the roadway. This compound ferments underfoot and is then bombarded by that dead blue light that pours out of television screens" (170). What emanates from this toxic combination of mass culture, radioactive gases, and drugs is "an insidious chemical gas that slowly leaches the human spirit out of these kids. It attacks and destroys the hippocampus so that these kids have no future and no cultural memory. Without a hippocampus they are forced to live in the eternal now" (170). These descriptions invoke Frederic Jameson's notion of post-modern "schizophrenia," where the postmodern/schizophrenic subject "is reduced to an experience of pure material signifiers, or, in other words, a series of pure and unrelated presents in time" (*Postmodernism*, 27). The in-habitants of Potrero Hill evidence a similar presentness in their consump-tion as a result of their exposure to the toxic waste dump of mass culture that is their environment.

These effects are not limited to only this hill, or even the United States. Such iconization and flattening occurs storyworld-wide: "The high-fives and low-fives of a celebrating Brazilian basketball team began here as back-street gestures of satisfaction or recognition" (169). Similarly, "Ghetto and barrio fashions, sources of probable cause in Oakland, would, in time, be found draped over the long, lithe bodies of starving French models" (169). Just as Calvin and the children of Potrero Hill are robbed of any cultural context or substance, global capitalism and the exporting of U.S. mass cul-ture flattens the context of these translated "signs" so that they too become substance-less, context-less icons.

But in being the site of these forces' concentration, Potrero Hill simul-taneously signals their unraveling. Like the heterotopic spaces before it, Potrero Hill robs these forces of their necessary invisibility, making mani-fest their operation and effect on those exposed to it. When Calvin "Biscuit Boy" Thibault returns to Potrero Hill after his acquittal, his former home is completely unfamiliar:

> Now he saw with new eyes, eyes like a starlight scope, tuned to foreign spectrums. Now he saw what he had never seen be-fore: roaming squads of fatherless boys, single mothers living on C-rations, marauding bands of tiny mercenaries proudly wearing their insignia of rank and assignment. On the side of the hill he saw the killing zone where four boys had gone down. Biscuit Boy gazed upon his own hill of birth and saw dimly what had once been his own impoverished life. (300)

Crystallized here again is that heterotopic mirroring effect: Calvin sees himself where he was but where now he no longer is. He is now the reflec-tion in the mirror that contrasts and counteracts his former positioning in reality. More to the point, Calvin is aware of this change. The new light be-hind his eyes is a new self-awareness. No longer is he the bookless, wordless, thoughtless boy Jesse first encountered. And along with that self-awareness comes an explicit awareness of the corrupting desire that infects this space and its inhabitants.

> Desire was there, leaking from the drainpipes and heading for the ocean untreated. Desire was leaping electrically down the wires that dangled from all the rusting antennas that clotted the rooftops. Desire was being pumped into gas tanks and rammed violently into the chambers of cheap weapons. Desire was being smoked in crack pipes and injected into the crooks of arms. (300)

The nakedness of this desire is only now apparent to Calvin. Exposed are its toxic and narcotic, deadly and numbing effects. Calvin's newfound recognition of this fact is a mark of his own transformation from one succumbing to those desires and the society that propagates them to someone who can recognize them for what they are and leave them behind. In Calvin, *Gods Go Begging* provides the first evidence of a new consciousness within and of its world. Like Zeferino at the end of *The Silver Cloud Café*, Calvin comes to a new understanding of his world, realizing how its dominant forces and society both victimize and marginalize people and cultures of difference.

*Gods Go Begging*'s other protagonist, Jesse Pasadoble, likewise transforms toward a new consciousness, but further revealing is how the novel suggests through him a possibly new world altogether. Through Jesse, the novel's two primary times and spaces conjoin and ultimately collapse into each other. What *Gods Go Begging* ultimately suggests through their simultaneous collapse is the birth of a new world within the novel as well as new possibilities in the consciousness of its readers.

At his introduction, Jesse appears, like Calvin and even Zeferino, to have succumbed to the narrow-minded and blinkered possibilities of his world. Much of this effect appears as the post-traumatic effect of his experiences in Vietnam. For one, he subscribes to the limits Amos Flyer critiques through his speedometer metaphor. "All that had been amputated was his ability to give or receive love" (39). As the narrator later describes, "That power had been replaced by something else: a soul sickness; a hunger for beauty but only at a distance" (45). Contradictorily, Jesse's truncated feelings coincide with a longing to express more that goes unfulfilled. This trauma, not surprisingly, negatively affects his relationship with Carolina. He wishes for "one sweet, mortal moment without the constant accompaniment of percussive anger and a grinding bass line of grief" (159). His very wish demonstrates how he has yet to achieve such a moment. From Carolina's perspective, Jesse "could never give in to the moment. He could never lose control" (307). To her, Jesse limits himself. To lose control would be to experience beyond that limited range of zero to sixty; so too would achieving that one perfect moment with Carolina. Jesse, then, like his world, is static. He remains bound within a certain range of experience, always wanting more but never achieving it.

Similarly, Jesse in the present has lost his ability to imagine. Jesse, in the past, possessed this faculty, as demonstrated by his participation in his platoon's storytelling exercises. These "supposings" served as a distraction from the reality of war around them. But as the novel's sixth chapter, "Mexicans in Space," demonstrates, they also allowed Jesse and his fellows to imagine a world alternative to the one they inhabit. Jesse's supposing begins with what he identifies as the essential difference between Mexico and the United States: "Mexico is a mestizo culture, a racially mixed *cultura* and the United States is not" (113, original italics). In Jesse's alternative history, "the *Mayflower* washes up onto the beach at Veracruz" (115–116). Today, "there would be a huge self-mortification theme park on the island" (116–117). On the other hand, the "Mexicans would have established a Border Patrol to keep those stern, pasty-faced people at bay" (117). Furthermore, Cortez's "supposed" landing at Plymouth Rock would have resulted in his slaughter by the Iroquois and a North America that was "Russian-Indian and French-Indian today" (117). More importantly, a series of invasions and oppressions—from Moctezuma to the Spanish Inquisition to slavery—would never have occurred. "The Industrial Revolution would have begun in the wide streets of Tenochtitlán city" (118). Jesse continues: "Without the Inquisition, Spain might have experienced the Renaissance" (119). Ultimately, Jesse's supposing culminates in the creation of M.A.S.A., "the Mexican Aeronautical Space Agency" (111). In these imaginings, Jesse postulates a world that corrects the wrongs of history. The repressions and oppressions of ethnic people are not only absolved but also replaced by technological advancement and innovation. Far from being marginalized by normative, mainstream society, they are that mainstream society, one that is European, Mexican, and Native American.

By the novel's present, Jesse has lost this imaginative ability to "suppose." The stories he shares in the novel's present with his fellow defense attorneys participate in, rather than counter, the cruel irony and cynicism of his world. Though there is a "common healing" described as a part of these stories, their manifest content concerns those victims of their world's cruelty, especially those victims from places like Potrero Hill (29). Be it the story of one client who wears the various articles stolen during his burglary to the trial, the story of the one who revealed his incriminating scar to the court over his lawyer's objections, or even the one of the second-story man mauled by a Bengal tiger after he stepped on its tail, these stories all point to the clients' ignorance, which allows them to be exploited and targeted by the dominant desires and forces of their world. The verdict in the trial of another of Jesse's clients, Bao Vung, who "should be sentenced for the truth of his crime, not for his stupidity," is Jesse's own personal story to contribute to these tellings, as it is yet another instance of this world's cruelty that Jesse has himself become cynically inured to (149). The narrative he tells can only replicate this cruelty.

Instead, it is Jesse's own narrative in *Gods Go Begging* that proves counter to the (hi)story of his world. Through Jesse's transformation, the novel likewise "supposes" a new world. This process begins when Jesse first visits Potrero/Tourette's Hill, which robs him, like Zeferino before, of the control that has been so much a part of his post-Vietnam experience:

> As they reached the first intersection, Jesse began to feel that a sharp, involuntary twitch had developed in his right hand. It began as a small tug on his wrist muscles but soon grew into a violent, twitching spasm that contorted the muscles of his upper arm. Jesse gritted his teeth and grabbed his right hand with his left. No matter how much force he exerted he was unable to control it.
>
> Suddenly the word "shit!" burst from his tensed lips, then "mother-fucker!" Jesse had no idea what impulse might have prompted those words. (167)

Jesse's immediate reaction to these effects is to exclaim "I was cursing like a soldier" (167). The end of this exclamation is telling, because Jesse can be seen as returned to his state as a soldier, that state of being exposed to what lies beyond the narrow range of experience delimited by his world. He loses control, something he has not done since the war. Specifically, Jesse feels the burden of his world's discomfort, concentrated as that desire is in this space. Similarly, in the connection Jesse makes here, his present starts to fold into his past and the novel's two localities into each other.

These two times become simultaneous in the climax of the novel, Jesse's summation to the jury in Calvin's trial, an act of storytelling or supposing that brings to a close, metaphorically, the cycle of history dominating the novel's world. Jesse tells how as Persephone dials 911 on a pay phone in the present, Amos, her husband, makes his call for an airstrike in the past. Mai, in San Francisco, rushes out of the Amazon Luncheonette toward Persephone as her husband Trin runs toward his opponent, Amos, in Laos. The killing shots delivered into Persephone coincide with the shots providing cover for Trin's assault. Both Mai and Trin scream "Tien Lan!" as they each fling themselves upon the body of their targets. In this instant, the husbands and wives see each other. Persephone and Amos speak each other's names into their phonesets and hear their own spoken (287–288). At this point, the two times and spaces have come together; they coincide, fold, and collapse into each other. They exist in the "same microsecond" and the "same place" so that each husband and wife can not only see but also hear each other.

And in this moment of simultaneity, the novel suggests the end of one cycle and birth of another. That the jury comes back with a verdict of not guilty on all counts is its first sign. Calvin's story will not be one to tell in the lawyers' cafeteria, or at least not for the traditional reason. It is an exception to that logic and irony. It is a story of hope, not cynicism, of survival, not destruction. So too is Jesse's story. He has been freed from his similar cynicism and the destructive path that made him as much a product of this world as anyone else. As Jesse describes toward the end of the novel, he and Calvin (as well as the still-existent chaplain) are "survivors on the hill. They were the boys who had pulled through. Neither of them would ever go back to the hill" (317–318). Not only that, but immediately after this declaration, the novel's narrator describes the ascent of "an Afro-Mexican deep-space probe launched from a newly supposed world" (318). The more egalitarian world Jesse once imagined as a distraction from the violence and pressure of the Vietnam War is, within the novel's world, a reality. The still-surviving chaplain likewise sees the M.A.S.A. satellite, as do other homeless veterans. It is there for those to see it, that world of justice and hope, not only for the novel's characters, but for its reader as well. In the image of the M.A.S.A. satellite, *Gods Go Begging* asks its reader the same question Ted for Short asked Zeferino at the end of *The Silver Cloud Café*: Do you believe in another world? It challenges its reader to transform, to break out of a cycle and into something new, specifically a new, inclusive understanding replacing the conventional and constricting one once dominant in the novel's imagined world.

# Conclusion

The hope for something new, particularly a new understanding or conception of cultural difference, that ends Véa's *Gods Go Begging* is particularly apt given the novel's publication in 1999, and thus both at the end of the twentieth century and on the cusp of the twenty-first. The fulfillment of that hope is, at best, ambiguous.

Some of the same problematic rhetorics of difference simply took on new forms in this millennium's first decade. Previously, this study elaborated others' critique of cultural studies: that it denied texts their special transcendence by, in a sense, dragging them down into processes of history, power, and sociopolitics (see Farrell 23). Today, the opposite is lamented. As Slavoj Žižek summarizes, as a consequence of the 9/11 attacks, the opponents of cultural studies "proclaimed the end of the American 'holiday from history'—the impact of reality shattering the isolated tower of the liberal tolerant attitude and the Cultural Studies focus on textuality." As he goes on, "Now, we are forced to strike back, to deal with real enemies in the real world" (Žižek). Once seen as too implicated with these processes, cultural studies is cast as too divorced from history and reality. Cultural studies theorists and critics are isolated and insular, withdrawn from history by means of a retreat to the textual. Such a move becomes an intellectual luxury that can no longer be afforded after the 9/11 attacks.

The same is true, I would argue, when it comes to the discussion of race and ethnicity in the new decade. During President Obama's candidacy and, even more acutely, after his election, the idea that his ascension was evidence of America having become a "post-racial society" began to be floated. That is, his election demonstrated how institutional racism was ended. If true, such a change would indeed be worthy of celebrating. But such a claim, in addition to its factual inaccuracy, belies an all-too-familiar agenda. It gets touted as a reason to end the discussion of racism and racial inequities and perhaps, along with those, gender, class, and sexual inequities. It is, quite simply, Rorty's argument dressed up in different clothes. In the same way that he and Farrell argue that we should stop talking about race and gender and ethnicity and sexuality and class because they are not "transcendent" or "human values," those asserting this post-racial idea similarly call for these topics to be dismissed because we, as a society, have now "moved beyond" them. Not terribly unlike the assumed cosmopolitanism Brennan castigated, these voices of a post-racial society assume such a thing to exist due to new conditions, thus releasing themselves and ourselves from the obligation to actively work toward racial and ethnic equality.

These examples exhibit how the problematic rhetoric of difference contextualizing this study's treatment of Chicano/a fiction has not yet gone away. Like the epistemological categories represented in Véa's *The Silver Cloud Café*, this rhetoric has simply adapted, its advocates finding additional ways in which to deploy it. Too, the thorny relationship of the literary text to sociopolitical reality remains. In both those critiques advanced by Rorty and Farrell, and those noted by Žižek, textuality and reality appear contradictorily related. The textual is either too conflated with extant reality and processes, or it is a "vacation" from these, a retreat, an escape. These critiques point to a need to rethink the relationship between the literary/textual and the sociopolitical/experiential. Or, if not to rethink, to more fervently assert the complex relationship between these different ontological realms, which such extreme representations elide.

I would like to think that *Of Space and Mind* contributes to this effort. For one, the narratives and ethics belonging to persistence and transformation add to, complicate, and perhaps even push us beyond those of resistance, which was shown earlier to be based in the same oppositional logic as the above and earlier critiques. Resistance seems in some ways best suited to the goals of early civil rights and nationalist movements, where what is at stake is a recognition of those differently raced, ethnically identified, classed, gendered, and sexed peoples and cultures. The sort of identity-in-difference that is so much a part of the resistance narrative seems particularly suited for demanding such basic and essential recognition.

Yet, I wonder if the rhetoric of difference has not surpassed the logic of resistance, meant here again as a conception of difference and not sociopolitical action. There is another change in our public rhetoric and thus its accompanying logic. The ongoing debates over gay marriage and immigration policy base themselves less in an assertion of difference than in one of similarity. What these groups and their advocates fight for are the same rights that heterosexual couples and U.S. citizens possess. Furthermore, their demand for that similarity is what dominant U.S. society finds dangerous and fears. Within such a context, the resistance paradigm, based as it is in a logic of opposition, contestation, and distance, would seem rather to feed into the racist and "comfortable" understandings lamented by Véa and the other authors in this study. A paradigm that fosters such a separatist and conflictual conception of difference would seem more to impede the achievement of these aims than facilitate them. The value I find in the narratives and ethics suggested by Castillo, Islas, Rechy, Véa, and Viramontes results from how they suggest different ways of conceiving difference, ways that might better challenge those comfortable understandings that continue to hold sway (or attempt to), which resistance, in its way, might be said to feed.

Additionally, the preceding discussion also avers a relationship between literature and experience also made necessary by those critiques. The literary text affects how we think about reality and experience. The identification of persistence and transformation not only serves to demonstrate how they exist within the body of Chicano/a literature, but also how they demonstrate this impact of literary texts on extant reality. As Hogan explains, "Authors do not simply live in ordinary culture. It is their job to make culture. Literature itself is part of culture. Moreover, it is not just some isolated part. Literature is one of the primary means by which a culture represents to itself the ambient acts and ideas of daily life" (*Empire* 2). Such a function of literature goes back to the works of Homer. *The Odyssey*, for example, depicts proper and improper host/guest relations in multiple scenes. Polyphemus the Cyclops eats his "guest" and thus is a "bad host," for which his blinding is consequence and punishment. Penelope's suitors are improper "guests" and so are slaughtered when Odysseus, their "host," returns. Here, again, the ethical implications of the text are stark. Nowadays, we perhaps do not view literature as so directly guiding how we live, or defining what is an ethical life, but that does not mean literature has lost that ethical imperative, only that it has perhaps lain dormant as other emphases have been theorized and pursued.

This study, then, might be considered an effort to reassert that ethical function. Furthermore, it does so in an effort to defuse those criticisms that might interfere with its work as well as that of cultural studies. This study parallels cultural studies in its interest in the sociopolitical conjunction of the textual, that conjunction occurring through literary aesthetics. The emphasis here, then, should not be read as asserting a New Critical formalism. Neither is this effort meant to accomplish the "domesticization" of sociopolitical action feared and lamented by Ahmad. Rather, the literary text stands as a means (and by no means the only means) by which we develop and change our understanding of our extant world and, in the particular case of this project, the differences with which we cohabit this world. Robert Wright contends that we "are potentially moral animals . . . but we aren't naturally moral animals. To be moral animals, we must realize how thoroughly we aren't" (344). If we accept Wright's contention that we possess the capacity for morality if not the actuality, then perhaps texts, like those in this study, that challenge our moral and ethical positioning—and, more generally, how we think—can provide in some perhaps small, perhaps large way the opportunity for self-reflection, demonstrating, like the Foucauldian heterotopic mirror, both what we are and what we are not.

# Notes

## INTRODUCTION

1. Several critics critique Anzaldúa for her discourse of indigenism. María Josefina Saldaña-Portillo sees Anzaldúa as failing to live up to the potential of her mestizaje. She states that "if Anzaldúa's borderland undoes the artificial duality of a border . . . it does so in the service of recognizing the material violence of such artificial constructs . . . [and] could proceed to resituate the Chicano/a as mestizo, the Mexican as mestizo, and the Indian as Mexican within a transnational frame that would address the unequal power relations among such positionalities" (281). However, she faults Anzaldúa for failing to take "up her own provocative challenge to do this" and "quickly slip[ping] back into the conventional usage of the 'us' against the Anglo 'them'" that "rallies mestizaje to access an indigenous ancestry that legitimates a prior claim to the Southwest for Chicanas and Chicanos" that ignores "contemporary Native American inhabitants of the Southwest and their very different mytho-genealogies" (281). Similarly, in *Blood Lines: Myth, Indigenism, and Chicana/o Literature*, Sheila Contreras notes Rafael Pérez-Torres who "overviews" these critiques of Anzaldúa before attempting his recuperation of her from them (183, n. 16).

2. Classic examples of such effects would, of course, include the influence of Harriet Beecher Stowe's *Uncle Tom's Cabin* on abolitionist efforts, as well as the reforms to the meat-packing industry prompted by outrage stemming from Upton Sinclair's *The Jungle*. While clearly not all literary texts have such a pronounced real-world effect, these do speak to the power of all literary texts to influence their readers' minds, which is a fundamental assumption of this study.

3. James Phelan provides a sense of how this dynamic process of reader and textual interaction occurs:

> Texts are designed by authors in order to affect readers in particular ways, that those designs are conveyed through the language, technique, structures, forms, and dialogic relations of texts as well as the genres and conventions readers use to understand them, and that

reader responses are a function, guide, and text of how designs are created through textual and intertextual phenomena. Methodologically, this view of the relationship among author, text (including the narrator), and the reader means that the interpreter may begin the interpretive inquiry from any one of these points on the rhetorical triangle, but the inquiry will at some point consider how each point both influences and can be influenced by the other two. (18)

## CHAPTER 2

1. José David Saldívar's discussion of Rechy's novel occurs within what the former describes as "the megaspatial view of Los Angeles as it actually exists" enumerated in Mike Davis's *City of Quartz*. As Saldívar notes, much of what we see in *The Miraculous Day of Amalia Gómez* eerily parallels what Davis describes about the "real" Los Angeles (see, for example, Davis's description of the LAPD's descent on a street carnival in 1986 [258–260] and Amalia's description of her own similar experience [Rechy 44]). However, Saldívar's reliance on Davis as a lens through which he views Rechy's novel problematizes his treatment. First, one can attribute Saldívar's neglect of other aspects of the novel's storyworld to this reliance. Second, Saldívar, perhaps inadvertently, reduces Rechy's novel to an illustration of what Davis describes and concomitantly offers the novel as an explanation of how the real Los Angeles has developed. In making such a claim, Saldívar falls under the critiques offered by Frederick Aldama and Marcial González, who criticize the confusion of literary texts "with a simply direct or 'objective' transcription of reality . . . that conflates fiction with ontological fact" (Aldama 28; see also González 282–285 for a critique of *Border Matters* among other works of Chicano/a literary criticism that so "romanticize" borderlands experience).

2. What precisely her country is is a matter of some debate. As Roberta Fernández points out, though Viramontes has publicly stated "that the woman in the story is from El Salvador, there is nothing in the text to place her there" (78). Furthermore, Viramontes makes an explicit reference to the "contras" of Nicaragua, "whose violence she was forced to flee" (78). This inconsistency leads Ana Patricia Rodríguez to read the woman as possibly "from Nicaragua, El Salavador, or Guatemala" and so she takes the woman as more generally symbolic of "Central American women" (397). However, though this might be the best we can make of the inconsistent information given in the story, Rodríguez's reading is itself contradictory within the context of her article, as her treatment of "The Cariboo Café" is grounded in correcting moves by Chicano/a writers to generalize the political and historical struggles of Central American peoples with their own.

3. Furthermore, Rodríguez goes on to describe the owner's attitude toward the refugee woman inaccurately. She writes, "To the 'American' owner, she is not only one of those who 'arrived in the secrecy of night, as displaced people often do' . . .

but also a freeloader" (399). Though the owner does in fact complain about the possibility of having to give her and the children a free meal, the first part of this description is not in his voice/words. These are part of the opening lines of the story, told in an unidentified third-person voice, and are not evocative of the owner's specific attitudes.

4. Moore's problematic treatment of the fragmentation in "The Cariboo Café" is attributable to her interpretation of its use as "postmodern." In doing so, she reduces the text's workings to the sort of vagaries de la Campa criticizes as "raving polysemy": that the ambiguities and uncertainties created in a writer like Jorge Luis Borges, when reduced to simply postmodern "play," ignore what may be very material and political reasons/interpretations (de la Campa 19). Similarly, by treating fragmentation in Viramontes's story as more of a postmodern aesthetic, Moore is not able to deal with its larger political/historical significance.

5. The absence of the newspaperman also proves eerily similar to how the refugee woman describes people in Central America as "disappeared," giving a further ominous feel to Sonya's environment.

6. Rodríguez bases this claim on how the women in "The Cariboo Café," and the other works she discusses, are "often key figures for contesting dominant narratives" and "reveal masculine investments across national, political, and economic borders, . . . develop[ing] more feminist, more humanitarian counter narratives." These qualities "demand" for these texts "inclusion in the U.S. Latino testimonio tradition" (390). However, this claim glosses over one problematic fact: "The Cariboo Café" is a work of fiction, not a *testimonio.* Even given recent questions about the authenticity of *testimonios,* centered most often on Rigoberta Menchú's seminal work, one cannot include a wholly fictional text like "The Cariboo Café" into this tradition without generalizing the tradition to the point of uselessness, a move that again seems oddly contradictory given Rodríguez's concerns over how Central American narratives have been absorbed into a U.S. Latino/a narrative.

## CHAPTER 3

1. Similarly inherent in Rechy and Viramontes is a failure or collapse of community. Amalia has no community: her friend Rosario has been disappeared, she has broken up with her current boyfriend after learning about his sexual advances toward her daughter, and this, plus the further revelation of her son's homosexuality, drives a wedge between her and both her children that remains unresolved at novel's end. And though Viramontes's use of La Llorona and the *testimonio* traditions functions to signal a similarity and communion between her characters, that community, obviously, is never realized within the world of "The Cariboo Café" because of the story's tragedy.

2. Alaimo convincingly parallels the image of the "It's a Small World" ride at Disneyland to multiculturalism. Both reduce cultures to "colorfully dressed child-

like performers who affirm the message that we are all so different, yet all the same, as the viewers, riding safely in their little train through the world of cultures get to be entertained by them but remain untouched, unchallenged, emerging into daylight at the end of the tunnel, safe from them all" (163).

3. Linda Hutcheon's notion of the "ex-centric"—under which she tropes class, race, gender, sexual orientation, and ethnicity—can be included in this critique. Hutcheon generalizes and aestheticizes the "marginal perspective" of such differences as part of postmodernism's general undermining of the subject and a "postmodern paradox" of "decentralized community" (see Hutcheon 11–12).

4. In fact, I would argue that Antonio's understanding of his world is more akin to the problematic kind of cosmopolitanism that Brennan decries. His identity will be composed of the forces and influences that make up his experience on the llano that for him *is* the world. Thus, if he were to extend himself into more global conditions, it would be with the self-assured view of himself as the world, making him a center and the rest of the world his periphery/alterity, thus again replicating a problematic binary understanding that is, again, consistent with the resistance narrative.

5. See also Carlston 130–131, where she notes the lack of female children in *La Maravilla* and uses Lola to demonstrate how her outburst and wholesale rejection are born of Buckeye Road's deleterious effects on her. Not only does Carlston parallel the omission of women's stories from Chicano literature prior to the 1970s to Lola, but also to the differentiating effect of gender on one's relation to culture.

6. As Aldama explains, the U.S. military/industrial complex is a kind of "Othering machine": "[T]he society of the spectacle is an ideological construct that makes visible an Other (in this case, Arabs) and/or magically erases this Other (in this case, the Chicana) for the exploitative and oppressive machine of capitalism to continue to operate" (*Postethnic Criticism*, 81).

7. Delgadillo provides a list of these experiences: "Castillo writes the lives not only of the four sisters and their mother, but also includes the stories of doña Felicia, María, Esmeralda, Helena, Rita de Belén, Mrs. Torres, doña Severa, garment workers on strike, workers suffering toxic poisoning at work, Navajo women trying to save future generations from uranium contamination, the many suffering from A.I.D.S. and more" (912).

## CHAPTER 4

1. Anzaldúa describes, near the end of the prose section of *Borderlands/La Frontera*, how the mestiza develops "a tolerance for contradictions, a tolerance for ambiguity." Furthermore, she "has a plural personality, she operates in a pluralistic mode—nothing is thrust out, the good the bad and the ugly, nothing rejected, nothing abandoned. Not only does she sustain contradictions, she turns the ambivalence into something else" (101).

## CHAPTER 5

1. The qualification here is based on Patrick Colm Hogan, who points out the limitations of decrying all binaries in his discussion of hybridity in Homi Bhabha. Hogan demonstrates how Bhabha himself falls prey to the very binarism he decries and thus exhibits how such sweeping demonizations and valorizations are untenable:

> The apartheid system of South Africa made distinctions among Africans, coloreds, and whites. Thus it was not binaristic. Was it, therefore, alright? Of course not. Conversely, it is highly binaristic to say that Nazi genocide and American slavery was bad and that opposition to these practices was good. Should we condemn people who make such statements because they are binaristic? Should we prefer hybrid, middle positions—for example, the view that Jews should have been confined to work camps, but not exterminated . . . ? Similarly are we to celebrate the "in-betweeness" of colonial collaborationists or quislings? (Hogan, *Empire* 5)

In Véa, binaristic thinking is clearly decried, but this declaration is no more general than the storyworld or text itself.

# Works Cited

Abrams, M. H. *A Glossary of Literary Terms.* 4th ed. Fort Worth: Harcourt, 1999.

Ahmad, Aijaz. *In Theory: Classes, Nations, Literatures.* London: Verso, 1992.

Alaimo, Stacy. "Multiculturalism and Epistemic Rupture: The Vanishing Acts of Guillermo Gómez-Peña and Alfredo Véa Jr." *MELUS* 25.2 (2000): 163–185.

Aldama, Frederick Luis. *Postethnic Narrative Criticism: Magicorealism in Oscar "Zeta" Acosta, Ana Castillo, Julie Dash, Hanif Kureishi, and Salman Rushdie.* Austin: University of Texas Press, 2003.

———. *Brown on Brown: Chicano/a Representations of Gender, Sexuality, and Ethnicity.* Austin: University of Texas Press, 2005.

———, ed. *Critical Mappings of Arturo Islas's Fictions.* Tempe, Ariz.: Bilingual Review Press, 2005.

Anaya, Rudolfo. *Bless Me, Ultima.* New York: Warner Books, 1999.

Anderson, Douglas. "Displaced Abjection and States of Grace: Denise Chávez's *The Last of the Menu Girls.*" *American Women Short Story Writers: A Collection of Critical Essays.* Ed. Julie Brown. New York: Garland, 1995. 235–250.

Anzaldúa, Gloria. *Borderlands/La Frontera: The New Mestiza.* 2nd ed. San Francisco: Aunt Lute, 1999.

Appiah, Kwame Anthony. *Cosmopolitanism: Ethics in a World of Strangers.* New York: Norton, 2007.

Aranda, José Jr. *When We Arrive: A New Literary History of Mexican America.* Tucson: University of Arizona Press, 2003.

Arteaga, Alfred. *Chicano Poetics: Heterotexts and Hybridities.* Cambridge: Cambridge University Press, 1997.

Baudrillard, Jean. "The Precession of Simulacra." *A Postmodern Reader.* Ed. Joseph Natoli and Linda Hutcheon. Albany: State University of New York Press, 1993. 342–375.

Bjornson, Richard. "Cognitive Mapping and the Understanding of Literature." *Sub-Stance* 30 (1980): 51–62.

Black, Debra B. "Times of Conflict: *Bless Me, Ultima* as a Novel of Acculturation." *Bilingual Review* 25.2 (2000): 146–162.

Brady, Mary Pat. *Extinct Lands, Temporal Geographies: Chicana Literature and the Urgency of Space.* Durham, N.C.: Duke University Press, 2002.

Brennan, Timothy. *At Home in the World: Cosmopolitanism Now.* Cambridge: Harvard University Press, 1997.

———. "Cosmo-Theory." *South Atlantic Quarterly* 100.3 (2001): 659–691.

Bruce-Novoa, Juan. "Canonical and Noncanonical Texts." *Americas Review* 14.3–4 (1986): 119–135.

Caminero-Santangelo, Marta. "'Jason's Indian': Mexican Americans and the Denial of Indigenous Ethnicity in Rudolfo Anaya's *Bless Me, Ultima.*" *Critique* 45.2 (2004): 115–128.

Cantú, Roberto. "Borders of the Self in Alfredo Véa's *The Silver Cloud Café.*" *Studies in Twentieth Century Literature* 25.1 (2001): 210–245.

Carbonell, Ana María. "From Llorona to Gritona: Coatlicue in Feminist Tales by Viramontes and Cisneros." *MELUS* 24.2 (1999): 53–74.

Carlston, Erin G. "'Making the Margins Chaos': Romantic and Antiromantic Readings of *La Maravilla.*" *Aztlán* 30.2 (2005): 113–135.

Castillo, Ana. *So Far from God.* New York: Penguin, 1993.

———. *Sapogonia: An Anti-Romance in 3/8 Meter.* New York: Anchor Books, 1994.

Cervantes, Lorna Dee. "Freeway 280." *Emplumada.* Pittsburgh: University of Pittsburgh Press, 1981. 39.

Chávez, Denise. *The Last of the Menu Girls.* Houston: Arte Público Press, 1986.

Cohn, Dorrit. *Transparent Minds: Narrative Modes for Presenting Consciousness in Fiction.* Princeton: Princeton University Press, 1978.

Contreras, Sheila. *Blood Lines: Myth, Indigenism, and Chicana/o Literature.* Austin: University of Texas Press, 2008.

Davis, Mike. *City of Quartz: Excavating the Future in Los Angeles.* New York: Random House, 1992.

———. *Magical Urbanism: Latinos Reinvent the U.S. City.* London: Verso, 2000.

Davis, Todd, and Kenneth Womack, eds. "Preface: Reading Literature and the Ethics of Criticism." *Mapping the Ethical Turn: A Reader in Ethics, Culture, and Literary Theory.* Ed. Todd Davis and Kenneth Womack, Charlottesville: University Press of Virginia, 2001.

de la Campa, Román. *Latin Americanism.* Minneapolis: University of Minnesota Press, 1999.

Delgadillo, Theresa. "Forms of Chicana Feminist Resistance: Hybrid Spirituality in Ana Castillo's *So Far from God.*" *Modern Fiction Studies* 44.4 (1998): 888–916.

DeSoto, Aureliano Maria. "On the Trail of the Chicana/o Subject: Literary Texts and Contexts in the Formation of Chicana/o Studies." *Multiethnic Literature and Canon Debates.* Ed. Mary Jo Bona and Irma Maini. Albany: State University of New York Press, 2006. 41–60.

"El Plan Espiritual de Aztlán." *Aztlán: Essays on the Chicano Homeland.* Ed.

Rudolfo Anaya and Francisco A. Lomeli. Albuquerque: University of New Mexico Press, 1991. 1–5.

Farred, Grant. "Cultural Studies: Literary Criticism's Alter Ego." *The Institution of Literature*. Ed. Jeffrey J. Williams. Albany: State University of New York Press, 2002. 77–94.

Farrell, Frank B. *Why Does Literature Matter?* Ithaca, N.Y.: Cornell University Press, 2004.

Fernández, Roberta. "'The Cariboo Café': Helena Maria Viramontes Discourses with Her Social and Cultural Contexts." *Women's Studies* 17.1–2 (1989): 71–85.

Fluck, Winfried, and Thomas Claviez, eds. "Introduction." *Yearbook of Research in English and American Literature* 19 (2003): ix–xii.

Folks, Jeffrey F. *From Richard Wright to Toni Morrison: Ethics in Modern and Postmodern American Narrative*. New York: Peter Lang, 2001.

Foucault, Michel. "Of Other Spaces." *Diacritics* 16 (1980): 22–27.

Gómez-Vega, Ibis. "Debunking Myths: The Hero's Role in Ana Castillo's *Sapogonia*." *Americas Review* 22. 1–2 (1994): 244–258.

Gonzales, Manuel G. *Mexicanos: A History of Mexicans in the United States*. 2nd ed. Bloomington: Indiana University Press, 2009.

González, Marcial. "A Marxist Critique of Borderlands Postmodernism: Adorno's *Negative Dialectics* and Chicano Cultural Criticism." *Left of the Color Line: Race, Radicalism, and Twentieth Century Literature of the United States*. Ed. Bill V. Mullen and James Smethurst. Chapel Hill: University of North Carolina Press, 2003. 279–297.

Grossberg, Lawrence. *Bringing It All Back Home: Essays on Cultural Studies*. Durham, N.C.: Duke University Press, 1997.

Gupta, Akhil, and James Ferguson. "Culture, Power, Place: Ethnography at the End of an Era." *Culture, Power, Place: Explorations in Critical Anthropology*. Ed. Akhil Gupta and James Ferguson. Durham, N.C.: Duke University Press, 1997. 1–29.

Harlow, Barbara. "Sites of Struggle: Immigration, Deportation, Prison, and Exile." *Criticism in the Borderlands: Studies in Chicano Literature, Culture, and Ideology*. Ed. Hector Calderón and José David Saldívar. Durham, N.C.: Duke University Press, 1991. 149–165.

Harvey, David. *The Condition of Postmodernity: An Enquiry into the Origins of Cultural Change*. Cambridge, Mass.: Blackwell, 1990.

Hinojosa, Rolando. "Sometimes It Just Happens That Way; That's All." *The Valley*. Ypsilanti, Mich.: Bilingual Press, 1983. 55–70.

Hogan, Patrick Colm. *Cognitive Science, Literature and the Arts: A Guide for Humanists*. New York: Routledge, 2003.

———. *Empire and Poetic Voice: Cognitive and Cultural Studies of Literary Tradition and Colonialism*. Albany: State University of New York Press, 2004.

Hogue, W. Lawrence. *Race, Modernity, Postmodernity: A Look at the History and the Literatures of People of Color Since the 1960s*. Albany: State University of New York Press, 1996.

Hutcheon, Linda. *A Poetics of Postmodernism: History, Theory, Fiction*. Routledge, 1988.

Islas, Arturo. *La Mollie and the King of Tears*. Albuquerque: University of New Mexico Press, 1996.

———. *Arturo Islas: The Uncollected Works*. Ed. Frederick Aldama. Houston: Arte Público Press, 2003.

Jameson, Fredric. "Cognitive Mapping." *Marxism and the Interpretation of Culture*. Ed. Cary Nelson and Lawrence Grossberg. Urbana: University of Illinois Press, 1988. 347–360.

———. *Postmodernism, or, The Cultural Logic of Late Capitalism*. Durham, N.C.: Duke University Press, 1991.

Johnson, Kelli Lyon. "Violence in the Borderlands: Crossing to the Home Space in the Novels of Ana Castillo." *Frontiers* 25.1 (2004): 39–58.

Kanoza, Theresa M. "The Golden Carp and Moby Dick: Rudolfo Anaya's Multi-Culturalism." *MELUS* 24.2 (1999): 159–171.

Kaup, Monika. *Rewriting North American Borders in Chicano and Chicana Narrative*. New York: Peter Lang, 2001.

Kort, Wesley A. *Place and Space in Modern Fiction*. Gainesville: University Press of Florida, 2004.

Lanza, Carmela Delia. "Hearing the Voices: Women and Home and Ana Castillo's *So Far from God*." *MELUS* 23.1 (1998): 65–79.

Lynch, Kevin. *The Image of the City*. Cambridge, Mass.: M.I.T. Press, 1960.

Maddox, Richard. "Bombs, Bikinis, and the Popes of Rock 'n' Roll: Reflections on Resistance, the Play of Subordinations, and Liberalism in Andalusia and Academia, 1983–1995." *Culture, Power, Place: Explorations in Critical Anthropology*. Ed. Akhil Gupta and James Ferguson. Durham, N.C.: Duke University Press, 1997. 275–290.

McDowell, Linda. *Gender, Identity and Place: Understanding Feminist Geographies*. Minneapolis: University of Minnesota Press, 1999.

McHale, Brian. *Postmodernist Fiction*. New York: Methuen, 1987.

———. "*En abyme*: Internal Models and Cognitive Mapping." *A Sense of the World: Essays on Fiction, Narrative, and Knowledge*. Ed. John Gibson, Wolfgang Huemer, and Luca Pocci. New York: Routledge, 2007. 189–205.

Moore, Deborah Owen. "La Llorona Dines at the Cariboo Café: Structure and Legend in the Work of Helena Maria Viramontes." *Studies in Short Fiction* 35.3 (1998): 277–286.

Morton, Donald. "Transforming Theory: Cultural Studies and the Public Humanities." *Critical Studies* 23 (2004): 25–47.

Neate, Wilson. *Tolerating Ambiguity: Ethnicity and Community in Chicano/a Writing*. New York: Peter Lang Press, 1998.

Newton, Adam Zachary. *Narrative Ethics*. Cambridge, Mass.: Harvard University Press, 1995.

Padilla, Genaro M. "Myth and Comparative Nationalism: The Ideological Uses of Aztlán." *Aztlán: Essays on the Chicano Homeland*. Ed. Rudolfo Anaya and Francisco A. Lomeli. Albuquerque: Academia/El Norte, 1989. 111–134.

Palmer, Alan. *Fictional Minds*. Lincoln: University of Nebraska Press, 2004.

Phelan, James. *Living to Tell About It: A Rhetoric and Ethics of Character Narration*. Ithaca, N.Y.: Cornell University Press, 2005.

Pisarz-Ramírez, Gabriele. "Bilingual, Interlingual-Language Identity Construction in Mexican-American Literary Discourse." *Holding Their Own: Perspectives on the Multi-Ethnic Literatures of the United States*. Ed. Heike Raphael-Hernandez. Tübingen, Germany: Stauffenburg, 2000. 67–75.

Rechy, John. *The Miraculous Day of Amalia Gómez*. New York: Grove Press, 1991.

Rodríguez, Ana Patricia. "Refugees of the South: Central Americans in the U.S. Latino Imaginary." *American Literature* 73.2 (2001): 387–412.

Rorty, Richard. "The Inspirational Value of Great Works of Literature." *Raritan* 16.1 (1996): 8–17.

Ryan, Marie-Laure. "Cognitive Maps and the Construction of Narrative Space." *Narrative Theory and the Cognitive Sciences*. Ed. David Herman. Stanford, Calif.: CSLI Publications, 2003. 214–242.

Saeta, Elsa. "Ana Castillo's *Sapogonia*: Narrative Point of View as a Study in Perception." *Confluencia* 10.1 (1994): 67–72.

Saldaña-Portillo, María Josefina. *The Revolutionary Imagination in the Americas and the Age of Development*. Durham, N.C.: Duke University Press, 2003.

Saldívar, José David. *Border Matters: Remapping American Cultural Studies*. Berkeley: University of California Press, 1997.

Saldívar, Ramón. *Chicano Narrative: The Dialectics of Difference*. Madison: University of Wisconsin Press, 1990.

Saldívar-Hull, Sonia. "Feminism on the Border: From Gender Politics to Geopolitics." *Criticism in the Borderlands: Studies in Chicano Literature, Culture, and Ideology*. Ed. Hector Calderón and José David Saldívar. Durham, N.C.: Duke University Press, 1991. 203–220.

Skenazy, Paul. "Borders and Bridges, Drugs and Drugstores: Toward a Geography of Time." *San Francisco in Fiction: Essays in a Regional Literature*. Ed. David Fine and Paul Skenazy. Albuquerque: University of New Mexico Press, 1995. 198–216.

Socolovsky, Maya. "Borrowed Homes, Homesickness, and Memory in Ana Castillo's *Sapogonia*." *Aztlán: A Journal of Chicano Studies* 24.2 (1999): 73–94.

Tierney, William G. "Beyond Translation: Truth and Rigoberta Menchú." *International Journal of Qualitative Studies in Education* 13.2 (2000): 103–113.

Toyosato, Mayumi. "Grounding Self and Action: Land, Community, and Survival in *I, Rigoberta Menchú*, *No Telephone to Heaven*, and *So Far from God*." *Hispanic Journal* 19.2 (1998): 295–311.

Véa, Alfredo. *La Maravilla.* New York: Penguin, 1993.
————. *The Silver Cloud Café.* New York: Penguin, 1996.
————. *Gods Go Begging.* New York: Penguin, 1999.
Viramontes, Helena María. "The Cariboo Café." *The Moths and Other Stories.* Houston: Arte Público Press, 1985. 61–75.
Walter, Roland. "The Cultural Politics of Dislocation and Relocation in the Novels of Ana Castillo." *MELUS* 23.1 (1998): 81–97.
Wright, Robert. *The Moral Animal: Evolutionary Psychology and Everyday Life.* New York: Random House, 1994.
Žižek, Slavoj. "Welcome to the Desert of the Real." Re: Constructions: Reflections on Humanity and Media after Tragedy. http://web.mit.edu/cms/recon structions/interpretations/desertreal.html. Accessed April 14, 2006.
Zoran, Gabriel. "Towards a Theory of Space in Narrative." *Poetics Today* 5.2 (1984): 309–335.
Zunshine, Lisa. *Why We Read Fiction: Theory of Mind and the Novel.* Columbus: Ohio State University Press, 2006.

# *Credits*

# Index

Lightning Source UK Ltd.
Milton Keynes UK
UKHW041247070422
401165UK00010B/236